ICSE Exams 2026

AF819936

All in One

GEOGRAPHY

Class 9

ICSE Exams 2026

All in one®

GEOGRAPHY

Class 9

Author
Farah Sultan
(M.A. Geography, B.Ed)

arihant
SUCCESS AND NOTHING LESS

ARIHANT PRAKASHAN

(School Division Series)

卐 *ADMINISTRATIVE & PRODUCTION OFFICES*

Regd. Office

'Ramchhaya' 4577/15, Agarwal Road, Darya Ganj, New Delhi -110002
Tele: 011- 47630600, 43518550; Fax: 011- 23280316

卐 *Head Office*

Kalindi, TP Nagar, Meerut (UP) - 250002, Tel: 0121-7156203, 7156204

卐 *SALES & SUPPORT OFFICES*

Agra, Ahmedabad, Bengaluru, Bareilly, Chennai, Delhi, Guwahati, Hyderabad, Jaipur, Jhansi, Kolkata, Lucknow, Nagpur & Pune.

PO No : TXT-XX-XXXXXXX-X-XX

Published By Arihant Publications (India) Ltd.

For further information about the books published by Arihant, log on to www.arihantbooks.com or e-mail at info@arihantbooks.com

Follow us on

卐 *PRICE* ₹220.00

PRODUCTION TEAM

Publishing Managers	*Cover Designer*	*Inner Designer*
Mahendra Singh Rawat & Keshav Mohan	Salman Shaikh	Ankit Tyagi
Project Head	*Page Layouting*	*Proof Reader*
Shivam Gupta	Jashoda	Priya

Index *cum* Study Planner

One Book- Endless Features

to Help you Succeed

Chapter Inside

At the start of each chapter, all the Chapter topics have been listed, so that students may know what they are going to study.

CHAPTER
01

Earth as a Planet

SYLLABUS

Earth as a Planet Shape of the Earth • Earth as the home of humankind and the conditions that exist.

The Earth is the third planet out of eight planets present in the Solar System revolving around the Sun which are Mercury, Venus, Earth, Mars, Jupiter, Saturn, Uranus and Neptune.

The Earth

The Earth came into existence around 4.6 billion years ago. The distance between the Sun and the Earth is about 150 million km. The Earth moves in an elliptical orbit around the Sun and the orbit of the Earth around the Sun lies between the planets Venus (Earth's twin) and Mars.

Quick Revision

At the end of each chapter, Quick Revision is given. It contains crux of the chapter in pointer form that provides the quick revision of the whole chapter.

Complete Theory in Each Chapter

Each chapter has Complete, Easy to Understand and Simplified theory covering latest syllabus. Theory is developed in such a way that it is suitable for all types of learners.

QUICK Revision

- Sun is a star and belongs to the 'Milky Way or Akash Ganga Galaxy'.
- Earth is the fifth largest planet and the third planet from the Sun.
- Earth is called 'a living planet', as it is the only planet supporting life on it.
- Earth is also known as 'blue planet' or 'watery planet' due to the presence of 71% of water on its surface.
- Greek philosopher Pythagoras was the first one to say that the Earth is spherical in shape and rotates around the Sun on its axis.
- The spherical shape of the Earth is supported by the proofs like shape of all terrestrial bodies, sunrise and sunset, circumnavigation of the Earth, sighting of a ship, circular

Check Your LEARNING...

1. Who said for the first time that the Earth is spherical in shape and rotates around the Sun on its axis?
2. During the lunar eclipse the shadow of which planet falls on the Moon's surface?
3. What is the direction of the Earth's rotation?

Check Your Learning

A set of 3-5 Questions given in between the text, helps students to remain connected with the text while studying. They can instantly assess themselves for their understanding.

One Book- Endless Features

to Help you Succeed

Chapter Practice

Chapter Practice have all types of questions that are asked in the examinations such as Multiple Choice Questions, Short Questions and Long Questions.

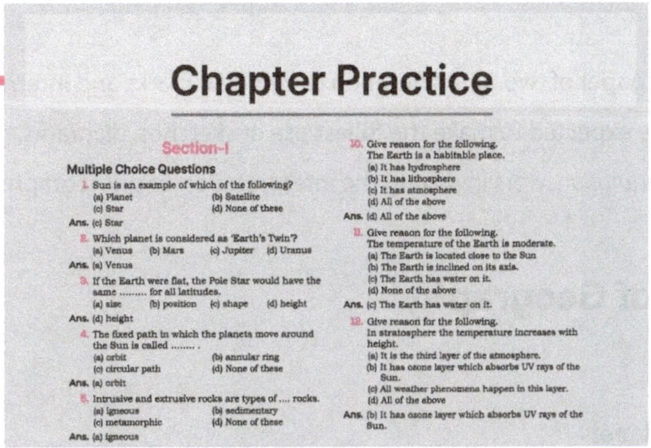

Chapter Practice

Section-I

Multiple Choice Questions

1. Sun is an example of which of the following?
   (a) Planet (b) Satellite
   (c) Star (d) None of these

Ans. (c) Star

2. Which planet is considered as 'Earth's Twin'?
   (a) Venus (b) Mars (c) Jupiter (d) Uranus

Ans. (a) Venus

3. If the Earth were flat, the Pole Star would have the same .... for all latitudes.
   (a) size (b) position (c) shape (d) height

Ans. (d) height

4. The fixed path in which the planets move around the Sun is called ....
   (a) orbit (b) annular ring
   (c) circular path (d) None of these

Ans. (a) orbit

5. Intrusive and extrusive rocks are types of .... rocks.
   (a) igneous (b) sedimentary
   (c) metamorphic (d) None of these

Ans. (a) igneous

10. Give reason for the following.
    The Earth is a habitable place.
    (a) It has hydrosphere
    (b) It has lithosphere
    (c) It has atmosphere
    (d) All of the above

Ans. (d) All of the above

11. Give reason for the following.
    The temperature of the Earth is moderate.
    (a) The Earth is located close to the Sun
    (b) The Earth is inclined on its axis.
    (c) The Earth has water on it.
    (d) None of the above

Ans. (c) The Earth has water on it.

12. Give reason for the following.
    In stratosphere the temperature increases with height.
    (a) It is the third layer of the atmosphere.
    (b) It has ozone layer which absorbs UV rays of the Sun.
    (c) All weather phenomena happen in this layer.
    (d) All of the above

Ans. (b) It has ozone layer which absorbs UV rays of the Sun.

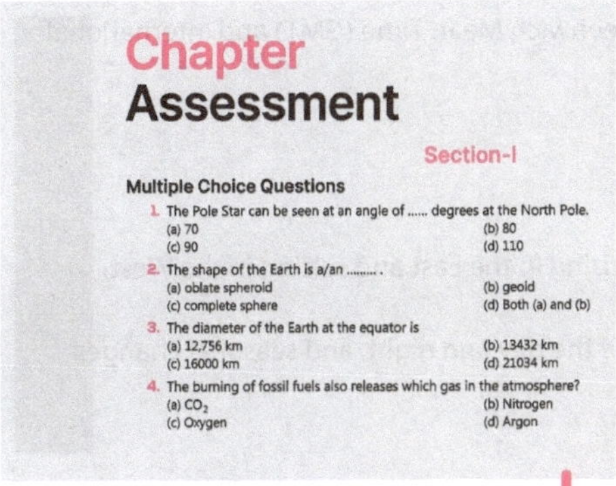

Chapter Assessment

Section-I

Multiple Choice Questions

1. The Pole Star can be seen at an angle of ...... degrees at the North Pole.
   (a) 70 (b) 80
   (c) 90 (d) 110
2. The shape of the Earth is a/an ....
   (a) oblate spheroid (b) geoid
   (c) complete sphere (d) Both (a) and (b)
3. The diameter of the Earth at the equator is
   (a) 12,756 km (b) 13432 km
   (c) 16000 km (d) 21034 km
4. The burning of fossil fuels also releases which gas in the atmosphere?
   (a) CO_2 (b) Nitrogen
   (c) Oxygen (d) Argon

Sample Question Papers

To make students practice of examination in real sense, there are 3 Sample Question Papers at the end. All these Sample Question Papers are exactly prepared on the latest syllabus & pattern of examination.

Chapter Assessment

It is the Assessment Exercise for the Complete Chapter.

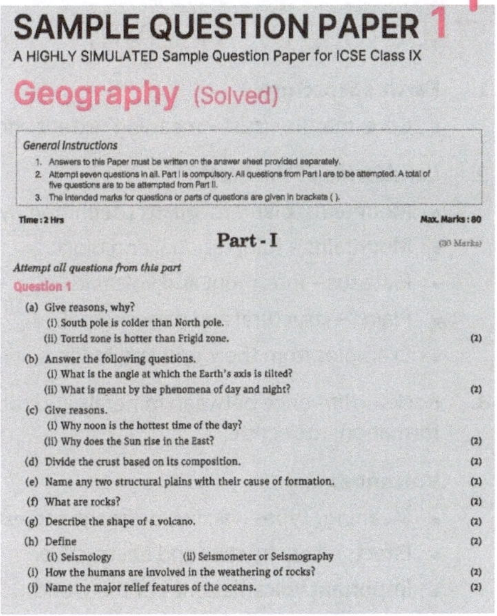

SAMPLE QUESTION PAPER 1

A HIGHLY SIMULATED Sample Question Paper for ICSE Class IX

Geography (Solved)

General Instructions

1. Answers to this Paper must be written on the answer sheet provided separately.
2. Attempt seven questions in all. Part I is compulsory. All questions from Part I are to be attempted. A total of five questions are to be attempted from Part II.
3. The intended marks for questions or parts of questions are given in brackets ( ).

Time : 2 Hrs **Max. Marks : 80**

Part - I

(30 Marks)

Attempt all questions from this part

Question 1

(a) Give reasons, why?
  (i) South pole is colder than North pole.
  (ii) Torrid zone is hotter than Frigid zone. (2)

(b) Answer the following questions.
  (i) What is the angle at which the Earth's axis is tilted?
  (ii) What is meant by the phenomena of day and night? (2)

(c) Give reasons.
  (i) Why noon is the hottest time of the day?
  (ii) Why does the Sun rise in the East? (2)

(d) Divide the crust based on its composition. (2)

(e) Name any two structural plains with their cause of formation. (2)

(f) What are rocks? (2)

(g) Describe the shape of a volcano. (2)

(h) Define (2)
  (i) Seismology (ii) Seismometer or Seismography

(i) How the humans are involved in the weathering of rocks? (2)

(j) Name the major relief features of the oceans. (2)

Latest Course Structure

There will be one paper of two hours duration carrying 80 marks and Internal Assessment of 20 marks.

Candidates will be expected to make the fullest use of sketches, diagrams, graphs and charts in their answers.

Questions may require answers involving the interpretation of photographs of geographical interest.

Principles of Geography

OUR WORLD

1. **Earth as a planet**
   - Shape of the Earth. Earth as the home of humankind and the conditions that exist.
2. **Geographic grid - Latitudes & Longitudes**
   - Concept of latitudes: main latitudes, their location with degrees, parallels of latitude and their uses.
   - Concept of longitudes - Prime Meridian, time (local, standard and time zones, Greenwich Mean Time (GMT) and International Date Line (IDL). Eastern and Western hemisphere.
   - Using latitudes and longitudes to find location. Calculation of time.
   - Great Circles and their use.
3. **Rotation and Revolution**
   - Rotation – direction, speed and its effects (occurrence of day and night, the Sun rising in the East and setting in the West, Coriolis effect)
   - Revolution of the Earth and its inclined axis – effects: the variation in the length of the day and night, and seasonal changes with Equinoxes and Solstices.

STRUCTURE OF THE EARTH

1. **Earth's Structure**
   - Core, mantle, crust – meaning, extent and their composition.
2. **Landforms of the Earth**
   - Mountains, plateaus, plains (definition, types and their formation):
   - Mountains – fold, residual and block.
   - Plateaus – intermont and volcanic.
   - Plains – structural and depositional.
   - Examples from the world and India.
3. Rocks - difference between minerals and rocks, types of rocks: igneous, sedimentary, metamorphic, their characteristics and formation; rock cycle.
4. **Volcanoes**
   - Meaning, Types – active, dormant and extinct.
   - Effects – constructive and destructive.
   - Important volcanic zones of the world.

5. **Earthquakes**

- Meaning, causes and measurement.
- Effects: destructive and constructive.
- Earthquake zones of the World

6. **Weathering and Denudation**

- Meaning, types and effects of weathering.
- Types: Physical Weathering – block and granular disintegration, exfoliation; Chemical Weathering–oxidation, carbonation, hydration and solution; Biological Weathering – caused by humans, plants and animals.
- Meaning and agents of denudation; work of river and wind.
- Stages of a river course and associated land forms – V-shaped valley, waterfall, meander and delta.
- Wind – deflation hollows and Sand dunes.

HYDROSPHERE

- Meaning of hydrosphere.
- Tides - formation and pattern.
- Ocean Currents – their circulation pattern and effects. (Specifically of Gulf Stream, North Atlantic Drift, Labrador Current, Kuro Shio and Oya Shio.)

ATMOSPHERE

1. **Composition and structure of the atmosphere**

- Troposphere, Stratosphere, Ionosphere and Exosphere; Ozone in the Stratosphere, its depletion. Global warming and its impact.

2. **Insolation**

- Meaning of insolation and terrestrial radiation.
- Factors affecting temperature: latitude, altitude, distance from the sea, slope of land, winds and ocean currents.

3. **Atmospheric Pressure and Winds**

- Meaning and factors that affect atmospheric pressure.
- Major pressure belts of the world.
- Factors affecting direction and velocity of wind – pressure gradient, Coriolis Effect.
- Permanent winds – Trades, Westerlies and Polar Easterlies
- Periodic winds - Land and Sea breezes, Monsoons
- Local winds - Loo, Chinook, Foehn and Mistral
- Variable winds - Cyclones and Anticyclones
- Jet Streams- Meaning and importance

4. **Humidity**
   - Humidity – meaning and difference between relative and absolute humidity
   - Condensation – forms (clouds, dew, frost, fog and mist)
   - Precipitation - forms (rain, snow and hail)
   - Types of rainfall – relief/orographic, convectional, cyclonic/ frontal with examples from the different parts of the world.

POLLUTION

(a) Types - air, water (fresh and marine), soil, radiation and noise.

(b) Sources
- Noise: Traffic, factories, construction sites, loudspeakers, airports.
- Air: vehicular, industrial, burning of garbage.
- Water: domestic and industrial waste.
- Soil: chemical fertilisers, bio medical waste and pesticides.
- Radiation: X- rays; radioactive fallout from nuclear plants.

(c) Effects - on the environment and human health.

(d) Preventive Measures

Carpools, promotion of public transport, no smoking zone, restricted use of fossil fuels, saving energy and encouragement of organic farming.

NATURAL REGIONS OF THE WORLD

- Location, area, climate, natural vegetation and human adaptation.
- Equatorial region, Tropical Grasslands, Tropical Deserts, Tropical monsoon, Mediterranean, Temperate Grasslands, Taiga and Tundra.

MAP WORK

On an outline map of the World, candidates will be required to locate, mark and name the following:

1. The major Natural Regions of the world - Equatorial, Tropical Monsoon, Tropical Deserts, Mediterranean type, Tropical Grasslands, Temperate Grasslands, Taiga and Tundra.
2. The Oceans, Seas, Gulfs and Straits - all Major Oceans, Caribbean Sea, North Sea, Black Sea, Caspian Sea, South China Sea, Mediterranean Sea, Gulf of Carpentaria, Hudson Bay, Persian Gulf, Gulf of Mexico, Gulf of Guinea, Bering Strait, Strait of Gibraltar, Strait of Malacca.
3. Rivers – Mississippi, Colorado, Amazon, Paraguay, Nile, Zaire, Niger, Zambezi, Orange, Rhine, Volga, Danube, Murray, Darling, Hwang Ho, Yangtse Kiang, Ob, Indus, Ganga, Mekong, Irrawaddy, Tigris, Euphrates.
4. Mountains – Rockies, Andes, Appalachian, Alps, Himalayas, Pyrenees, Scandinavian Highlands, Caucasus, Atlas, Drakensburg, Khinghan, Zagros, Urals, Great Dividing Range.
5. Plateaus – Canadian Shield, Tibetan Plateau, Brazilian Highlands, Patagonian Plateau, Iranian Plateau, Mongolian Plateau.

CHAPTER 01

Earth as a Planet

SYLLABUS

Earth as a Planet Shape of the Earth • Earth as the home of humankind and the conditions that exist.

Our Solar System is a part of an extremely large galaxy called **the Milky Way** or **the Akash Ganga**. The Solar System consists of the planets, the satellites that revolve around the planets and other celestial bodies called asteroids, comets and meteorites.

The Earth is the third planet out of eight planets present in the Solar System revolving around the Sun which are Mercury, Venus, Earth, Mars, Jupiter, Saturn, Uranus and Neptune.

The Earth

The Earth came into existence around 4.6 billion years ago. The distance between the Sun and the Earth is about 150 million km. The Earth moves in an elliptical orbit around the Sun and the orbit of the Earth around the Sun lies between the planets Venus (Earth's twin) and Mars.

The Sun is the nearest star to the Earth. It gives a very powerful force of gravity which holds the Earth and the other planets in their fixed elliptical path (called the orbit) around the Sun.

The Earth is the densest planet in the Solar System. It is the fifth largest planet. The Earth appears to be a small greenish blue marble ball from the distant space, with its blue oceans and polar ice caps.

The Earth is also known as the **blue planet** or **watery planet** due to the presence of abundance of water on it. The surface of the Earth consists of about 71% water and 29% land.

Shape of the Earth

Earlier it was believed that the Earth is flat and one might fall if one reaches to the edge of the Earth. However, the observations by the various research scholars gave a confirmation that the Earth is **spherical** in shape.

A famous Greek philosopher, **Pythagoras** was the first one to say that the Earth is spherical in shape and rotates around the Sun on its axis. Later other philosophers like Aryabhatta, Aristotle, Varahamihira and Copernicus also pointed that the Earth is spherical in shape, but it is not a perfect sphere. It possess a shape like an orange i.e. it is bulging at the equator and slightly flattened at the poles.

It is revealed from the evidence that the diameter of the Earth varies at the equator i.e. 12,756 km and at the poles i.e. 12,714 km. The difference in diameter is due to the **centrifugal force**[1] of the Earth's rotation. The Earth rotates at a great speed that it creates bulge at the equator and a compression at the poles.

1 **Centrifugal Force** It is the apparent outward force on a mass when it rotates.

That is why, its shape is described as a **oblate spheroid** or **geoid** which means an Earth-like shape.

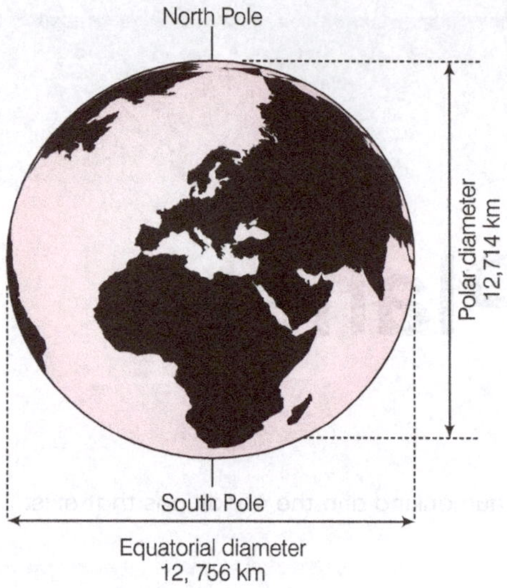

Shape of the Earth

Evidences of Spherical Shape of the Earth

- **The Spherical Shape of all the Celestial Bodies** The Sun, the Moon and the other planets in the Solar System are spherical in shape. Thus, being a part of Solar System, Earth is also believed to be spherical in shape.
- **Sunrise and Sunset** The sunrise and sunset are not always the same everywhere. If the Earth was flat, then everyone would see the sunrise and sunset at the same time. The Sun rises in the East and sets in the West. The rotation of the Earth is from West to East which is the primary reason why people in the East are able to see the Sun earlier than that of people living in the West.
- **Circumnavigation of the Earth** This evidence was given by **Magellan Ferdinand** who completed a round-the-world voyage in 1522. It proves that people travelling in different directions come back to the same point from where they started. Thus, Earth has a spherical shape.
- **Sighting of a Ship** When a person standing on the seashore watches an approaching ship, then only the upper part is visible at first. As the ship approaches nearer, rest of the parts become visible one by one. This is possible only if the shape of the Earth is curved and not flat. If the shape of the Earth was flat, then the entire ship would come in the view at once which never happens in reality. Thus, it proves that the Earth is curved in shape.
- **Circular Horizon** The **horizon**[2] looks circular whether seen from the top of a building, a mountain, a plain surface or any other place. A clear view of the Earth's surface can be captured when viewed from a height. Such a situation is only possible if the body is spherical in shape.

  As the altitude increases, the circular horizon also increase. If the Earth was flat, then the circular horizon would have been similar from every place.
- **Lunar Eclipse** It is the situation when the Sun, the Moon and the Earth are aligned, with the Earth in the middle of the Sun and the Moon. During a lunar eclipse, the shadow of the Earth falls on the Moon's surface. The shadow of Earth on the Moon appears as an arc of a circle. Thus, the circular shadow of Earth proves that the shape of the Earth is spherical.

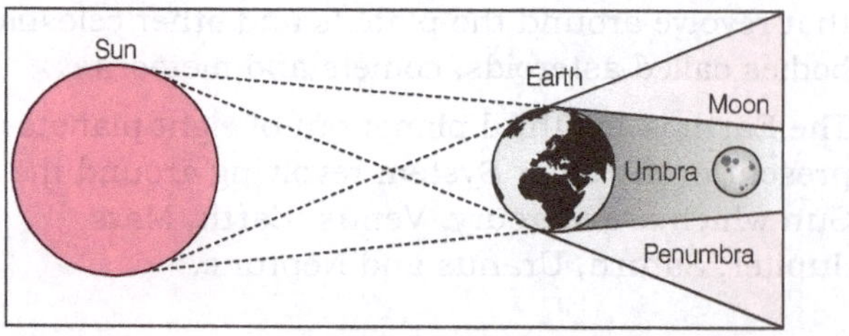

Tot al Lunar Eclipse

- **Aerial Photographs** The photographs of the Earth sent by the artificial satellites clearly shows the spherical shape of the Earth having flattened poles. **Jean Baptiste Delambre** (1749-1822), a French astronomer discovered the flattening of the Earth at the poles.
- **Pole Star** At the North Pole, the Pole Star can be seen at an angle of 90°. It lies in line with the axis of the Earth. As we move towards the equator, angle of Pole Star decreases. At the equator, the angle is 0°. This can happen only in an arc of a circle. If the Earth was flat, then the Pole Star would have the same height from all latitudes.

2 **Horizon** It refers to the line at which the Earth's surface and the sky appear to meet.

- **The Bedford Level Experiment** To identify the shape of the Earth, an experiment was carried out in England in the Bedford Level canal area. In this experiment, three poles of equal length were fixed at intervals of 5 km and had the same height above the water in the canal. When the poles were viewed from one end of the canal, the middle pole looked slightly higher.

  If the Earth had a flat surface, it could not have happened. After this, similar experiments were conducted at different places and got the same result. This experiment demonstrated that the surface of the Earth was curved.

Earth as a Unique Planet

The Earth is a unique planet due to its following features

- It is the only planet which supports life.
- It is a home to a large variety of living organisms and plants.
- It is the planet that has atmosphere which is essential for supporting life.

Check Your LEARNING...

1. Who said for the first time that the Earth is spherical in shape and rotates around the Sun on its axis?
2. During the lunar eclipse the shadow of which planet falls on the Moon's surface?
3. What is the direction of the Earth's rotation?

Earth as a Home of Humankind

Earth is considered as a home of humankind because it includes various conditions that are suitable for the existence of life, like spheres of the Earth, favourable location and temperature and life-giving cycles on the Earth. These conditions are

Spheres of the Earth

The Earth is composed of mainly three spheres which are important to sustain life on the Earth. These are

(i) Lithosphere (ii) Hydrosphere
(iii) Atmosphere

(i) Lithosphere

The solid crust of the rocks on the surface of the Earth is called lithosphere. This sphere consists of rocks named **igneous rocks**, **sedimentary rocks** and metamorphic rocks and has many layers.

Lithosphere has also a layer of soil which has been formed by weathering of rocks and other minerals. As plants and vegetation grow into the soil thus, it sustains life on the Earth.

(ii) Hydrosphere

It is the total amount of water on the Earth. The Earth contains about 71% of water on its surface in the form of oceans, seas, lakes and rivers which gives blue colour to the planet.

The temperature of the Earth is moderate because of water bodies present on it. These water bodies, especially oceans help in setting up a water circulation system known as **water cycle**[3]. This cycle maintain a proper balance between evaporation, condensation and precipitation without which life would not be possible.

The effect of water can also be seen by the fact that it absorbs enormous amount of heat without causing much change in its temperature. Water bodies absorb enormous amount of heat during day time and make the Earth fairly cool. At night, the water bodies release this heat and along with other atmospheric effects keep most of the surface from freezing at night.

(iii) Atmosphere

The Earth is surrounded by an envelop of air called atmosphere. It is a tasteless, odourless and colourless layer of gases. Air is elastic, compressible and mobile on the Earth.

The Earth's atmosphere contains life supporting gases which consist of **21% of oxygen, 78% of nitrogen** and less than **1% of carbon dioxide, argon** and **other gases** along with water vapour upto the extent of 1600 km.

The Sun is the ultimate source of energy, light and heat of the Earth. The Earth's atmosphere receives heat in the form of solar radiation and loses heat by the terrestrial radiation. Thus, this process maintains a **balance of heat** on the Earth and keeps it

3 **Water Cycle** It is a natural phenomenon in which water from seas, rivers and lakes evaporates into the atmosphere where it condenses and falls back as precipitation.

warm which is important for sustaining life on the Earth. Also, the Ozone present in the atmosphere absorbs the harmful ultraviolet rays of the Sun.

Biosphere

Biosphere is the life zone of the Earth which has an interaction between the atmosphere, lithosphere and hydrosphere. Biosphere provides all the necessities for all the species living on Earth, i.e. light, heat, water, food and habitat.

Biosphere consists of a thin layer of around 15 km from the deepest ocean trench to the highest mountain peak. It extends to a depth of just 3 m below the ground and about 200 m deep in ocean waters which consists both marine and freshwater life.

Biosphere is a network of all interrelated ecosystems found on and below the Earth's surface. In biosphere, life develops, transformed and exchange energy within and between different ecosystems. Within the biosphere, life is found chiefly in two forms i.e. the plant kingdom and the animal kingdom.

Favourable Location and Temperature

The Earth lies between the orbits of the Venus and the Mars. It is located at an optimum distance from the Sun of about 150 million km. Thus, it is neither too hot nor too cold and this makes life possible on the Earth.

The average temperature on Earth's surface is about 17°C on the side that faces towards the Sun which is favourable temperature for the living organisms. The other two terrestrial planets i.e. Mercury and Venus are very hot while the remaining planets are very cold.

The rotation of the Earth on its axis helps in maintaining temperature between day and night. Due to constant rotation of Earth, no region remains constantly in sunlight. This helps in maintaining temperature of the Earth.

Life-Giving Cycles on the Earth

There are different life-giving cycles which help to sustain life on the Earth. These are

Nutrition Cycle

This is an important cycle which shows the interdependence of all living things on the Earth. Nutrient cycle is operated through the food chain and other processes like photosynthesis, transpiration, respiration, etc. In this cycle, living things are divided into producers, consumers and decomposers.

Plants are the primary producers which produce food through photosynthesis. Energy originates from primary producers. Then there are other levels of consumers like herbivores and carnivores. These depend on the producers for their life.

The energy flows from primary producers to herbivorous and from herbivorous to carnivorous. After this, all living beings undergo decomposition by the action of decomposers. Man is at the top of this cycle who can modify his own environment and create changes in the levels of the food chain.

Carbon Cycle

The cyclic movement of carbon from the atmosphere to the organisms and from organisms to the atmosphere is known as carbon cycle. This cycle maintains carbon balance on the Earth and if this balance disturbs, it may lead to Global Warming.

Carbon is the basic raw material of all life forms on the Earth. It is present in all living beings. Plants use atmospheric Carbon Dioxide (CO_2) in the presence of sunlight and chlorophyll to make food by the process of photosynthesis. From plants, carbon moves from one level to another level of food chain.

Plants and consumers get decomposed after their death by the decomposers like bacteria and fungi. This results in the formation of fossil fuels containing huge amounts of carbon. During the process of respiration, all living beings use atmospheric oxygen and release carbon dioxide back into the atmosphere.

CO_2 is also released in the atmosphere by the burning of fossil fuels. In this way, carbon from CO_2 taken by plants from the environment through photosynthesis is returned to the environment by different processes like respiration, decomposition and burning of fossil fuels.

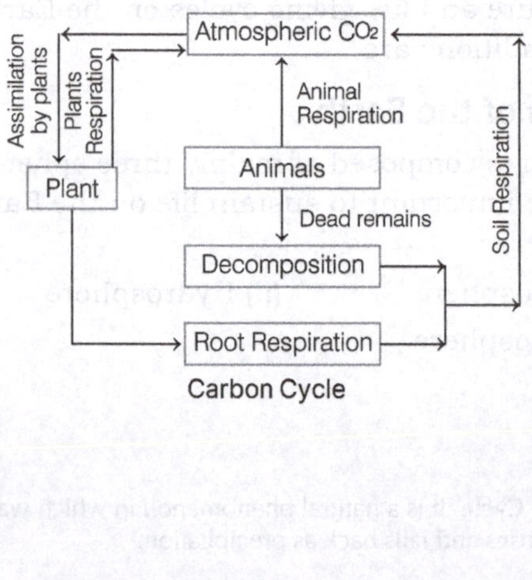

Carbon Cycle

Nitrogen Cycle

Earth's atmosphere has around 78% of nitrogen gas. Plants take nitrogen in the form of nitrates from the soil. Then, it moves from one level to another level of the food chain. After that, nitrogen returns to the soil through manure, excreta and earthly remains of plants, animals and micro-organisms.

Oxygen Cycle

Oxygen is a life giving gas in the atmosphere as all living beings depend on it. It is used to release energy from the food that living beings eat. It is also used together with carbon, hydrogen and nitrogen to build new molecules in the body. The green plants release oxygen into the atmosphere during photosynthesis by using carbon dioxide released by animals and humans.

Check Your LEARNING...

1. What proportion of Earth's surface is covered with water?
2. With which two elements the lithosphere's crust has been formed?
3. What is the percentage of oxygen in the Earth's atmosphere?
4. Which is the lowest layer of the atmosphere?

QUiCK Revision

- Sun is a star and belongs to the 'Milky Way or Akash Ganga Galaxy'.
- Earth is the fifth largest planet and the third planet from the Sun.
- Earth is called 'a living planet', as it is the only planet supporting life on it.
- Earth is also known as 'blue planet' or 'watery planet' due to the presence of 71% of water on its surface.
- Greek philosopher Pythagoras was the first one to say that the Earth is spherical in shape and rotates around the Sun on its axis.
- The spherical shape of the Earth is supported by the proofs like shape of all terrestrial bodies, sunrise and sunset, circumnavigation of the Earth, sighting of a ship, circular horizon increases with increase in altitude, location of Pole Star in the universe, lunar eclipse and satellite photographs.
- Earth is the unique planet in the solar system which supports the life. Atmosphere, hydrosphere and Lithosphere of Earth are formed in such a manner that it supports the life.
- The realms of the Earth made life possible on the Earth such as Biosphere. It is the narrow zone of contact between land, water and air where life exists. The biosphere is divided into the planet and animal kingdom.
- The Earth is located at an optimum distance from the Sun of about 150 million km.
- There are many life-giving cycles which help to sustain life on the Earth such as nutrition cycle, carbon cycle, nitrogen cycle and oxygen cycle.

Chapter Practice

Section-I

Multiple Choice Questions

1. Sun is an example of which of the following?
   (a) Planet (b) Satellite
   (c) Star (d) None of these

Ans. (c) Star

2. Which planet is considered as 'Earth's Twin'?
   (a) Venus (b) Mars (c) Jupiter (d) Uranus

Ans. (a) Venus

3. If the Earth were flat, the Pole Star would have the same .... for all latitudes.
   (a) size (b) position (c) shape (d) height

Ans. (d) height

4. The fixed path in which the planets move around the Sun is called ....
   (a) orbit (b) annular ring
   (c) circular path (d) None of these

Ans. (a) orbit

5. Intrusive and extrusive rocks are types of .... rocks.
   (a) igneous (b) sedimentary
   (c) metamorphic (d) None of these

Ans. (a) igneous

6. The three layers of the Earth from the surface to the centre constitute the ....
   (a) interior (b) crust (c) core (d) seal

Ans. (a) Interior

7. Coal, natural gas and petroleum are examples of
   (a) fossils fuel (b) mineral
   (c) gas (d) rock

Ans. (a) fossils fuel

8. Which of the following is the proof to find out the spherical shape of the Earth?
   (i) Sunrise and Sunset
   (ii) Circumnavigation of the Earth
   (iii) Sighting of a ship

   Codes
   (a) Only (i) (b) Only (iii)
   (c) Only (iii) (d) All of these

Ans. (d) All of these

9. Give reason for the following.
   The Earth is called a unique planet.
   (a) The Earth is neither too hot nor too cold
   (b) Presence of water
   (c) Presence of oxygen
   (d) All of the above

Ans. (d) All of the above

10. Give reason for the following.
    The Earth is a habitable place.
    (a) It has hydrosphere
    (b) It has lithosphere
    (c) It has atmosphere
    (d) All of the above

Ans. (d) All of the above

11. Give reason for the following.
    The temperature of the Earth is moderate.
    (a) The Earth is located close to the Sun
    (b) The Earth is inclined on its axis.
    (c) The Earth has water on it.
    (d) None of the above

Ans. (c) The Earth has water on it.

12. Give reason for the following.
    In stratosphere the temperature increases with height.
    (a) It is the third layer of the atmosphere.
    (b) It has ozone layer which absorbs UV rays of the Sun.
    (c) All weather phenomena happen in this layer.
    (d) All of the above

Ans. (b) It has ozone layer which absorbs UV rays of the Sun.

13. Which of the following statements is incorrect?
    (i) The horizon looks flat whether seen from the top of a building or mountain.
    (ii) Lunar eclipse is the situation when Sun comes between Earth and Moon.
    (iii) The shadow of the Earth on the Moon appears as a triangular.

    Codes
    (a) Only (i) (b) Only (ii)
    (c) Only (iii) (d) All of these

Ans. (d) All of these

14. Match the following.

List-I	List-II
A. Ozone layer	1. Troposphere
B. Weather phenomena	2. Stratosphere
C. Ionosphere	3. Presence of helium
D. Exosphere	4. Thermosphere

Codes

	A	B	C	D		A	B	C	D
(a)	1	2	3	4	(b)	2	1	4	3
(c)	3	4	1	2	(d)	4	3	2	1

Ans. (b)

15. Match the following.

	List-I		List-II
A.	Troposphere	1.	Second layer of the atmosphere
B.	Stratosphere	2.	Lowest layer of the atmosphere
C.	Mesosphere	3.	Fourth layer of the atmosphere
D.	Thermosphere	4.	Third layer of the atmosphere

Codes

	A	B	C	D		A	B	C	D
(a)	1	2	3	4	(b)	1	2	3	4
(c)	3	4	1	2	(d)	4	3	2	1

Ans. (c)

Section-II

Short Questions

1. What do you mean by Solar System?

Ans. The clusters of stars together with the planets and other heavenly bodies form the Solar System.

2. Where is the position of the Earth in reference to the Sun?

Ans. The position of the Earth in reference to the Sun is between Venus and Mars. The distance between the Sun and the Earth is about 150 million km.

3. Why is Earth known as a watery planet?

Ans. Earth is known as blue planet or watery planet due to the presence of 71% of water on its surface out of which, only 3% of water on the Earth is fresh water suitable for drinking.

4. Name the nearest star from the Earth. Why it is important for the Earth?

Ans. The nearest star from the Earth is the Sun.

It is important for the Earth because it is the main source of energy on the Earth.

5. What are the various sources of water on the Earth?

Ans. The various sources of water on the Earth comprises of water in the oceans, water in the frozen ice caps and glaciers, water vapour in the air and water in lakes, rivers and ponds.

6. Why Earth appears to be blue in colour?

Ans. The Earth appears to be blue in colour due to the presence of abundance of water on the Earth. Earth consists of about 71% of water.

7. Answer the following questions.
   (i) In which galaxy is the Solar System located?
   (ii) What is the reason for fixation of planets in the Solar System?

Ans. (i) The Solar System is located in the Milky Way Galaxy or the Akash Ganga.

(ii) The reason for fixation of planets in the Solar System is the gravitational force of the Sun which holds the planets in their fixed elliptical paths.

8. What do you mean by antipodal arrangement of Earth?

Ans. The antipodal arrangement means that the continents and oceans are roughly arranged in such a way that land on one side of the globe is balanced by water on the opposite side of the globe.

9. Answer the following questions.
   (i) Define the term lithosphere.
   (ii) This sphere consists of which rocks?

Ans. (i) The solid crust of the rocks on the surface of the Earth is called lithosphere.

(ii) Lithosphere consists of rocks named igneous rock, sedimentary rocks and metamorphic rocks.

10. What is the density of first 20 km of the Earth's crust?

Ans. Lithosphere is the first layer of the Earth's crust which is composed of Silicon and Aluminium. The density of the Earth's crust is about 2.7 g/cm^3.

11. Define the term hydrosphere.

Ans. The word 'Hydros' means 'water' and 'sphere' means area. Hydrosphere includes the vast oceans that cover about 71 % of the Earth's surface. Fish and other organisms are rich source of food from hydrosphere.

12. Define the term atmosphere.

Ans. The Earth is surrounded by an envelop of air which is called atmosphere. It is a tasteless, odourless and colourless layer of gases. Air is elastic, compressible and mobile on the Earth.

13. What are the contents of Earth's atmosphere?

Ans. The Earth contains gases like oxygen, nitrogen with the traces of carbon dioxide, argon and other gases along with water vapour.

14. Answer the following questions.
   (i) Which layer of the atmosphere contains ozone layer?
   (ii) What is the other name of this layer?

Ans. (i) Stratosphere is the layer of atmosphere which contains ozone layer.

(ii) Stratosphere is also called 'the zone of uniform temperature'.

15. Answer the following questions.
   (i) What do you mean by realms of the Earth?
   (ii) Which sphere they form?

Ans. (i) The Earth is composed of the lithosphere, hydrosphere and atmosphere. They are called 'the realms of the Earth'.

(ii) Lithosphere, hydrosphere and atmosphere combine together to form the Biosphere.

16. How is the word biosphere formed?

Ans. The word biosphere has been formed by the Greek word 'bios' means life and the Latin word 'sphaera' means total range.

17. How is life found in the biosphere?

Ans. Life is found as plant kingdom or animal kingdom in the biosphere. The biosphere extends from the deepest root systems of trees to the dark environment of ocean.

Long Questions

1. Explain the following.

(i) The spherical shape of all the celestial bodies.

(ii) Circumnavigation of the Earth.

(iii) Sighting of a ship.

Ans. (i) The Sun, the Moon and the other planets of the Solar System are spherical in shape.
Since Earth also belongs to the same Solar System, it should also be spherical. Thus, Earth is also believed to be spherical in shape without being an exception.

(ii) Circumnavigation of the Earth means to go around the Earth. It is a proof that the Earth is spherical in shape as people travelling in different directions come back to the same point from where they started. This proof was given by Magellan Ferdinand's round-the-world expedition. Magellan with his ship called Victoria, completed his round-to-the-world expedition and came back to the same point from where he started.

(iii) Refer chapter theory page no. 2.

2. How Pole Star and aerial photographs provide proofs that the Earth has spherical shape?

Ans. The proofs provided by Pole Star and aerial photographs are

- **Pole Star** The Pole Star is visible from the North pole at an angle of 90°. It lies approximately aligned with the Earth's axis of rotation. The angle of the Pole Star decreases on moving towards the equator. On reaching the equator, its angle becomes 0°. Such situation happens only in an arc of a circle. Thus, proving that Earth has a spherical shape.
- **Aerial Photographs** Photographs of the Earth sent by the artificial satellites clearly show the spherical shape of the Earth having flattened poles.

3. Give any three proofs of the spherical shape of the Earth.

Ans. Refer to chapter theory page no. 2.

4. Explain the oblate spheroid shape of the Earth.

Ans. Oblate spheroid shape means the Earth is slightly flattened at the poles and has a bulge at the Equator. Although the Earth appears to be spherical, but after the measurement of the size of the Earth, it is said to have an oblate spheroid shape.
The slight bulge at the Equator of the Earth is due to the tremendous rotation speed of the Earth. Since the Earth possesses a spherical shape, the force of gravity at all the places is almost equal.

5. Why is Earth known as a 'unique planet'?

Ans. Earth is known as a 'unique planet' due to following reasons

- It is the only planet where life exists.
- Due to its appropriate distance from the Sun, the Earth has a favourable temperature of 18-20°C.
- It is the only planet having abundance of water on it which is necessary for the human survival.
- It has a biosphere that provides us with food, shelter, clothing and minerals.
- There is absence of poisonous gases and it has an oxygen rich environment.
- The presence of atmosphere acts as a blanket protecting the Earth from extreme temperatures.

6. Explain the planetary relations of the Earth.

Ans. Earth being a unique planet maintains a special relationship with the Sun and the Moon in the Solar System. The Earth revolves around the Sun and the Moon revolves around the Earth.
The rotation of the Earth on its axis causes day and night, the changes in the seasons, the changes in the tides, etc. Since the Earth keeps on rotating and only half of the Earth is able to receive the rays of the Sun at any point of time which is causing day, the rest half remains in darkness causing night.

7. Explain about the favourable location and temperature of the Earth.

Ans. The Earth lies between the orbits of the Venus and the Mars. It is located at an optimum distance from the Sun of about 150 million km. Thus, it is neither too hot as Venus nor too cold as the outer planets.
The average temperature on Earth's surface is about 17°C on the side that faces towards the Sun which is favourable temperature for the living organisms. The rotation of the Earth on its axis helps in maintaining temperature between day and night.

8. Briefly explain the following.

(i) Hydrosphere (ii) Lithosphere (iii) Atmosphere

Ans. (i) **Hydrosphere** It is the total amount of water on the Earth. More than 71% of the Earth's surface is occupied by water and is present in the oceans, rivers, lakes, ice on glaciers, underground water and water vapour in the air.

(ii) **Lithosphere** It is the solid part of the Earth that forms the outermost layer of the Earth. It is mainly made up of rocks and thin layers of soil that provides support to the living organisms.

(iii) **Atmosphere** It is the layer of gases surrounding the Earth. The Earth's Atmosphere contains life supporting gases which consist of 21% of oxygen, 78% of nitrogen and less than 1% of carbon dioxide, argon and other gases along with water vapour upto the extent of 1600 km.

9. Briefly discuss about the spheres of the atmosphere.

Ans. Refer to chapter theory page no. 3-4.

Chapter Assessment

Section-I

Multiple Choice Questions

1. The Pole Star can be seen at an angle of ...... degrees at the North Pole.
   (a) 70 (b) 80
   (c) 90 (d) 110
2. The shape of the Earth is a/an ....
   (a) oblate spheroid (b) geoid
   (c) complete sphere (d) Both (a) and (b)
3. The diameter of the Earth at the equator is
   (a) 12,756 km (b) 13432 km
   (c) 16000 km (d) 21034 km
4. The burning of fossil fuels also releases which gas in the atmosphere?
   (a) CO_2 (b) Nitrogen
   (c) Oxygen (d) Argon

Section-II

Short Questions

1. Which powerful force holds the planets into its orbit?
2. What is essential for the existence of life on the Earth?
3. The Aurora Borealis is visible in which part of the Earth?
4. Define geoid.
5. Differentiate between troposphere and ionosphere.
6. Give reasons.
   (i) Earth is called a living planet.
   (ii) Earth is a watery planet.
   (iii) Ionosphere is important for communications.

Long Questions

1. Give one word for the following.
   (i) Earth-like planet (ii) The living components on Earth
   (iii) Sphere of water
2. Explain the following.
   (i) Stratosphere (ii) Exosphere
3. What do you understand by lunar eclipse? Explain.

CHAPTER 02

Geographic Grid : Latitudes and Longitudes

SYLLABUS

Geographic grid - Latitudes & Longitudes • Concept of latitudes : main latitudes, their location with degrees, parallels of latitude and their uses. • Concept of longitudes : Prime Meridian, time (local, standard and time zones, Greenwich Mean Time (GMT) and International Date Line (IDL). • Eastern and Western hemisphere. • Using latitudes and longitudes to find location. • Calculation of time. • Great Circles and their use.

Geographic Grid

It is a system designed to depict any location on Earth by laying a horizontal and vertical grid over the Earth's layout. It is a matrix that shows intersection of horizontal and vertical lines by using two co-ordinates i.e. latitude and longitude.

The horizontal lines which run East to West and are parallel to the equator are called **latitudes** and the vertical lines which run North to South passing through the poles are called **longitudes**. The point at which these lines intersect is the exact location of a place on the Earth.

In the 3rd century BCE, **Eratosthenes**, a Greek philosopher, was the first who proposed a system of latitude and longitude for a map of the world. He calculated the circumference of the Earth. The grid on the globe works in the similar way as x-axis and y-axis are used on a graph. Thus, x-axis represents latitude and y-axis represents longitude.

Lines of Latitude

These are the imaginary lines that can be defined as the angular distance of a place located on the North or South of the equator.

These are measured as an angle whose apex is at the center of the Earth i.e. on the equatorial plane. Some characteristic features of the latitudes are

- The lines of latitude run from East to West dividing the Earth into two equal halves at the Equator.
- These lines join all places having the same latitude towards North and South of Equator.
- The latitudes are also calculated with reference to the Zenith Distance. Zenith is the point directly (vertically) above a particular location. Zenith distance is the angular distance between the Zenith and arc of a vertical circle that is perpendicular to the horizon.
- Latitude can also be found by measuring the vertical angle of the pole star from a point.
- There are total 180 parallel lines of latitude located at an angular distance of 1°. Of this, 90 are located in the Northern hemisphere and 90 are located in the Southern hemisphere.
- The latitudes form circles on the globe as each latitude is a full circle, but only Equator is the Great Circle.
- The radius of the latitudes is maximum at the Equator and reduces on moving towards the poles.

- In each hemisphere at 60° latitude, the length of the circle is half the length of the Equator and at poles, these lines are merely dotted.
- The distance between each latitude is approximately 111 km. This approximate value is calculated by dividing the circumference of Earth (i.e. approx 40000 kms by 360° (40000/360 = 111 km).
- The latitudes are expressed in degrees, minutes and seconds. This is used for determining the exact location more precisely. Earth as a whole represents 360°. Each degree is split into 60 parts, each part is being 1/60 of a degree. These parts are called **minutes**. Each minute is split into 60 parts, each part is being 1/60 of a minute. These parts are called **seconds**. For example, 40°20' 50" means 40 degrees, 20 minutes and 50 seconds.

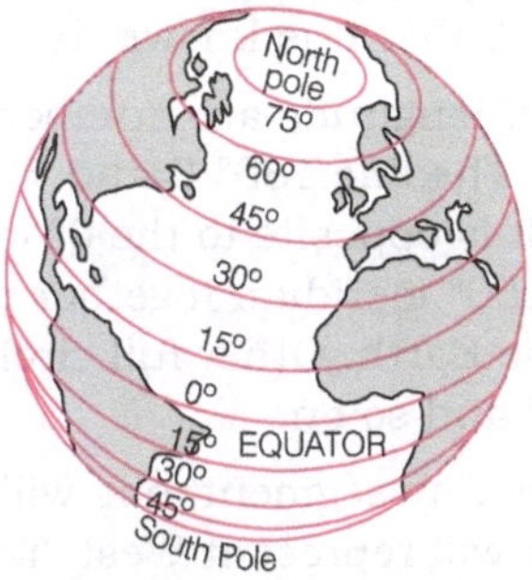

Lines of Latitude

Parallels of Latitude

As the latitudes run parallel to each other and to the Equator they are collectively called parallels of latitude. There are 180 parallels of latitudes at 1° interval, of which the main parallels of a latitude are

The Arctic Circle

It is located at approximately 66.5° North latitude or North of the Equator. This circle of latitude stretches through eight countries, which includes the United States of America, Canada, Greenland, Iceland, Norway, Sweden, Finland and Russia.

The Arctic Circle marks the beginning area where the Sun does not rises during winter season and not sets during summer season. It also marks the polar region surrounding the North pole.

The Tropic of Cancer

It is located at approximately 23.5° North latitude or North of the Equator. This line of latitude is the Northern boundary of the area referred to as the 'tropics' or tropical zone.

During the summer season, the Sun is located immediately above the Tropic of Cancer at noon on **21st June** and make it the longest day in the Northern hemisphere.

Tropic of Cancer passes through countries like Algeria, Niger, Libya, Egypt, Saudi Arabia, UAE, India, Bangladesh, Myanmar, China, etc.

The Equator

It is located at 0° latitude. It is an imaginary line on the Earth's surface that is equidistant from the North pole and South pole, dividing the Earth into the Northern hemisphere and Southern hemisphere.

These hemispheres are located opposite to each other. The seasons on the Earth are opposite in the Northern and Southern hemisphere.

The Equator has the same length as the circumference of the Earth. The approximate distance between a pole and the Equator is almost 1/4th of the total circumference of the Earth i.e. about 10000 km.

The Tropic of Capricorn

It is located at approximately 23.5° South latitude or South of the Equator. This line of latitude is the Southern boundary of the area referred as the tropics. This line marks the point farthest to the South at which the Sun is directly upward in the sky at noon.

22nd December in the winter day marks the longest day in the Southern hemisphere. Tropic of Capricon passes through countries like Argentina, Australia, Botswana, Brazil, Chile, Madagascar, Mozombique, Namibia, Paraguay, etc.

The Antarctic Circle

It is located at approximately 66.5° South latitude or South of the Equator. This line or circle of latitude marks the starting point of the Southern area known as the Antarctic. The circle consists of only one continent, Antarctica. There is no permanent residence found in Antarctica.

North and South Pole

Northpole is located at an angular distance of 90° North of the Equator. The North pole is at the Northernmost point of the Earth. The area around it is very cold. South pole is located at an angular distance of 90° South of the Equator.

The South pole is at the Southernmost point on the Earth. The area around it is very cold.

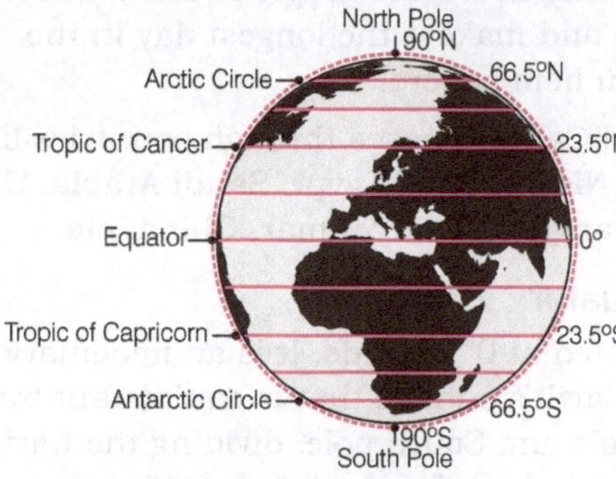

Parallels of Latitude

Check Your LEARNING...

1. What are the lines of latitude?
2. What is the angle of latitude at the Equator?
3. What is the length of the Equator?
4. Name two countries, through which Tropic of Capricorn passes.

Lines of Longitude

Longitude is defined as the angular distance of a place, from East or West of the **Prime Meridian**. Prime Meridian is used for locating the places in the East and West directions of the Earth.

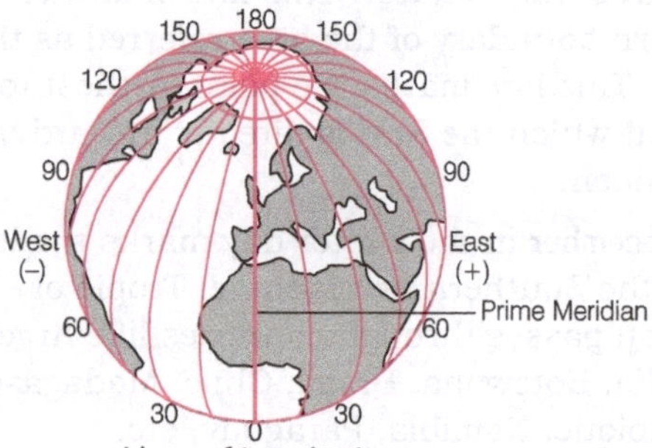

Lines of Longitude

Prime Meridian

It is a meridian (a line of longitude) in a geographical co-ordinate system at which longitude is defined to be 0°. It passes through the Old Royal Observatory at Greenwich in London and thus, it is known as **Greenwich Meridian.**

The lines of longitude in the East of Prime Meridian are denoted as °E and those to the West are denoted as °W. There are total 360 lines of longitude each at an angle of 1°.

Eastern and Western Hemisphere

The Prime Meridian divides the Earth into the Eastern and Western hemispheres. The Eastern and Western hemispheres are geographical terms which are used for half of the Earth that is East of the Prime Meridian (Eastern hemisphere) and West of the Prime Meridian (Western hemisphere).

Continents like Europe, Asia, Africa and Australia lie in the Eastern Hemisphere, whereas North and South America lie in the Western hemisphere.

Meridians of Longitude

The lines of longitude are known as **meridians of longitude**. The term meridian is derived from the Latin word 'meridianum' meaning noon. As the Sun passes through the meridian at noon, all the places lying on the particular meridian will have noon at the same time.

All the meridians of longitude intersect or join at two places i.e. North and South pole. All longitudes are semicircle and equal in length. Two longitudes make a full circle i.e. 360°. It is known as Great Circle.

All meridians of longitude are numbered between 0° to 180°E or W. The line 180° E and W is the same meridian and it is opposite to the 0° longitude. Thus, 0° and 180° meridian together make a full circle round the Earth. Other full circles will be 1° - 179°, 2° - 178° and so on.

The two lines in any segment, one will represent the East and other will represent West. The sum of two lines will always be 180°. There is maximum distance between two longitudes at the equator i.e. 111 km which decreases towards poles.

Time Zones

A time zone is a geographical area which observes a uniform standard time. It refers to any of 24 regions divided by Prime Meridian (0° longitude) where the same standard time has been adopted. Each meridian of longitude shows a particular time zone on Earth.

Each time zone is 15° of longitude wide (with local variations) and the local time is one hour earlier than the zone immediately to the East on the map. The time for a whole zone can be determined by taking the central meridian as the base.

The Earth has been divided into 24 time zones according to the number of hours in a day. Due to vast East to West longitudinal extent, many countries have more than one time zones, e.g. Russia and USA have 11 time zones, Australia has 8 time zones, Canada has 6 time zones, etc. France has the maximum time zones in the world i.e. 12 time zones because it has several overseas territories.

Local Time

Local time of any place can be identified when Sun is overhead at noon. When it is 12 noon at longitude, all the place on that longitude will have the same time. Each place at a different longitude has its own local time.

As the Earth rotates on its axis, it covers 360° longitudes in 24 hours. Therefore, it covers 15° longitudes in an hour. The difference in the time is of 4 minutes between each longitude. Thus, if it is 12 noon at 0° longitude, it will be 4 minutes past 12 at the longitude 1° to the East.

Each hour has 60 minutes. So, it can be stated that at 15° E longitude, the time will be 1 PM and as one move from 0° to 15° W, the time will be one hour less than 12 PM, as the Earth rotates from West towards the East.

This can be memorised by the EGA-WLS formula, where EGA stands for **East Gain Add** and WLS stands **West Lose Subtract**. So, each 1° longitude towards East will gain 4 minutes and each 1° longitude towards West will lose 4 minutes.

For example, the longitude of Patna is 85° E and that of Delhi is 77" E. If it is 12 noon at Delhi, it must be 32 minutes past 12 noon at Patna at the same time. As 85° E - 77" E= 8° longitude difference, thus 1° longitude = 4 minutes and 8° longitude = 32 minutes which is to be added as Patna lies to the East of Delhi.

Greenwich Mean Time

Greenwich Mean Time (GMT) or Prime Meridian (0° meridian) is the mean solar time which passes through the Royal Observatory in Greenwich, London. It is the starting point for dividing the Earth's surface into time zones.

GMT was formerly used as the International Civil Time Standard. The GMT is followed as the base international time by all of the countries since 1884.

Indian Standard Time

The uniform time based on a central meridian is called the standard time. The standard time is needed as it will be difficult to maintain railway and flight timings. This is because different locations have different local time, so each country adopts a time that becomes the standard time throughout the country.

Majority of countries adopt their standard time from their central meridian. For example, India has accepted the meridian of 82.5° E for calculating their standard time, which passes through Mirzapur near Allahabad.

This meridian is 5 hours 30 minutes ahead of GMT. The other two countries that have adopted the same meridian are Nepal and Sri Lanka. It is necessary that the standard time is always divisible by $7\frac{1}{2}°$ or 15°.

International Date Line

It is an imaginary line of longitude which passes through the Pacific Ocean on the Earth's surface located at about 180° East or West of the Greenwich Meridian.

If one count up longitudes to 180° to the East or West from the Prime Meridian, the longitude of 180° West and 180° East will be same line. So, 180° longitude is called neither East nor West as it is both. Thus, it has been selected for counting dates on the globe and is known as International Date Line (IDL).

In order to remove the confusion of the different dates within a same country, the International Date Line bends and goes zig-zag at the Bering Strait between Siberia and Alaska and at Fiji, Tonga, New Zealand and some other islands. On crossing the International Date Line from East to West, a day is added, whereas on crossing the International Date Line from West to East, a day is subtracted.

This happens due to the time difference of 12 hours (180° 4 mins) from either side of the meridian. Thus, when moving from East to West direction, 12 hours are added and while moving from the West to East direction, 12 hours are subtracted.

For example, when a person is travelling from United States to Japan, he/she is travelling in East of International Date Line towards the West. Thus, if he/she start travelling on a Wednesday, the day would immediately change to Thursday as soon as he/she crosses the International Date Line.

Uses of Latitude and Longitude

Locating Places on the Earth and Measuring Distance

With the help of both latitude and longitude one can find accurate location of any place, e.g. Delhi can be anywhere between 28° 64' N latitude. But the exact location of Delhi can be located at the point where this latitude intersects the longitude at 77° 21' E.

The distance of the places are calculated with reference to the Equator at right angle to the place, e.g. the latitude of Delhi is 28.44° North (approximately). As we know, 1° latitude = 111 km. Thus, the distance of New Delhi from equator can be calculated as 28.44 × 111 = 3156.84 km.

Measuring Climatic Conditions of a Location

Latitudes also help in estimating the temperature or climate of a particular place. The latitudes divide the Earth into three different **heat zones** based on the sunlight received by each zone. These are

(i) **Frigid Zone** The frigid climate zones include the areas within the Arctic and Antarctic circles, extending from 66.5° North and South latitude to the poles, respectively. They are characterised by a short, cool summer and long bitterly cold winter, as these regions receive the extreme slanting Sun rays particularly during the winter months.

The North frigid zone lies in the North of the Arctic Circle and South frigid zone lies in the South of the Antarctic Circle. Each frigid zone covers 4.12% of the Earth's surface.

(ii) **Temperate Zone** The temperate climate zone falls between 23.5° and 66.5° North and South latitudes. Temperate climate zones experience warm to hot summers and cool winters, with great temperature variations throughout the year. These zones are neither too hot nor too cold.

The four annual seasons i.e. spring, summer, autumn and winter occur in these zones. The North temperate zone lies between the Arctic Circle and the Tropic of Cancer and South temperate zone lies between the Tropic of Capricorn and the Antarctic Circle. Each of the temperate zone in North and South covers 25.99% of Earth's surface.

(iii) **Tropical or Torrid Zone** The torrid climate zone stretches from the Tropic of Cancer at 23.5° North latitude to the Tropic of Capricorn at 23.5° South latitude, with the Equator centered within this zone. These latitudes mark the Northern and Southern extremes in which the sun seasonally passes directly overhead.

This zone receives direct rays of the Sun throughout the year thus, it is the hottest zone of the Earth. Summers are long and humid and winters are short and warm.

This zone covers 39.78% of the Earth's surface.

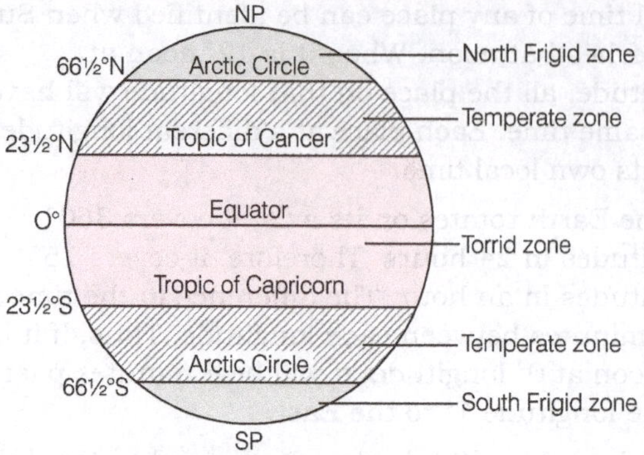

Heat Zones of the Earth

Calculation of Time

The longitude also helps in the calculation of time of a place as towards East of GMT, 4 minutes will be added on each degree of longitude and towards West of GMT, 4 minutes will be subtracted. This can be understood through the following examples.

Example 1 Calculate the time of 40° E when it is noon at GMT.

As, 1° = 4 minutes

Then, 40° = 40 × 4 = 160 minutes

or 2 hours 40 minutes.

As, 40° E is East of GMT,

So, 2 hours 40 minutes are added to 12 noon.

∴ It is 2:40 pm on 40° E longitude.

Example 2 Calculate the time of New York, if it is 8 pm on GMT.

New York is located 74° W longitude

As, 1° = 4 minutes

Then, 74° = 74 × 4 = 296 minutes

or 4 hours 56 minutes.

As New York is West of GMT and it is 8 pm on GMT

Then, the time is subtracted.

8 – 4 hours 56 minutes

∴ It is 3 : 04 pm in New York.

Great Circles

A great circle is the largest possible circle that can be drawn around a sphere. It is on the center of a sphere. The great circles represent the shortest distance between two points anywhere on the Earth's surface. Because of this, great circles have been important in navigation for hundreds of years, but their presence was discovered by ancient mathematicians.

All the meridians of longitude on Earth are great circles. Meridians including the Prime Meridian, are the North-South lines, use to describe exactly where we are on the Earth. All these lines of longitude meet at the poles, cutting the Earth nearly in half.

Among parallels of latitudes, the Equator is the only great circle of the Earth as if the Earth is cut right on its Equator, it will get divided into two equal halves. However, rest of the parallel of latitudes are small circles as they do not divide the Earth into two equal halves. A small circle has its own centre other than the centre of the globe and its radius is shorter than the radius of the globe.

Uses of Great Circles

- In geography, the use of great circles is for navigation because they represent the shortest distance between two points on a sphere.
- It is very economical to use great circle routes as they save time as well as fuel.
- Except frigid zones i.e. Arctic and Antarctic regions, sailors use great circle routes for safe navigation through seas.
- Great Circle routes are used especially for places having opposite locations. For example, routes between ports across the Pacific Ocean, the Atlantic Ocean and the Indian Ocean.
- These routes are also used in meteorology to determine climate and weather forecast of a place.

Check Your LEARNING...

1. Which longitude is known as Prime Meridian?
2. How much time is taken by the Earth when it rotates on its axis to cover 360° longitudes?
3. Which standard meridian has been accepted by the Indian Government?
4. Mention any one use of great circles.

QUiCK Revision

- The grid system has been developed for locating places on the Earth.
- The two co-ordinates of the geographical grid are longitude and latitude.
- The vertical lines on the globe are called longitude and the horizontal lines are called the latitude.
- The lines of latitude are the imaginary lines that can be defined as the angular distance of a place located on the North or South of the equator.
- The main latitudes on the globe are Arctic circle, Tropic of Cancer, Equator, Tropic of Capricorn, Antarctic circle, North pole and South Pole.
- The Arctic Circle is located at approximately 66.5° North latitude or North of the Equator.
- The Tropic of Cancer is located at approximately 23.5° North latitude or North of the Equator.
- The Equator of the Earth (0° latitude) is an imaginary line on the Earth's surface, dividing the Earth into the Northern hemisphere and Southern hemisphere.
- The Tropic of Capricorn is located at approximately 23.5° South latitude or south of the Equator.
- Antarctic is the line or circle of latitude which marks the starting point of the southern area.
- Northpole and Southpole is located at an angular distance of 90° North and South of the Equator respectively.
- The Prime Meridian passes through the Old Royal Observatory at Greenwich near London and thus, it is also known as Greenwich Meridian. It is taken as standard time for London.
- There are total 360 lines of longitude each at an angle of 1°. These lines are also known as meridians of longitude.
- The Prime Meridian and the 180° longitude divide the Earth into two hemispheres i.e. the Eastern hemisphere and the Western hemisphere.
- A time zone refers to any of 24 regions divided by longitudes where the same standard time has been adopted.
- The uniform time based on a central meridian is called the standard time.
- India has accepted the meridian of 82.5° E for calculating their standard time. This meridian is 5 hours 30 minutes ahead of GMT.
- The International Date Line (IDL) is an imaginary line of longitude passes through the Pacific ocean on the earth's surface located at about 180° East or West of the Greenwich Meridian.
- With the help of latitude and longitude one can find accurate location of any place.
- On the basis of sunlight received by each zone, latitudes divides the Earth into three different heat zones i.e. frigid zone, temperate zone and tropical or torrid zone.
- Longitude helps in the calculation of time of a place as toward East of GMT 4 minutes will be added on each degree of longitude.
- A great circle is the largest possible circle that can be drawn around a sphere. Equator is the only latitude that forms great circle while all the meridians of longitude form great circles.

Chapter Practice

Section-I

Multiple Choice Questions

1. What is the name of the imaginary line which runs on the globe and divides it into two equal parts?
(a) Pole (b) Axis
(c) Equator (d) None of these

Ans. (c) Equator

2. Who proposed the system of latitudes and longitudes on the world map for the first time?
(a) Plato (b) Eratosthenes
(c) Wegener (d) Lord Wavell

Ans. (b) Eratosthenes

3. All imaginary circles are known as the parallels of latitude because
(a) these lie parallel to Prime Meridian.
(b) these lie parallel to the Equator.
(c) these lie parallel to International Date Line.
(d) None of the above

Ans. (b) these lie parallel to the Equator.

4. Earth is slightly flattened at the ....
(a) North Pole
(b) Middle
(c) South Pole
(d) North and the South Poles

Ans. (d) North and the South Poles

5. Prime Meridian passes through which city?
(a) Paris (b) London
(c) Birmingham (d) Liverpool

Ans. (b) London

6. The total number of longitudes are ....
(a) 240 (b) 360
(c) 150 (d) 180

Ans. (b) 360

7. Longitudes divide the Earth into how many time zones?
(a) 12 (b) 16 (c) 20 (d) 24

Ans. (d) 24

8. What time does Earth take, rotating from one degree longitude to next longitude?
(a) 4 minutes (b) 15 minutes
(c) 10 minutes (d) None of these

Ans. (a) 4 minutes

9. The local time of 82°30' E longitude is taken as a standard throughout India. It is known by which name?
(a) Local time of India
(b) Indian Standard Time (IST)
(c) Both (a) and (b) (d) None of these

Ans. (b) Indian Standard Time (IST)

10. Which of the following zone is situated between 66.5° and poles?
(a) Torrid zone (b) Temperate zone
(c) Frigid zone (d) All of these

Ans. (c) Frigid zone

11. Give reasons for the following.
21st June is the longest day in the Northern hemisphere.
(a) The Sun is located overhead the Tropic of Cancer.
(b) The Sun is located overhead the Tropic of Capricorn.
(c) The Sun is located overhead the Antarctic Circle.
(d) The Sun is located overhead the Arctic Circle.

Ans. (a) The Sun is located overhead the Tropic of Cancer.

12. Give reasons for the following.
Russia has 11 time zones.
(a) Russia is a vast country.
(b) Russia has many overseas territories.
(c) Prime Meridian passes near the Russia.
(d) None of the above

Ans. (a) Russia is a vast country.

13. Give reasons for the following.
France has maximum number of time zones.
(a) France is the largest country of the world.
(b) France has several overseas territories.
(c) France is located near the International Date Line.
(d) None of the above

Ans. (b) France has several overseas territories.

14. Give reasons for the following.
Frigid zone is the coldest zone on the Earth.
(a) This region receives the extreme slanting Sun rays.
(b) This region is located near the tropics.
(c) This region receives maximum rain.
(d) None of the above

Ans. (a) This region receives the extreme slanting Sun rays.

15. Which of the following statements is correct?
(i) The circumference of Earth is 30000 km.
(ii) The latitudes are expressed in degrees, minutes and seconds.
(iii) There are 180 parallel lines of latitude on the Earth.

Codes
(a) Only (i) (b) Only (ii)
(c) (ii) and (iii) (d) All of these

Ans. (c) (ii) and (iii)

16. Which of the following statements is incorrect?
(i) Earth as a whole represents 360°.
(ii) Latitudes are used for determining the exact location more precisely.
(iii) France has 2 time zones.

Codes
(a) Only (i) (b) Only (ii)
(c) Only (iii) (d) All of these

Ans. (c) Only (iii)

17. Match the following.

List-I	List-II
A. Tropic of Cancer	1. 0° Longitude
B. Tropic of Capricorn	2. 0° Latitude
C. Equator	3. 23.5° S
D. Prime Meridian	4. 23.5° N

Codes

	A	B	C	D		A	B	C	D
(a)	1	2	3	4	(b)	2	1	4	3
(c)	3	4	1	2	(d)	4	3	2	1

Ans. (d)

18. Match the following.

List-I	List-II
A. Arctic Circle	1. 66.5° S
B. Antarctic Circle	2. 66.5° N
C. International Date Line	3. 40000 km
D. Circumference of the Earth	4. 180°

Codes

	A	B	C	D		A	B	C	D
(a)	1	2	3	4	(b)	2	1	4	3
(c)	3	4	1	2	(d)	4	3	2	1

Ans. (b)

19. Match the following.

List-I	List-II
A. North frigid zone	1. Between Tropic of Cancer and Capricorn
B. South frigid zone	2. Between 23.5° N and 66.5° N latitudes
C. Tropical zone	3. Between Arctic and North Pole
D. North temperate zone	4. Between Antarctic and South Pole

Codes

	A	B	C	D		A	B	C	D
(a)	1	2	3	4	(b)	2	1	4	3
(c)	3	4	1	2	(d)	4	3	2	1

Ans. (c)

Section-II

Short Questions

1. What is a geographical grid?

Ans. The geographical grid is a system designed to depict any location on Earth by laying a vertical and horizontal grid over the Earth's layout.

2. How do you locate places using the geographic grid of Earth?

Ans. To depict any location on Earth, the geographic grid uses two co-ordinates i.e. latitude and longitude. The vertical lines on the globe are called longitudes and the horizontal lines are called the latitudes. The point at which these lines intersect is the exact location.

3. What is geographic co-ordinate system?

Ans. Geographic co-ordinate system is a system that enables every location on the Earth to be specified by a set of numbers, letters or symbols.

4. Answer the following questions.
(i) Why the lines of latitude are also known as parallels?
(ii) State any one feature of these lines.

Ans. (i) All the lines of latitude lie parallel to the equator and thus, they are also known as the parallels.
(ii) A feature of lines of latitude is that two latitudes never meet each other.

5. Answer the following questions.
(i) Define the lines of latitude.
(ii) State the unit of measurement of latitudes.

Ans. (i) The lines of latitude are the imaginary lines, that can be defined as the angular distance of a place located on the North or South of the equator, measured as an angle whose apex is at the centre of the Earth, on the equatorial plane.
(ii) The unit of measurement of latitudes is a degree.

6. Answer the following questions.
(i) How are the latitudes divided?
(ii) Where is the maximum radius of latitude?

Ans. (i) There are total 180 parallels of latitude located at an angular distance of 1°, 90 of which are located in the Northern hemisphere and 90 are located in the Southern hemisphere.

(ii) The radius of latitudes is maximum at the Equator.

7. Answer the following questions.

(i) What do you understand by 11° 30′ 40″?

(ii) What does this (11°30′40″) represent ?

Ans. (i) 11°30′ 40″ means the latitude position i.e. 11 degrees 30 minutes and 40 seconds.

(ii) It represents the location of a place.

8. Name the five main latitudes on the globe.

Ans. The five main latitudes on the globe are

(i) The Arctic Circle
(ii) The Tropic of Cancer
(iii) The Equator
(iv) The Tropic of Capricorn
(v) The Antarctic Circle

9. Answer the following questions.

(i) Define Equator.

(ii) State its one feature.

Ans. (i) The equator of the Earth is an imaginary line on the Earth's surface that is equidistant from the North pole and South pole.

(ii) Equator divides the Earth into two hemispheres i.e. Northern and Southern hemisphere.

10. What is the distance between the poles and the equator?

Ans. The approximate distance between the pole and the equator is almost one-fourth of the total circumference of the Earth.

11. What is the variance in the radius of latitude as we move from the Equator to the poles?

Ans. The radius of the latitudes is maximum at the Equator and reduces on moving towards the poles. Therefore Equator forms largest circle, while reduces in poles.

12. Why Equator is more hotter than poles?

Ans. The Equator receives direct sunlight of high intensity, as the rays travels straight and covers less space in comparison with poles, which receives slanting rays. Therefore, Equator is more hotter than poles.

13. State how much difference is between Earth's original circumference and circumference at the Equator.

Ans. The original circumference of the Earth is 40000 km and at the equator, it is 40075 km. The difference between these two circumferences is 75 km approx.

14. What do you mean by an Antarctic?

Ans. The line or circle of latitude that marks the starting point of the frigid zone in the Southern area is known as Antarctic. 66.5° S is known as Antarctic Circle.

15. What is the importance of latitudes ?

Ans. The lines of latitudes are important to use

(i) for measuring and locating the places on the Earth.

(ii) for identifying the climatic conditions of the Earth.

16. Name the five heat zones of the Earth.

Ans. The five heat zones of the Earth are

(i) The North Frigid zone
(ii) The North Temperate zone
(iii) The Torrid zone
(iv) The South Temperate zone
(v) The South Frigid zone

17. Why frigid zone is colder than other zones?

Ans. Frigid zone is colder primarily because it receives far less solar radiation than the tropics and mid-latitudes. At either pole, the Sun never rises overhead beyond 23.50° polewards due to tilt of Earth's axis as compared to other zones that receive more degrees of heat.

18. How do the seasons vary in the Northern and Southern hemisphere?

Ans. The seasons on the Earth are opposite in the Northern and Southern hemisphere. If there is summer in Northern Hemisphere, it will be winter in Southern hemisphere and *vice-versa*. This is because the Earth is tilted and not straight. During half of the year Northern hemisphere receives more heat and in another half of the year Southern hemisphere receives more heat.

19. Define longitude.

Ans. A longitude is defined as the angular distance of a place, East or West of the Prime Meridian measured as an angle whose apex is at the center of the Earth.

20. What do you understand by line of reference?

Ans. Line of reference is an arbitrary fixed line from which co-ordinates of a point are computed. It is important to locate a place in map or a globe.

21. Answer the following questions.

(i) What do you mean by Prime Meridian?

(ii) What is the use of Prime Meridian?

Ans. (i) A Prime Meridian is a meridian (a line of longitude) in a geographical co-ordinate system at which longitude is defined to be 0°.

(ii) Prime Meridian is used as a line of reference for locating the places in East and West directions.

22. Why do the places on a meridian have same time at noon?

Ans. As the Sun passes the meridian at noon, all the places lying on perpendicular meridian will have noon at the same time. The reason for this is that the Sun is equally overhead from all the places.

23. Why is the length of the longitudes equal?

Ans. The length of all the meridians of longitude is equal as they all are the semi circles that join the North pole and the South pole.

24. What is the similarity between the distance of the longitudes and the radius of the latitudes?

Ans. The distance of the longitudes and the radius of the latitudes decreases as we move towards the poles. The reason behind this is that the length of circle decreases towards pole.

25. Why is the Prime Meridian known as Greenwich Meridian?

Ans. The Prime Meridian passes through the Old Royal Observatory at Greenwich in London and thus, it is known as Greenwich Meridian.

26. Why did some countries choose more than one time zone?

Ans. Some countries have chosen more than one time zone due to having vast geographical and longitudinal extent of their country, e.g. Russia.

27. Which country has the maximum number of time zones in the world?

Ans. France has the maximum number of time zones in the world i.e. 12 due to having overseas territories. USA and Russia have the second highest time zones with 11 for each.

28. How time is changed at each 1° longitude ?

Ans. Time changes at each 1° longitude is 4 minutes and 1 hour at each 15° longitude. It is so because the Earth rotates 1° in 4 minutes.

29. Answer the following questions.
(i) What is a standard time?
(ii) Which countries have same standard time as of India?

Ans. (i) The uniform time based on a central meridian is called the standard time of a country.
(ii) Nepal and Sri Lanka have same standard time as of India.

30. Answer the following questions.
(i) What are tropics?
(ii) How many tropics are there?

Ans. (i) The lines of latitude in the Northern and Southern boundaries of the torrid zone are known as tropics.
(ii) There are mainly two tropics i.e. the Tropic of Cancer and the Tropic of Capricorn.

31. Which meridian has been accepted by India for calculating its standard time?

Ans. The Indian Government has accepted the meridian of 82.5° E for calculating their standard time. This meridian is 5 hours 30 minutes ahead of GMT.

32. Why Indian Standard Time is 5 hours 30 minutes ahead from Greenwich Mean Time (GMT)?

Ans. Indian Government has accepted central meridian 82.5° E longitude as its standard time. As each longitude of 1° East of Greenwich adds 4 minutes time, thus being on Eastward location Indian Standard Time (IST) is 5 hours 30 minutes ahead from Greenwich. For example, $82.5 \times 4 = 330$ minutes while, means 5 hours 30 minutes.

33. Answer the following questions.
(i) How do meridians make a circle?
(ii) Give an example of it.

Ans. (i) Each meridian is a semicircle. Therefore, when one meridian joins with another meridian exactly opposite to it then it, makes a full circle.
(ii) An example of meridians making a circle is 0° Prime Meridian and 180° longitude and 1° longitude and 179° longitude which make a complete circle i.e. Great Circle.

34. Answer the following questions.
(i) Why do all the longitudes make great circle?
(ii) Which latitude makes a great circle?

Ans. (i) All the meridians of the longitude form great circles as they all are equal and join the North pole and the South pole.
(ii) The 0° latitude makes a great circle.

Long Questions

1. (i) Write the important features of the latitudes.
(ii) How are the latitudes expressed? Explain with example.

Ans. (i) Refer to chapter theory page no. 10 and 11.
(ii) The latitudes are expressed in degrees, minutes and seconds. This is used for determining the exact location more precisely. In a full circle, there are 360°. Each degree is split up into 60 parts, each part being 1/60 of a degree. These parts are called minutes. Each minute is split up into 60 parts, each part being 1/60 of a minute. These parts are called seconds.

2. Briefly describe any three major latitudes.

Ans. The three major latitudes are
(i) **The Arctic Circle** It is located at approximately 66.5° N latitudes, or 66.5° N of the equator. This circle of latitude stretches through eight countries.
(ii) **The Tropic of Cancer** It is located at approximately 23.5° N latitude of the Equator. This line of latitude is the Northern boundary of the area referred to as the tropics or torrid zone.

(iii) **The Equator** It is an imaginary line on the Earth's surface that is equidistant from the North pole and South pole, dividing the Earth into the Northern hemisphere and Southern hemisphere.

3. Describe the methods for locating places on the Earth and measuring distance with the help of latitude and longitude.

Ans. Refer to chapter theory page no. 13-14.

4. What do you mean by the lines of latitude and how these lines are used in measuring and locating places on the Earth? Explain with an example.

Ans. The lines of latitude are the imaginary lines that can be defined as the angular distance of a place located on the North or South of the equator. These are measured as an angle whose apex is at the center of the Earth i.e. on the equatorial plane.

These lines are used in measuring and locating places on the Earth. It becomes very easy for us to locate a place in North or South of the equator which is known as absolute location. The distance of the places are measured with reference to the equator at the right angle of the place. For example, the line of latitude for New Delhi is 28.644° North (approx). It is also known that 1° latitude on the map is 111 kms. Thus, the distance of New Delhi from the equator can be calculated as 28.644×111=3179.48 kms.

5. Briefly describe the three heat zones of the Earth.

Ans. Refer to chapter theory page no. 14.

6. Briefly discuss about Eastern and Western hemispheres.

Ans. Refer to chapter theory page no. 12.

7. Give reasons, why?

(i) South pole is colder than North pole.

(ii) Torrid zone is hotter than Frigid zone.

Ans. (i) South pole is colder than North pole because South pole lies on the top of a very thick ice sheet i.e. 9000 feet in elevation above mean sea level.

In comparison, North pole lies in the middle of the Arctic Ocean, where surface of floating ice is only one feet or so above the surrounding sea. Being a heat reservoir, the Arctic Ocean warms the cold atmosphere in the winter and draws heat from the atmosphere in the summer.

(ii) Torrid zone also known as tropical zone lies between 23.5° N i.e. Tropic of Cancer to 23.5° S, i.e. Tropic of Capricorn. These areas are near the Equator which is the hottest place on the Earth because it receiving direct rays of the around the year. Thus, the intensity of heat is more in this zone that makes this zone hottest and humid on the Earth.

8. Differentiate between latitude and longitude.

Ans. Differences between latitude and longitude are

Latitude	Longitude
It is the geographic co-ordinate which determines the distance of a point North-South of the Equator.	It is the geographic co-ordinate that determines the distance of a point East-West of the Prime Meridian.
Lines are parallel to each other.	Lines are not parallel to each other, but converge at the North and South poles.
Lines are used for measuring distance.	Lines are used for measuring local time.

9. Differentiate between the Equator and the Prime Meridian.

Ans. Differences between the Equator and the Prime Meridian are

Equator	Prime Meridian
It is the imaginary circle, which cuts the spherical Earth exactly in the middle into two equal halves.	It is the vertical line that marks the 0° longitude measurement on the Earth and intersects the latitude lines.
It is a horizontal line.	It is a vertical line.
It separates the Earth into Northern hemisphere and Southern hemisphere.	It separates the Earth into two hemispheres i.e. Eastern and Western hemispheres.

10. Why do we have different time zones on the Earth? Explain in brief.

Ans. We have different time zones on the Earth due to following reasons

- As the Earth rotates on its axis, different parts of the Earth receives sunlight or darkness giving us day and night.
- If we had one single time zone for the Earth, noon would be the middle of the day in some places, but it would be morning, evening and the middle of the night in other places. Since different parts of the Earth experience daylight at different times, we need different time zones. For example, as the Earth rotates on its axis, it moves about 15° every 60 minutes. After 24 hours, it completes a full circle rotation of 360°. So, each time zone is 15° of longitude wide.

11. How is the local time calculated?

Ans. The local time is calculated through meridians. The lines of longitude are also known as meridians. When it is 12 noon at a longitude, all the places on the same longitude will have the same time i.e. it will be 12 noon. As the Earth rotates on its axis it covers 360° longitudes in 24 hours. Therefore, we can say that it covers 15° longitudes in an hour. The difference in the time is of 4 minutes between the longitudes.

Thus, we can say that if it is 12 noon on 0° longitude, it will be 4 minutes past 12 at the longitude 1° to the East. As each hour has 60 minutes so, it can be stated that at 15° E longitude, the time will be 1 pm. As we move from 0° to 15° W, the time will be one hour less than 12 pm as the Earth rotates from West towards the East.

12. Why Indian Standard Time is important for us?

Ans. Indian Standard Time (IST) is important due to the following reasons

- India is a large country and has a difference of 2 hours from Gujarat in the West to Assam in the East.
- IST helps us in organising a uniform schedule for transport like railways and airways.
- IST provides a standard time for the entire country so, that the local time differences can be managed easily.

13. (i) What are great circles ?
(ii) How these circles are important?

Ans. (i) Great circles are the largest possible circles that can be drawn around a sphere.
All spheres have great circles. The great circle represents the shortest distance between two points anywhere on the surface of the Earth.

(ii) The great circles are important due to its uses. The great circle can be used for the following purposes

- The great circles are used in the navigation between two points on the sphere.
- The navigator uses these circles because these great circle routes are very economical which saves time and fuels of the navigator.

Chapter Assessment

Section-I

Multiple Choice Questions

1. The distance between each latitude is around
(a) 11km (b) 90 km
(c) 111 km (d) 121km

2. The time of India is ahead of England by
(a) 2 hours
(b) 5 hours and 30 minutes
(c) 3 hours (d) None of these

3. Latitudes are which type of line on the Globe?
(a) Slanting lines (b) Horizontal lines
(c) Vertical lines (d) Diagonal lines

4. Which of the following is an imaginary line on the Earth?
(a) Prime Meridian (b) Equator
(c) International Date Line (d) All of these

Section-II

Short Questions

1. Name the following.
(i) 0° latitude (ii) 0° longitude

2. What is the original circumference of the Earth?

3. How can we write 11 degrees 30 minutes 50 seconds into geographical term?

4. What do you understand by the term 'local time'?

5. Why are lines of latitude called parallels of latitude?

6. What is meant by meridian?

7. Name two important lines of latitude.

8. What is tropical zone?

9. What is the International Date Line?

10. Name two countries which have more than two time zones.

Long Questions

1. Why longitudes are important for us? Explain in brief.

2. Differentiate between North pole and South pole.

3. Differentiate between standard time and local time.

4. Discuss about Indian Standard Time (IST).

5. How International Date line is important for us?

6. Give reasons, why?
(i) Longitudes towards East gain time.
(ii) All meridians are great circles.

CHAPTER

03

Rotation and Revolution

SYLLABUS

Rotation and Revolution Rotation – direction, speed and its effects (occurence of day and night, the Sun rising in the East and setting in the West, Coriolis effect)
• Revolution of the earth and its inclined axis effects : the variation in the length of the day and night and seasonal changes with Equinoxes and Solstices.

All the planets including the Earth rotates on their own axis and revolves around the Sun on the fixed path called **orbit**. The movements of the Earth is known as rotation and revolution. These movements of the Earth around the Sun causes day and night, change of seasons, effect on ocean currents, etc. These are also called motions of the Earth.

Rotation

Rotation of the Earth is defined as the Earth rotating on its own axis from West to East. A complete rotation of the Earth on its axis makes a day i.e. 24 hours (approx).

The characteristics of rotation of the Earth are

- The time required by Earth to complete its one rotation from West to East on its axis is 23 hours, 56 minutes and 4.09 seconds. This is roughly estimated as 24 hours. This period of rotation of the Earth is known as **a sidereal day**.
- The Earth always remains tilted towards the pole star in the celestial sphere while moving around the Sun.
- The speed of the Earth's movement at the Equator is 1670 km per hour. This is the speed required by Earth to cover its complete circumference in 24 hours. This speed gradually reduces while moving towards the pole.

Effects of Earth's Rotation

- **The Sun and other Celestial Bodies seem to move from East to West** Due to the rotating direction of the Earth from West to East, everything on Earth appears to be moving from East to West (i.e. in opposite direction). For example, while sitting in a train one can experience the object like the trees and the buildings moving in an opposite direction.

  The Earth always moves from West to East therefore the Sun always appears to be rising in the East. Thus, when the direction of the rising Sun is known, it becomes easy to figure out all the other directions.
- **Occurrence of Day and Nights** The occurrence of day and night on the Earth are caused due to the rotation of the Earth. The part of the Earth that faces the Sun has day and the opposite part on the Earth experiences night. This phenomena of day and night can be seen easily by the **circle of illumination.**

There are three phases of the Sun in a day i.e dawn, noon and dusk.

- **Duration of Day and Night** The duration of the day and night is not equal at all the places on the Earth. It always vary due to the inclination of the axis of the Earth. The length of the days also varies with the latitude.
- **Sunrise and Sunset** Due to the rotation of the Earth, each and every part of the Earth faces the Sun at some time or the other. The part of the Earth when receives Sun's rays during rotation, experience sunrise and when it moves away from the Sun's rays, it experience sunset.
- **Temperature Variation** The temperature of the Earth also varies as the part of the Earth that receives the rays of the Sun in the day is hotter, while the part of the Earth that does not receive the Sun rays is cooler during the night. The rotational period makes the variation of temperature moderate between day and night.
- **Effect on Movement of Water and Oceans** The rotation of the Earth also affects the movement of water in the oceans. The tides in the ocean get diverted due to the rotation of the Earth. The high and the low tides occur at an interval of 12 hours 56 minutes in a day and are caused by the **gravitational pull**[1] of the Sun and the Moon.
- **Variation in Time** The time at various places varies for each degree of longitude by four minutes. This results in a variation of time at different places.
- **Coriolis Effect** Due to the Earth's rotation, the ocean currents and the air moves clockwise and are deflected towards the right in the Northern hemisphere and towards the left and anti-clock wise in the Southern hemisphere. This effect is known as coriolis effect. It was first described by a French scientist **Gustave Coriolis** in 1835.
- **Atmospheric Changes** Due to the speed of Earth's rotation, atmospheric changes occur as it deflects the cyclonic winds, monsoon winds and trade winds in different direction in Northern and Southern hemisphere.
- **Centrifugal Force** The speed of Earth's rotation create **centrifugal force**[2] which makes the Earth bulging at the equator and flattened at the poles.

Check Your LEARNING...

1. What is the meaning of orbit?
2. At what angle the Earth is tilted on its axis?
3. What time is required by the Earth to complete its one rotation on its axis?
4. At what time intervals the high and the low tides occur?

Revolution

The movement of the Earth around the Sun in an elliptical orbit is known as revolution. The characteristics of revolution of the Earth are

- The Earth takes 365.25 days to complete its revolution once. This is roughly taken as 365 days which is a calendar year or Earth year.

  As one revolution of the Earth is 1/4th day more than a calendar year of 365 days, an extra day is added to the calendar year after every four years. This extra day is added to the month of February and the year consists of 366 days. This year with an extra day is known as **leap year**.
- The revolution of the Earth is in the same direction as rotation i.e. from the West to the East.
- The Earth revolves around the Sun at an average speed of about 100,000 kms per hour or 29.8 kms per second. But this varies according to the path of the orbit.
- When the Earth comes nearer to the Sun, the gravitational pulls makes the Earth move faster, whereas it moves slower when it moves away from the Sun as the gravitational pull reduces.
- According to the **Kepler's Law of Planetary Motion**, the Earth moves the fastest when it is in the perihelion and slowest when it is in the aphelion.

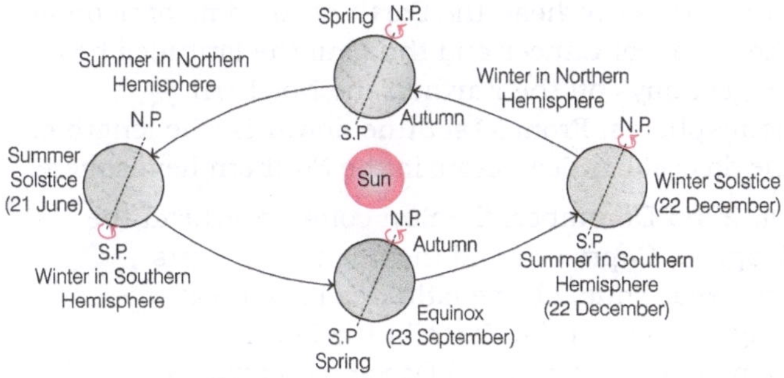

Revolution

1 **Gravitational** Pull It is magnetic pull that a celestial body (for example Earth, Sun, Planets) exerts on an object near to it.

2 **Centrifugal Force** An outward force acting on a rotating object.

Aphelion and Perihelion

The Earth moves around the Sun on its orbit which is elliptical in shape. Due to this elliptical shape of the orbit the distance between Earth and Sun varies. For the first six months of the year i.e. from 3rd January till 4th of July, the Earth moves away from the Sun. On the 4th of July, the Earth is at its farthest point from the Sun at a distance of about 152 millions kms. This position of the Earth is known as **aphelion**.

For the rest of the six months, the Earth comes closer to the Sun. On 3rd January, the Earth is nearest to the Sun at a distance of about 147 millions kms. This position of the Earth is known as **perihelion**.

Effects of Earth's Revolution

Change in Seasons

Different seasons are caused due to revolution of the Earth around the Sun. When the direct Sun's rays fall, the amount of heat is concentrated at one place or small areas as compared to slanting Sun's rays which cover large area. Thus, the areas which receive slanting Sun rays are less warm because heat is distributed over large place.

These differences in heating of the Earth results in the four seasons i.e. Spring, Summer, Autumn and Winters. With the change in the temperature at various places, the seasons also keeps on changing gradually. This phenomena of change of seasons is continuous with the movement of the Earth.

Variance in the Length of the Day and Night

The variation in the length of the day and night are due to the revolution of the Earth. As the Earth moves away from the Sun, its rays reach the Earth's surface as the parallel rays.

On 21st June every year, the Earth is in the position where the North pole is tilted towards the Sun. The Sun comes overhead the Earth at the time of noon at the Tropic of Cancer and thus, all the latitudes have longest days on the Earth in the Northern hemispheres. From 21st June onwards, the length of the days starts decreasing in the Northern hemisphere.

On 22nd December, the Sun comes overhead the Tropic of Capricorn and the phenomena gets reversed. Thus, all the latitudes have their longest days on the Earth in the Southern hemisphere. From 22nd December onwards, the length of the days starts decreasing in the Southern hemisphere.

On 21st March and 23rd September every year, the Sun is overhead at the time of noon at the Equator due to which all the places have equal days and nights. There is 12 hours of day and 12 hours of night.

Creation of the Heat Zones

The distribution of temperature is not uniform on the surface of the Earth due to its spherical shape and its revolution. The temperature on the Earth varies with the angle at which the Sun rays fall over it. Due to this variance of heat received by the Earth from the Sun, the Earth has been divided into three temperature zones, also known as heat zones. These are

(i) **Torrid Zone** It lies on both sides of the equator in between Tropic of Cancer (23½°N) to Tropic of Capricorn (23½°S). This region receives direct/vertical Sun rays, it thus experiences warm climate.

(ii) **Temperate Zone** It lies between Tropic of Cancer (23½°S) to Antarctic Circle (66½°S). This region receives slanting Sun rays, thus it experiences moderately warm climate.

(iii) **Frigid Zone** It lies in the polar regions i.e. beyond 66½° N and S. This region receives extremely slanting Sun rays, thus, it experiences extremely cold climate.

Equinoxes

The term equinoxes means equal nights. Equinoxes occur when the rotation axis of the Earth (i.e. the line from the North or South poles) is exactly parallel to the Sun. The length of day is exactly the same (12 hours) at all points on the Earth's surface on the equinoxes. On two occasion in a year, the days and nights are equal on the Earth because Earth's axis is inclined neither away from the Sun nor towards the Sun. These are

(i) **Spring or Vernal Equinox (21st March)** 21st March is called the day of vernal equinox, when the Sun's rays again fall vertically at the Equator and the day and night become equal. It occurs when the Sun crosses the equator moving from the Southern to the Northern hemisphere. In the Northern hemisphere, spring season begins on the Vernal equinox and the Southern hemisphere experiences autumn season.

(ii) **Autumn Equinox (23rd September)** 23rd September is called 'the day of autumnal equinox, when the Sun's rays fall vertically at the equator. On this day all places on the Earth have equal days and nights. It occurs when the Sun crosses the equator moving from the Northern to the Southern hemisphere.

In the Northern hemisphere, autumn begins on the autumn equinox and the Southern hemisphere experiences spring season.

Solstices

Solstice is derived from two Latin words, 'sol' meaning Sun and 'sistere' meaning stand still. Thus, the word solstice means that the Sun stand still. It is a position of earth in which the Sun is on maximum distance towards Northern hemisphere or Southern hemisphere, with respect to the Equator. This causes summer and winter solstices. Thus, the solstice occur twice in a year i.e. summer and winter.

(i) **Summer Solstice** The position of the Earth on 21st June every year is known as summer solstice. During summer solstice, the Sun is overhead the Tropic of Cancer.

On this day, the North pole is tilted towards the Sun and the South pole is tilted away from the Sun. The areas beyond the Arctic circle (66.5°N) experience 24 hours day light. This phenomenon is known as **Midnight Sun.** Norway is known as land of midnight Sun, as this phenomenon is clearly visible from Norway.

On summer solstice, the Northern hemisphere has the longest day and the shortest night. While the Southern hemisphere has the shortest day and the longest night. There is summer in the Northern hemisphere and winter in the Southern hemisphere during summer solstice.

(ii) **Winter Solstice** The position of the Earth on 22nd December every year is known as winter solstice. During winter solstice, the South pole is tilted towards the Sun and the North pole is away from the Sun. The Sun is directly overhead the Tropic of Capricorn.

On winter solstice, the Northern hemisphere has the shortest day and the longest night, while Southern hemisphere has longest day and shortest night.

The areas beyond the Antarctic Circle (66.5°S) experience 24 hours daylight. There is summer in the Southern hemisphere and winter in the Northern hemisphere during winter solstice.

Inclination of the Earth's Axis

The Earth's axis is tilted at an angle of 23.5° vertically and makes an angle of 66.5° horizontally with the orbital plane of the Earth. This tilting of axis is known as the inclination of the Earth's axis.

The tilt is measured from the axis that runs perpendicular to orbital plane. The tilt or slant is known as **obliquity angle.**

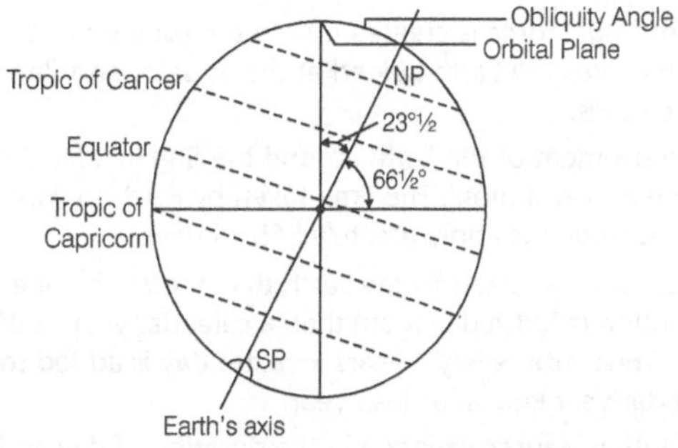

Inclination of Earth's axis

Effects and Significance of Earth's Inclined Axis

- Length of the day varies on the Earth due to tilted position of the Earth's axis. The temperature also varies with the change of day and night.
- The winters have longer nights and summers have longer days.
- During the time when the Northern hemisphere experiences longer nights, the Southern hemispheres experiences longer days and *vice-versa.*
- Due to the inclination of the axis, the North pole always remains inclined towards the sunlight and the South pole stays away from it for a long period of time.

- If the Earth had a vertical axis, then the length of the day and night would have been similar at all the places. There would also have been no variance in the temperatures and thus, no seasonal changes would have been there.

Check Your LEARNING...

1. How many days the Earth takes to complete its one revolution?
2. On which date the Earth is at its farthest point from the Sun?
3. On which date the Earth is at its nearest point from the Sun?
4. What do you mean by winter solstice?

QUiCK Revision

- The movement of the Earth on its axis is known as 'rotation'.
- The rotation of the Earth causes day and night, which means that only half of the Earth has day and half has night. This phenomena of the Earth of day and night can be seen easily by the circle of illumination.
- The Earth always moves from West to East and the Sun always appears to be rising in the East.
- Due to the Earth's rotation, the ocean currents and the air is deflected towards the right in the Northern hemisphere and towards the left in the Southern hemisphere. This is known as 'coriolis effect'.
- A centrifugal force is created due to the rotation of the Earth which makes the Earth bulged at the equator and flattened at the poles.
- The movement of the Earth around the Sun in a fixed orbit is known as 'revolution'. The time taken by Earth to complete one revolution is approximately 365.25 days.
- Since, the time taken by the Earth to complete its one revolution is 1/4th day more than a calendar year of 365 days. Thus, after every 4 years an extra day is added to the calendar year known as leap year.
- Revolution causes variation in the duration of day and night and alteration of the seasons. When the Northern hemisphere experiences longer nights, the Southern hemisphere experiences longer days and *vice-versa*.
- On the 4th of July, the Earth is at its farthest point from the Sun at a distance of about 152 million Kms. This position of the Earth is known as aphelion.
- On 3rd January, the Earth is nearest to the Sun at a distance of about 147 million kms. This position of the Earth is known as perihelion.
- Due to the variance in the heat received by the Earth from the Sun, the Earth has been divided into three temperature zones, also known as heat zones. These are torrid zone, temperate zone and frigid zone.
- On two days in a year, the days and nights are equal on the Earth. This phenomenon is known as equinox means equal-night. 23 September and 21 March are equinox.
- When Earth's axis is pointed directly toward or away from the Sun, then it is solstice. 21st June is summer solstice and 22nd December is winter solstice.
- The axis of the Earth is not parallel to the plane of revolution. It is inclined at an angle of 66.5 degrees with the plane of ecliptic and is tilted 23.5 degrees perpendicular to the plane.

Chapter Practice

Section-I

Multiple Choice Questions

1. Motion of the Earth on its axis in about 24 hours is called as
   (a) revolution (b) rotation
   (c) Both (a) and (b) (d) None of these

Ans. (b) rotation

2. What is orbital plane?
   (a) Plane formed by the axis
   (b) Plane formed by the orbit
   (c) Both (a) and (b)
   (d) None of the above

Ans. (b) Plane formed by the orbit

3. The circle that divides the globe into day and night is called
   (a) circle of darkness.
   (b) circle of day and night.
   (c) circle of illumination.
   (d) None of the above

Ans. (c) circle of illumination.

4. A year with 366 days is called
   (a) leap year (b) normal year
   (c) sideral year (d) None of these

Ans. (a) leap year

5. Leap year is repeated after ....
   (a) 4 years (b) 2 years (c) 3 years (d) 1 year

Ans. (a) 4 years

6. Which one of the following is the source of light on the Earth?
   (a) The Moon (b) The Sun
   (c) The Satellite (d) The Space

Ans. (b) The Sun

7. The minimum distance between the Sun and the Earth occurs on which day?
   (a) 22nd December (b) 22nd September
   (c) 21st June (d) 3rd January

Ans. (d) 3rd January

8. Cycle of the seasons is caused due to
   (a) rotation (b) revolution
   (c) gravitation (d) All of these

Ans. (b) revolution

9. Motion of the Earth around the Sun is known as
   (a) revolution (b) rotation
   (c) Both (a) and (b) (d) None of these

Ans. (a) revolution

10. On ...., the Northern hemisphere is tilted towards the Sun.
    (a) 21st January (b) 28th February
    (c) 21st June (d) 22th September

Ans. (c) 21st June

11. Give reason for the following.
    We do not feel the motions of the Earth.
    (a) According to the gravitational force everything is attached to the Earth.
    (b) Coriolis force is responsible for this.
    (c) Revolution makes everything stable on the Earth.
    (d) None of the above

Ans. (a) According to the gravitational force everything is attached to the Earth.

12. Give reason for the following.
    We always see the Sun rising in the East.
    (a) Moon's shadow is the responsible reason for this.
    (b) The Earth moves from West to East
    (c) Due to rotation of the Sun.
    (d) None of the above

Ans. (b) The Earth moves from West to East.

13. Give reason for the following
    Vertical rays are hotter than slanting rays.
    (a) Vertical rays cross longer distance from the Sun to the Earth.
    (b) Vertical rays cross shorter distance from the Sun to the Earth.
    (c) Vertical rays cover large distance from the Sun to the Earth.
    (d) None of the above

Ans. (b) Vertical rays cross shorter distance from the Sun to the Earth.

14. Give reason for the following
    The length of day and night is not equal at all places on the Earth.
    (a) Due to the straight axis of the Earth and the migration of the Sun between Tropic of Cancer and Arctic Circle.
    (b) Due to the tilted axis of the earth and the migration of the Sun between Tropic of Cancer and Capricorn.
    (c) Due to rotation of the Earth on its axis at a very fast speed.
    (d) All of the above

Ans. (b) Due to the tilted axis of the Earth and the migration of the Sun between Tropic of Cancer and Capricorn.

15. Give reason for the following.
    Norway is called the land of the midnight Sun.
    (a) Northern part of Norway is beyond the Arctic Circle.
    (b) Norway lies on the South Pole.

(c) Northern part of Norway is beyond the Antarctic Circle.
(d) All of the above

Ans. (a) Northern part of Norway is beyond the Arctic Circle.

16. What would have happened if the Earth did not rotate?
(i) Cold conditions on Earth's half portion.
(ii) Warm conditions on Earth's another half portion.
(iii) No life possible in such extreme conditions.

Codes
(a) Only (i) (b) Only (ii)
(c) (i) and (iii) (d) All of these

Ans. (d) All of these

17. Match the following.

	List-I	List-II
A.	Arctic circle	1. Fall equinox
B.	Vernal equinox	2. 22nd December
C.	Autumn equinox	3. 66.5° N
D.	Winter solstice	4. Spring equinox

Codes

	A	B	C	D		A	B	C	D
(a)	1	2	3	4	(b)	2	1	4	3
(c)	3	4	1	2	(d)	4	3	2	1

Ans. (c)

18. Match the following.

	List-I	List-II
A.	North frigid zone	1. Between Antarctic and South Pole
B.	South frigid zone	2. Between Arctic and North Pole
C.	Tropical zone	3. Between 23.5° N and 66.5° N latitudes
D.	North temperate zone	4. Between Tropic of Cancer and Capricorn

Codes

	A	B	C	D		A	B	C	D
(a)	1	2	3	4	(b)	2	1	4	3
(c)	3	4	1	2	(a)	4	3	2	1

Ans. (b)

Section-II

Short Questions

1. How does the Earth moves?

Ans. The movement of earth is marked by the rotation of Earth on its axis and its revolution around the sun on a fixed elliptical orbit.

2. Write any two effects of the movement of the Earth.

Ans. The two effects of the movement of the Earth are
(i) It causes day and night (due to rotation).
(ii) It causes change of seasons (due to revolution).

3. Why does the amount of heat varies from place to place?

Ans. The amount of heat and light varies from place to place due to the inclination of the Earth's axis. The region tilted towards the Sun receives more heat.

4. Answer the following questions.
(i) What is rotation of the Earth and in which direction it rotate?
(ii) State any one effect of rotation.

Ans. (i) Rotation is defined as the movement of the Earth on its own axis. Earth rotates on it axis from West to East direction.
(ii) The effect of rotation is that it causes day and night.

5. Answer the following questions.
(i) Define the Earth's axis.
(ii) Name the two end points of the Earth's axis.

Ans. (i) The Earth's axis is an imaginary line that passes through the centre of the Earth.
(ii) The two end points of the Earth's axis are North pole and South pole.

6. How is the phenomena of day and night observed?

Ans. The phenomena of the day and night can be seen easily by the circle of illumination. The portion which receives Sunlight experiences day while darker portion experiences night.

7. What do you understand by sidereal day?

Ans. The period of rotation of the Earth is known as a sidereal day. Sidereal time is measured with respect to the apparent motion of the fixed stars in the sky due to the Earth's rotation.

8. Where is the duration of day and night always same and why?

Ans. The duration of day and night at the Equator is always same. It is because the Equator receives vertical Sun's rays throughout the year and both the day and night are of 12 hours each.

9. Why is it easy to figure out the directions by observing the direction of the sunrise ?

Ans. The Earth always moves from West to East therefore, the Sun always appears to be rising in the East i.e. in the opposite direction. Thus, when the direction of the rising Sun is known, it becomes easy to figure out all the other directions.

10. Why does the temperature of Earth varies from place to place?

Ans. The temperature of the Earth varies as the part of the Earth that receives the rays of the Sun in the day is hotter, while the part of the Earth that does not receives the Sun's rays is cooler during the night.

11. What is the effect of rotation on oceans?

Ans. The rotation of the Earth affects the movement of water in the oceans. The tides in the ocean get diverted due to the rotation of the Earth. The high and the low tides are alternate in a day and are caused by the gravitational pull of the Sun and the Moon at different times of the day.

12. How much time varies at different places?

Ans. The time at various places varies for each degree of longitude by 4 minutes. This results in a variation of time at different places.

13. What is coriolis effect?

Ans. Coriolis effect is the effect in which due to the Earth's rotation, the ocean currents and the air are deflected towards the right in the Northern hemisphere and towards the left in the Southern hemisphere.

14. Answer the following questions.

(i) What is revolution?

(ii) How much time is taken by the Earth to complete one revolution?

Ans. (i) The revolution is defined as the movement of the Earth around the Sun.

(ii) The time taken by the Earth to complete one revolution is approximately 365.25 days.

15. What is the angle of inclination of the Earth's axis?

Ans. The Earth's axis is inclined at an angle of 66.5° and is tilted at 23.5° perpendicular to the plane.

16. What would have happened if the Earth had a vertical axis?

Ans. If the Earth had a vertical axis, then the length of the day and night would have been similar at all the places. There would have been no variance in the temperatures and thus, no seasonal changes would have been there.

17. Which is the coldest zone of the Earth?

Ans. Frigid zone is the coldest zone located on the poles of the Earth. The reason behind this is that this zone receives very little Sun's rays and the rays are slanting.

18. (i) What are equinoxes?

(ii) On which day the equinoxes occur?

Ans. (i) The term equinoxes means equal nights. Equinoxes occur when the rotation axis of the Earth (i.e. the line from the North or South poles) is exactly parallel to the Sun.

(ii) Equinoxes occur on 21st March i.e. spring or vernal equinox and on 23rd September i.e. autumn equinox.

19. On which days solstices occur?

Ans. The dates of maximum tilt of the Earth's equator correspond to the summer solstice and winter solstice. Summer solstice occurs on 21st June and winter solstice occurs on 22nd December.

20. Answer the following questions.

(i) What is the angle at which the Earth's axis is tilted?

(ii) What is meant by the phenomena of day and night?

Ans. (i) The Earth's axis is tilted at an angle of 23.5° from the vertical.

(ii) The rotation of the Earth causes day and night, which means that only half of the Earth has day and half has night.

Long Questions

1. What are the characteristics of rotation of the Earth?

Ans. Refer to chapter theory page no. 22.

2. Give a brief account of the effect of rotation of the Earth.

Ans. Following are the effects of the Earth's rotation

(i) Due to direction of rotation of Earth from West to East, the heavenly bodies like the Sun and the Moon appears to be moving in the East to West direction from any point of the Earth. Due to this, the people on the Earth sitting in a train experience the object like the trees and the buildings moving in an opposite direction.

(ii) The occurrence of day and night on the Earth are caused due to the rotation of the Earth. The part of the Earth that faces the Sun has day and the opposite part on the Earth experiences night. This phenomena of the Earth can be seen easily by the circle of illumination.

(iii) The Earth always moves from West to East and the Sun always appears to be rising in the East. Thus, when the direction of the rising Sun is known, it becomes easy to figure out all the other directions.

3. Give reasons.

(i) Why do we have leap year?

(ii) Why there is unequal day and night?

Ans. (i) Normally, our calendar years are made up of 365 days, but every four years a day is added to make it a 'leap year'. It is because, the Gregorian calendar is most widely used across the globe and it measures a year to be 365 days following the Earth's orbit around the Sun. However, the Earth takes about 365.25 days to complete its movement around the Sun and we normally ignore those 0.25 days or 6 hours every year. But every four years, these 6 hours are added to make a day of 24 hours to keep the calendar seasons synchronised with solar seasons.

(ii) There is unequal day and night because of the inclination of the Earth's axis. Due to this inclination, the orientation of the Sun changes over a period of time.

4. Answer the following questions.
(i) What is midnight Sun?
(ii) Why does midnight Sun occur?

Ans. (i) Midnight Sun is a natural phenomenon where one can see the Sun even at midnight. This phenomenon occurs near the Arctic and Antarctic circles.
(ii) The Earth has a tilt of about 23.5 degrees on its axis. Due to this axial tilt, the Sun does not set in the Arctic circle region and the North pole during the summer solstice. At times of winter solstice, the Antarctic circle region and the South pole, experience the same conditions, these conditions are known as midnight Sun.

5. Give reasons.
(i) Why noon is the hottest time of the day?
(ii) Why does the Sun rise in the East?

Ans. (i) Noon is the hottest time of the day because the Sun is at its highest point in the sky at noon and lower latitudes get vertical and intense Sun's rays. Thus, noon time receives more intense Sun's rays and called the hottest time of the day.
(ii) Due to rotation of the Earth from West to East, it appears that the Sun rises in the East and sets in the West.

6. What are the phases of the Sun?

Ans. The three phases of the Sun are
(i) The time when the Sun begins to rise is known as dawn. It is the period between sunrise and full day light.
(ii) At noon, the Sun reaches its highest peak which is also called zenith.
(iii) As the Sun begins to disappear, it is known as dusk. It is the period between sunset and complete darkness.

7. What are the effects of the speed of rotation?

Ans. The effects of the speed of rotation are
- Due to the speed of the Earth's rotation, the ocean currents and the air is deflected towards the right in the Northern hemisphere and towards the left in the Southern hemisphere. This effect is known as 'coriolis effect'.
- Due to the speed of rotation, atmospheric changes occur which is due to the deflection of the cyclones and anti-cyclones in both the hemispheres.
- A centrifugal force is created due to the speed of Earth's rotation which makes the Earth bulge at the equator and flattened at the poles.

8. A complete revolution of the Earth makes a calendar year. In this context answer the following questions.
(i) How much time is taken by the Earth to complete one revolution?
(ii) What is a leap year?
(iii) When do we have an extra day in the calendar?

Ans. (i) The Earth takes about 365.25 days to complete its revolution once. This is roughly taken as 365 days which is a calendar year or Earth year.
(ii) The year with an extra day is known as a leap year. In a leap year, there are total 366 days.
(iii) Since, the time taken by the Earth to complete its one revolution is 1/4th day more than a calendar year of 365 days. Thus, after every four years an extra day is added to the calendar year. This extra day is added to the month of February.

9. What are the characteristics of revolution?

Ans. Refer to chapter theory page no. 23

10. What are the effects of the inclination of the Earth's axis?

Ans. Following are the effects of the inclination of the Earth's axis
- **Variation in the Length of Day and Night** If the Earth had a vertical axis, then the length of the day and night would have been similar at all the places. This in reality does not happen as the Earth is tilted.
- **Alteration of the Seasons During the Year** The Earth completes its one revolution in a year in an ecliptical path. Due to the inclination of the axis, the North pole always remains inclined towards the polaris and the South pole stays away from it because of which the people on the Earth experience changes in the temperature and day and night.
- **Other Effects of the Inclination of the Earth's Axis** Due to inclination of the Earth's axis, the winters have longer nights and summers have longer days. During the time when the Northern hemisphere experiences longer nights, the Southern hemisphere experiences longer days and *vice-versa.*

11. Explain the variations of day and night throughout the year.

Ans. The variations of day and night throughout the year are
- As the Earth moves away from the Sun, its rays reach the Earth's surface as the parallel rays. On 21st June every year, the Sun is overhead the Earth at the noon at the Tropic of Cancer and all the latitudes have longest days on the Earth in the Northern hemisphere. From 21st June onwards, the length of the days starts increasing with the increasing latitude in the North of the equator.
- On 22nd December, the Sun comes overhead the Tropic of Capricorn and the phenomena gets reversed. All the latitudes have their longest days on the Earth in the Southern hemisphere. From 22nd December onwards, the length of the days starts decreasing in the Southern hemisphere.

- On 21st March and 23rd September every year, the Sun is overhead at the equator due to which all the places have equal days and nights. There is 12 hours of day and 12 hours of night.

12. Differentiate between aphelion and perihelion.

Ans. Differences between aphelion and perihelion are

Aphelion	Perihelion
It occurs when the Earth moves away from the Sun.	It occurs when the Earth comes closer to the Sun.
On 4th of July, the Earth is at its farthest point from the Sun.	On 3rd January, the Earth is nearest to the Sun.
The farthest distance of the Earth from the Sun is 152 million kms.	The nearest distance of the Earth from the Sun is 147 million kms.

13. Differentiate between summer solstice and winter solstice.

Ans. Difference between summer solstice and winter solstice are

Summer Solstice	Winter Solstice
The position of the Earth on 21st June, every year is known as summer solstice.	The position of the Earth on 22nd December every year is known as winter solstice.
During a summer solstice, the Sun is overhead at the Tropic of Cancer.	During a winter solstice, the Sun is directly overhead the Tropic of Capricorn.
On a summer solstice, the Northern hemisphere has the longest day and the shortest night.	On this day, the Northern hemisphere has the shortest day and the longest night.

14. Differentiate between autumn equinox and vernal equinox.

Ans. Differences between autumn equinox and vernal equinox are

Autumn Equinox	Vernal Equinox
23rd September is called the day of autumn equinox.	21st March is called the day of vernal equinox.
In the Northern hemisphere, autumn begins on the autumn equinox.	In the Northern hemisphere, spring begins on the vernal equinox.
The North pole begins to tilt away from the Sun.	The North pole begins to lean towards the Sun again.

15. Why are seasons in the Northern hemisphere opposite to those in the Southern hemisphere?

Ans. The seasons in the Northern hemisphere are opposite to those in the Southern hemisphere because of three factors, the tilt of the Earth's axis, its revolution around the Sun and both the hemisphere are on opposite sides of the Earth. If one side is illuminated, then the other side must be shadowed. So, the Earth alternates between Northern hemisphere tilted towards the Sun and Southern hemisphere tilted away from the Sun and *vice-versa*. It does so moving around Sun. Tilting towards the Sun makes summer season and tilting away from the Sun makes winter season. As the hemispheres are on opposite sides, if Northern hemisphere has summer the Southern hemisphere must have winter and *vice-versa*. In the same way, if one hemisphere has spring season the other must face autumn season.

16. Explain about summer solstice in the Northern hemisphere.

Ans. Refer to chapter theory page no. 25

17. What do you understand by winter solstice ?

Ans. Refer to chapter theory page no. 25.

Chapter Assessment

Section-I

Multiple Choice Questions

1. In which season Christmas is celebrated in Australia?
   (a) Winter season (b) Summer season
   (c) Autumn season (d) Spring season
2. When do equinoxes occur on the Earth?
   (a) 21st March
   (b) 23rd September
   (c) Both (a) and (b)
   (d) None of the above
3. Days and nights occur on Earth due to ....
   (a) rotation (b) revolution
   (c) Both (a) and (b) (d) None of these
4. What is meant by Equinox?
   (a) Neither of the poles is tilted towards the Sun
   (b) North Pole is tilted towards Sun
   (c) South Pole is tilted towards Sun
   (d) Both poles are tilted towards Sun

Section-II

Short Questions

1. What is meant by solstices?
2. Which is the longest and the shortest day in the Southern hemisphere?
3. What is the distance of Earth from the Sun on aphelion and perihelion?
4. What is the direction of rotation and revolution of the Earth?
5. Define the following.
   (i) Coriolis Effect (ii) Circle of illumination
6. Give reasons.
   (i) The people living in the East see the Sun before the people living in the West.
   (ii) The duration of day and night varies at different places.
7. Differentiate between summer and winter solstice
8. What is the Kepler's Law of Planetary Motion?
9. What is the difference between rotation and revolution of the Earth?

Long Questions

1. Describe the three phases of the Sun.
2. How inclination of the Earth's axis causes day and night?
3. What is the position of the Sun on the following days.
   (i) 22nd December
   (ii) 21st June
   (iii) 21st March
4. Where do the following heat zones lie? Also write their temperature.
   (i) Temperate zone
   (ii) Frigid zone
   (iii) Torrid zone
5. When do the equinoxes occur?
6. What would have been the effect on Earth if it had vertical axis?

CHAPTER

04

Structure of the Earth

SYLLABUS

Earth's Structure Core, mantle, crust-meaning, extent and their composition.

The study of origin of the Earth plays an important role in determining its chemical composition, structure, temperature, pressure and density at various depths inside the Earth. During Earth's formation, several layers also formed that covered its surface.

Sources about the Earth's Structure

The interior structure of the Earth is quite different to its outer structure. A part of the inner structure is liquid, while another part is very dense and is thick solid. It is not possible to study the Earth's interior directly, due to its greater depth, intense heat and pressure. Thus, there are certain direct and indirect sources of information that are used to study the interior of the Earth.

Direct Sources of Information

- **Mining** Surface rocks, obtained from mining areas are the most easily available source of information about the Earth.
- **Drilling** Going beyond 3-4 km in mines is not possible, as it is very hot at this depth. So scientists have taken up a number of projects to penetrate deeper depths to explore the conditions in the crustal portion.

These projects are Deep Ocean Drilling Project and Integrated Ocean Drilling Project. These projects have provided information through the analysis of materials collected at different depths.

- **Volcanic Eruption** When the molten material (magma) is thrown onto the surface of the Earth during volcanic eruption, it becomes available for source of information like depth, density and composition of the Earth.

Indirect Sources of Information

- **Meteors** The material and the structure observed in the meteors are similar to that of the Earth. Hence, this becomes a source of information about the interior of the Earth.
- **Gravitation** The gravitational force is not same at different latitudes on the surface. The gravity values also differ according to the mass of the material. The reading of the gravity at different places is also influenced by many other factors. When these readings differ from expected values, such a difference is called **gravity anomaly**. It gives information about the distribution of mass of the material in the Earth's crust.
- **Magnetic Field** Magnetic surveys provide information about the distribution of magnetic materials in the crustal portion and thus, provide information about the distribution of materials in this part.

- **Seismic Activity** It is one of the most important sources of information about the interior of the earth. It provides a complete picture of the layered interior of the Earth. The scientific instruments which record the seismic waves or earthquake waves, have enabled the scientists to know about the pressure, density and temperature of the interior of the Earth.

Earth's Structure

The Earth's interior is made up of several concentric layers. On the basis of physical properties and chemical composition of the Earth, it can be divided into three layers, the core (the innermost layer), the mantle and the crust (outermost layer).

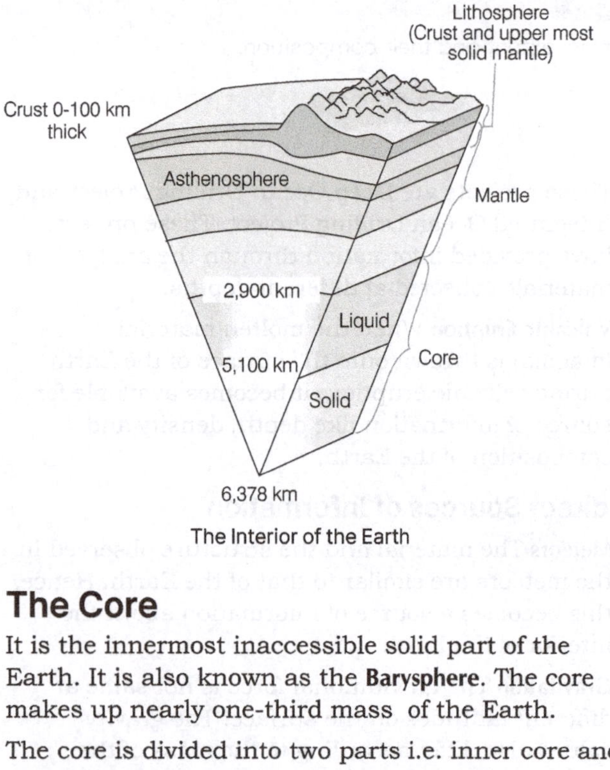

The Interior of the Earth

The Core

It is the innermost inaccessible solid part of the Earth. It is also known as the **Barysphere**. The core makes up nearly one-third mass of the Earth.

The core is divided into two parts i.e. inner core and outer core.

(i) **The outer core** It is a 2,200 km thick liquid core, due to the extremely high temperature that melts all the minerals and rocks. **S-waves**[1] disappear in the outer core which suggests that it is in a molten state. Magnetic electric current exists in the outer core which is known as magnetic field.

(ii) **The inner core** It is a 1,250 km thick solid core. The inner core is very dense and solid due to extreme pressure and density of all the layers lying above it.

Composition and Extent

The core is mainly composed of **iron** (Fe) and **nickel** (Ni) which is responsible for Earth's magnetism. The magnetic field is oriented towards North Pole and South Pole. Together they are known as **NiFe**.

The core is the thickest layer of the Earth having a thickness of 4671 kms. The average diameter of the core is about 6950 kms.

The temperature here ranges from about 4400° C to about 6000° C. The average density of core at the mantle-core boundary is about 5 g/cm^3 and at the centre of the Earth is about 13 g/cm^3.

The Mantle

The Earth's second layer is the mantle. The mantle is found between the crust and the core with its upper surface marked as **Mohorovicic Discontinuity**[2] and the lower surface marked as **Gutenberg Discontinuity**.

The mantle is divided into two layers

(a) **The Upper Mantle or the Asthenosphere** The upper mantle extends from the Mohorovicic Discontinuity to the depth of 700 kms. It is made up of mainly solid rocks and it is cooler. It is partially molten and has an average temperature of around 1100°C.

(b) **The Lower Mantle or the Mesosphere** The lower mantle extends from 700 kms to 2900 kms. It is made up of semi-molten rocks due to contact with the core. This layer has an average temperature of around 1900°C. Thus, it is hotter and denser than upper mantle due to increase in pressure and heat towards the core.

1 **S-waves** They are seismic body waves that shakes the ground back and forth. They are created by earthquake and they travel only in solid particles.

2 **Discontinuity** A plane or surface making a change in physical or chemical properties in soil or rock mass.

Composition and Extent

The mantle is the largest layer, composed of rocks, oxides and silicates under high pressure. It is mainly composed of magnesium and iron silicates in the upper mantle and nickel and iron in the lower mantle.

The depth of mantle is about 2900 kms. It has a density of 3.4 g/cm^3. It comprises 84% of Earth's volume. The temperature in this layer is high and ranges between 1000° C near its boundary with the crust to 3700° C near its boundary with the core. The pressure exerted by the upper layers keep the lower layers in almost solid state.

Gutenberg and Mohorovicic Discontinuity

The Gutenberg Discontinuity is the boundary between the mantle and core. It occurs within Earth's interior at a depth of about 2,900 km. Here, the density increases due to the change of the seismic waves. Gutenberg discontinuity is dense as it has a greater percentage of iron. Here, sudden change happens in seismic waves. The Primary waves decrease in velocity and the Secondary waves disappear completely.

The Mohorovicic Discontinuity or 'Moho' is the boundary between the crust and the mantle. It was discovered in 1909 by **Andrija Mohorovicic,** a Croatian **seismologist**[3]. It is 8 km thick under the oceans and about 32 km thick beneath the continents.

The Crust

The outer most layer of the Earth is the crust. It is the thinnest layer in comparison to the other layers. It is also known as **lithosphere**, derived from the word '*Lethos*' which means rocks.

The crust is divided into many pieces called plates. These plates float on the soft, plastic mantle which is located below the crust. They usually move along smoothly, but sometimes they stick and build up pressure. When such pressure is built up, the rock bends until it breaks. This results in various tectonic activities like earthquakes, volcanoes, formation of mountains, rift valley and ocean trenches.

The crust or lithosphere is believed to be made up of 15 such **tectonic plates**[4]. These are North American plate, Caribbean plate, South American plate, Scotia plate, Antarctic plate, Eurasian plate, Arabian plate, African plate, Indian plate, Philippine plate, Australian plate, Pacific plate, Juan de Fuca plate, Cocos plate and Nazca plate.

Composition and Extent

Crust has two types i.e. **oceanic crust** and **continental crust**. Oceanic crust is composed of basalt and continental crust is composed of lighter granite.

The crust is only about 5-10 kms thick under the oceans (oceanic crust) and about 35 kms thick under the continents (continental crust). The continental crust is thicker in the areas of major mountain systems. It is as much as 70 km thick in the Himalayan region. It comprises 1% of Earth's mass and contains all known life in the universe.

The oceanic crust has an average density of 2.7 g/cm^3 while the continental crust has an average density of 3 g/cm^3. The temperature of the upper part of the crust is as same as the atmospheric temperature. But it increases with depth, reaching from about 500 °C to 1,000 °C at the boundary with the underlying mantle.

Chemical Composition of the Crust

The Earth's crust mainly consists of the silica, aluminium and magnesium. Radio active minerals like thorium and uranium are also present in this layer, which are environment friendly source of energy.

The Earth's crust is generally divided into two parts i.e. **SiAl** and **SiMA.** SiAl is named after Silicon (Si) and Aluminium (Al) and SiMA is named after Silica (Si) and Magnesium (Mg). SiAl is the outer part or upper part of the crust whereas SiMA is the lower part of the crust. The rocks that form SiMA are heavier having a density of about 3 to 3.4 g/cm^3 as compared to the rocks that form SiAl.

Materials of the Earth's Crust

Earth's crust is composed of various types of rocks. The term 'rocks' refers to both hard materials like granite as well as soft and loose particles like sand, silt and clay.

Rocks are built from minerals and areas are heterogenous in composition. Minerals, in turn are formed from natural elements and compounds which are chemical in nature and are homogenous in form.

3 **Seismologist** A scientist who does research in seismology or causes and effect of earthquake.

4 **Tectonic Plates** Tectonic plates are massive, irregular shaped slab of solid rock, generally composed of both oceanic and continental lithosphere.

Geologists have identified many minerals in the Earth's crust. Most of them are made of only 8 elements which are

Elements	Abundance (by weight)
Oxygen	47
Silicon	28
Aluminium	8
Iron	5
Calcium	3.5
Sodium	3
Potassium	2.5
Magnesium	2

Check Your LEARNING...

1. Why meteors are important sources for studying Earth's formation?
2. What is the composition of the core of the Earth?
3. Give the meaning of the Mohorovicic Discontinuity.
4. What are the materials found inside the earth's crust?

QUiCK Revision

- Mining, drilling and volcanic eruption are the direct sources of information that are used to study the interior of the Earth.
- Meteors, gravitation, magnetic field, and seismic activity are the indirect sources of information to study the interior of the Earth.
- The Earth can be divided into three layers i.e. the crust (outermost layer), the mantle and the core (the innermost layer).
- The core lies below the mantle and is around the centre of the Earth. It is also known as the Barysphere.
- The core is mainly composed of Iron (Fe) and Nickel (Ni). Together they are known as 'NIFE'. It is the thickest layer of the Earth having a thickness of 4671 kms. The average diameter of the core is about 6950 km.
- The average density of the core varies from 5 gm per cubic cm to 13 gm per cubic cm. The temperature of the core varies between 4400 degree Celsius to 6000 degree Celsius.
- The Earth's second layer is the mantle. The mantle is found between the crust and the core with its upper surface marks as Mohorovicic discontinuity and the lower surface marked as Gutenburg discontinuity.
- The upper mantle extends from Mohorovicic discontinuity to the depth of 700 km.
- The lower mantle extends from 700 kms to 2900 kms.
- The depth of mantle is about 2900 kms with a varying density of 3.4 to 5 g per cubic cm.
- The crust is only about 3-5 miles (5-10 kms) thick under the oceans (oceanic crust) and about 25 miles (35 kms) thick under the continents (continental crust).
- The outermost layer of the Earth known as the crust or lithosphere is made up of mostly solid silicate rocks like basalt and granite.
- The continental crust is mainly composed of granite, whereas the oceanic crust consists of a volcanic lava rock called basalt.
- The Earth's crust is generally divided into two parts i.e. SiAl and SiMa.
- The crust is mainly composed of various types of rocks i.e. both hard and soft materials like granite and sand respectively.

Chapter Practice

Section-I

Multiple Choice Questions

1. Which one of the following is a direct source of information about the interior of the Earth?
   (a) Earthquake waves
   (b) Gravitational force
   (c) Volcanoes
   (d) Earth magnetism

Ans. (c) Volcanoes

2. The rock which is made up of molten magma is
   (a) igneous (b) sedimentary
   (c) metamorphic (d) All of these

Ans. (a) igneous

3. Which one of the following earthquake waves is more destructive?
   (a) P-waves
   (b) Surface waves
   (c) S-waves
   (d) None of the above

Ans. (b) Surface waves

4. The innermost layer of the Earth is ....
   (a) crust (b) core
   (c) mantle (d) asthenosphere

Ans. (b) core

5. The inner core of the Earth is made up of ....
   (a) copper (b) iron
   (c) nickel-iron (d) platinum

Ans. (c) nickel-iron

6. The thinnest layer of the Earth is ....
   (a) crust (b) mantle
   (c) inner core (d) outer core

Ans. (a) crust

7. Which one of the following describes the lithosphere?
   (a) Upper and lower mantle
   (b) Crust and core
   (c) Crust and upper mantle
   (d) Mantle and core

Ans. (c) Crust and upper mantle

8. Sudden movement of the lithosphere which causes mass destruction is ....
   (a) earthquake (b) volcano
   (c) Both (a) and (b) (d) None of these

Ans. (c) Both (a) and (b)

9. The minimum thickness of crust under the oceans is
   (a) 8 km (b) 2 km (c) 5 km (d) 10 km

Ans. (c) 5 km

10. The main mineral of continental mass is called SiAl and consists of
    (a) silicon and aluminium (b) silicon and magnesium
    (c) sulphur dioxide (d) selenium aluminate

Ans. (a) silicon and aluminium

11. Give reason for the following.
    The density gradually increases as we move towards the centre of the Earth.
    (a) It is due to the presence of heavy metals.
    (b) It is due to the presence of light metals.
    (c) It is due to the presence of mixed metals.
    (d) None of the above

Ans. (a) It is due to the presence of heavy metals.

12. Give reason for the following.
    The outer core is in liquid state.
    (a) Due to extremely high temperature.
    (b) Due to extremely high pressure.
    (c) Due to low movement of tectonic plates.
    (d) All of these

Ans. (b) Due to extremely high pressure.

13. Give reason for the following.
    The inner core is very dense.
    (a) There is extreme pressure in the inner core.
    (b) The density is very high in the inner core.
    (c) Temperature is extremely low in the inner core.
    (d) Both (a) and (b)

Ans. (d) Both (a) and (b)

14. Give reason for the following.
    Density increases at Gutenberg Discontinuity.
    (a) Iron is found in abundance in this layer.
    (b) The seismic waves change in this layer.
    (c) All types of minerals are found here.
    (d) Both (a) and (b)

Ans. (d) Both (a) and (b)

15. Give reason for the following.
    Crust layer of the Earth is termed as SiAl.
    (a) It is composed of Silica and Iron.
    (b) It is composed of only Iron.
    (c) It is composed of only magnesium.
    (d) It is composed of both Silica and Aluminium.

Ans. (d) It is composed of both Silica and Aluminium.

16. Which of the following statements is incorrect?
(i) The density gradually decreases as we move towards centre of the Earth.
(ii) The minerals are mostly formed till 100 km outside the Earth.
(iii) The study of meteors is the secondary source.

Codes
(a) Only (i) (b) Only (ii)
(c) (i) and (ii) (d) All of these

Ans. (c) (i) and (ii)

17. Which of the following statements is correct?
(i) Iron is a heavy metal.
(ii) Nickel which is present in the interior part of the Earth is a light metal.
(iii) The Earth's interior is made up of two layers.

Codes
(a) Only (i) (b) Only (ii)
(c) (ii) and (iii) (d) All of these

Ans. (a) Only (i)

18. Match the following.

List-I	List-II
A. Seismic waves	1. Volcanic eruption
B. Meteors	2. Molten rocks
C. Volcanoes	3. Inside the earth
D. Magma	4. Secondary source

Codes

	A	B	C	D		A	B	C	D
(a)	1	2	3	4	(b)	2	1	4	3
(c)	3	4	1	2	(d)	4	3	2	1

Ans. (c)

19. Match the following.

List-I	List-II
A. Temperature of Upper Mantle	1. 500°C to 1,000 °C at depth
B. Temperature of Lower Mantle	2. 4400° C to 6000° C
C. Temperature of Core	3. 1900° C
D. Temperature of Crust	4. 1100° C

Codes

	A	B	C	D		A	B	C	D
(a)	1	2	3	4	(b)	2	1	4	3
(c)	3	4	1	2	(d)	4	3	2	1

Ans. (d)

Section-II

Short Questions

1. What is the importance of the study of origin of the Earth?

Ans. The study of origin of the Earth plays an important role in determining its chemical composition, structure, temperature, pressure and density at various depths inside the Earth.

2. At what depth inside the Earth provides us information about the increasing temperature and pressure?

Ans. The interior of the Earth upto the depth of 3 to 4 km provides us information about the increasing temperature and pressure. These informations play important role in studying Earth's structure.

3. Describe the direct sources that inform about the Earth's interior.

Ans. The direct sources of information are
- The easiest source of information about the Earth's interior is provided by the rocks that we get from the mining areas.
- Molten magma coming out of the volcanoes are also direct sources of information.

4. Name the indirect sources that inform about the interior of the Earth.

Ans. The indirect sources that inform about the interior of the Earth are
- The temperature and pressure inside the Earth.
- The density of the different layers of the Earth.
- The behaviour of the earthquake waves.
- The evidence from the meteorites.

5. Which two radioactive minerals found on the upper layer of the Earth are energy sources?

Ans. On the upper layer of the Earth, the radioactive minerals like thorium and uranium are an important source of energy. They are environment friendly sources of energy.

6. How the pressure is important to know about the Earth's interior?

Ans. The outer layers of the Earth exert pressure on the layers inside the surface of the Earth. This pressure exerted by the layers has been used as a source of information to determine the structure and composition of the Earth.

7. How are meteorites used as a source of information about the interior of the Earth?

Ans. Meteors that reach the Earth's surface are important source of information. Meteors come from outside the Earth, but possess a similar material and structure as that of the Earth. Thus, they are used for getting information about the interior of the Earth.

8. Answer the following questions.
(i) What is the average diameter of the core?
(ii) What is the average density of the core of the Earth?

Ans. (i) The average diameter of the core is about 6950 km.
(ii) The average density of the core varies from 5 g/cm^3 to 13 g/cm^3.

9. Answer the following questions.
(i) What is the composition of core?
(ii) Name the thickest layer of the Earth.

Ans. (i) The core is divided into two parts i.e. inner core and outer core. The outer core is a 2,200 km thick liquid core, whereas the inner core is a 1,250 km thick solid core. The core is mainly composed of Iron (Fe) and Nickel (Ni). Together they are known as 'NiFe'.

(ii) Core is the thickest layer of the Earth having a thickness of 4671 kms.

10. What is Gutenburg Discontinuity?

Ans. The Gutenberg Discontinuity occurs within Earth's interior at a depth of about 2900 km. It is the boundary of the mantle and core.

11. What is Mohorovicic Discontinuity and who discovered it?

Ans. The Mohorovicic Discontinuity or 'Moho' is the boundary between the crust and the mantle. The Mohorovicic Discontinuity was discovered in 1909 by Andrija Mohorovicic, a Croatian seismologist.

12. Define the following
(i) Asthenosphere
(ii) Mesosphere

Ans. (i) **Asthenosphere** It is the upper mantle layer that extends from the Mohorovicic Discontinuity to the depth of 700 kms. It is made up of mainly solid rocks and has an average temperature of 1100° Celsius.

(ii) **Mesosphere** It is the lower mantle layer that extends from 700 kms to 2900 kms. It is made up of semi-molten rocks and has an average temperature of 1900° Celsius.

13. Divide the crust based on its composition?

Ans. The crust is divided into two categories i.e. SiAl and SiMA. SiAl stands for Silica (Si) and Aluminium (Al) and SiMA stands for Silica (Si) and Magnesium (Ma). The SiAl floats over SiMa due to its density. SiAl consists of the continents and SiMA consists of the oceans.

14. (i) What do you understand by density?
(ii) What is the average density of the Earth's crust?

Ans. (i) The density of a substance is the relationship between the mass of the substance and how much space it takes up.

(ii) The average density of the crust is less than 2.7 g/cm^3.

Long Questions

1. What are the direct sources of information about the interior of the Earth?

Ans. Refer to chapter theory page no. 33

2. How does the temperature provide us information about the interior of the Earth?

Ans. It is true that temperature provides us information about the interior of the Earth. It is known to us that as we move down below the surface of the Earth, the temperature keeps on increasing. It increases 1 degree for every 32 metres of descent. Increasing at this rate, the temperature at the center of the Earth will be extremely high.

At this temperature, the rocks and minerals do not remain solid inside the Earth's surface Thus, it is assumed that the volcanic eruptions take place from nearly 48 kms inside the Earth.

On the upper layers of the Earth, the radioactive minerals like thorium and uranium become an important source of heat for us. There is a sharp increase in the temperature as we go into the deeper depths from the surface.

3. Answer the following questions.
(i) How does the density varies at the various layers inside the Earth?
(ii) Explain the composition of the Earth's crust.

Ans. (i) The average density of the Earth is 5.5 g/cm^3. The surface layer of the Earth comprising of the minerals and rocks has a density of 2.7 g/cm^3. Thus, it can be said that the density of the materials inside the Earth is more than that of the layers on the outer surface. The density gradually increases as we move towards the center of the Earth due to the presence of heavy metals like iron and nickel. Therefore, the density is said to be varying at every layer inside the Earth's surface.

(ii) The outer most layer of the Earth is the crust. Crust has two types i.e. oceanic crust and continental crust. Oceanic crust is composed of basalt and continental crust is composed of lighter granite.

4. What are the features of the mantle?

Ans. The features of mantle are

- The mantle is the largest layer, composed of rocks, oxides and silicates under high pressure. It is mainly composed of magnesium and iron silicates in the upper mantle and nickel and iron in the lower mantle.
- The depth of mantle is about 2900 kms. It has a density of 3.4 g/cm^3. It comprises 84% of Earth's volume.
- The temperature of the mantle is high and ranges between 1000° C near its boundary with the crust to 3700° C near its boundary with the core. The pressure exerted by the upper layers keep the lower layers in almost solid state.

5. Write a short note on Mohorovicic Discontinuity.

Ans. Refer to chapter theory page no. 34.

6. Answer the following questions.
   (i) What are the contents of the Earth's crust?
   (ii) What is the average density of the two layers of the Earth's crust?
   (iii) How does the temperature varies in the Earth's crust?

Ans. (i) The Earth's crust consists of two types of rocks, namely granite and basalt. The continental crust is mainly composed of granite whereas, the oceanic crust consists of volcanic lava rock called basalt.

(ii) The continental crust has an average density of 2.7 g per cubic cm and the oceanic crust has an average density 3 g per cubic cm.

(iii) The temperatures of the crust vary from air temperature on top to about 500°C to 1000°C in the deepest parts of the crust.

7. What are the materials found in the Earth's crust?

Ans. Refer to chapter theory page no. 35 and 36.

8. Briefly explain the chemical composition of the crust or lithosphere.

Ans. Refer to chapter theory page no. 35.

Chapter Assessment

Section-I

Multiple Choice Questions

1. The third layer of the Earth which comes after mantle is known as ....
   (a) crust (b) asthenosphere
   (c) outer core (d) inner core
2. In which part of the Earth is NiFe found?
   (a) Crust (b) Mantle
   (c) Core (d) All of these
3. The outermost layer of the Earth is ....
   (a) asthenosphere (b) crust
   (c) trench (d) ridge
4. Silicates, feldspar, mica etc. are characteristics of which layer of the Earth?
   (a) Crust (b) Mantle
   (c) Inner core (d) Outer core

Section-II

Short Questions

1. What are seismic waves?
2. Write two characteristics of the Earth's crust.
3. Name the constituents of SiAl.
4. Mention any two features of core.
5. Mention any two features of lithosphere.
6. Define the following.
   (i) Barysphere
   (ii) Gutenburg Discontinuity
7. Differentiate between the following.
   (i) Inner core and outer core
   (ii) Mantle and crust

Long Questions

1. Describe the direct sources of information about the Earth's crust.
2. 'The Core of the Earth is also known as NiFe.' Explain.
3. Where do we find the following? Also name them.
   (a) SiAl
   (b) SiMA
   (c) Lithosphere
4. Answer the following questions.
   (i) What is the chemical composition of mantle?
   (ii) Where is the mantle located?
   (iii) What is the average temperature of this layer?
5. What are the major consequences of the movements of the Earth?
6. How does the temperature varies in the interior of the Earth?

CHAPTER

05

Landforms of the Earth

SYLLABUS

Landforms of the Earth Mountains, plateaus, plains (definition, types and their formation) :
• Mountains - fold, residual and block. • Plateaus - intermont and volcanic.
• Plains – structural and depositional • Examples from the world and India.

Landforms are natural physical features of the Earth's surface, for example, valleys, plateaus, mountains, plains, etc. One-fourth of the Earth's surface is covered by land. At some places, the land may be too high and at some places the land may be too low; some areas are lush green while some areas are dry and barren.

Factors Leading to Landform Development

- **Plate Tectonics** There are several tectonic plates beneath the Earth's surface. These plates float on the semi-molten asthenosphere and their horizontal movement is very slow. These plates push, collide or move away from each other. This movement creates disturbances in the sedimentary rock deposits lying in between two or more plates. When sedimentary rocks are compressed, it causes folding of the rocks. This process is responsible for the formation of mountains.
- **Epeirogenic Movement/Uplift and Submergence** The word epeirogenic has been derived from two Greek words 'Epeiros' which means 'continent' and 'genic' or 'genetic' which means 'building'. Epeirogenic movements are vertical movements which are also known as continent building movements. These movements act along the radius from the Earth's centre to the surface. These are characterised by large-scale uplift or subsidence of land area.

  These movements are caused by faulting or crack in the Earth's surface. These are responsible for the formation of block mountains, basins, rift valleys, etc.

  Both orogenic and epeirogenic forces are together known as **diastrophic forces** which originate deep inside the Earth. They act horizontally and vertically and produce reliefs features such as mountains, plateaus, plains, lakes and faults.
- **Exogenic Forces** Exogenic or external forces operate on the surface of the Earth and cause formation of landforms. These forces are weathering, mass movement, erosion and deposition of existing landforms. They form new landforms through process of erosion and deposition.

Types of Landforms on the Earth

The landforms can be broadly classified into three main types on the basis of the relief features such as

(i) Mountains (ii) Plateaus

(iii) Plains

(i) Mountains

A mountain is a landform that rises high above the surrounding terrain in a limited area. It has some kind of significant prominence. Mountains are considered to be steeper, taller and more prominent than hills.

Mountains can rise individually, but usually form in a series of mountains called a **mountain range** or a **chain of mountains.**

Some features of the mountains are

- Mountains are the landmasses that rises approx 900 m above the mean sea level.
- Some mountains have extensive chain of mountains that form mountain ranges, like the Andes in South Africa.
- Some mountain ranges like Himalayas in Asia, have been continuously growing and rising.
- Some mountain ranges like Aravalli in India, are the oldest fold mountain in the world.
- Most of the mountains are the source of many rivers. For example, the Himalayas are the source of Gangas, Indus, Jhelum, Beas and so on.

Formation of the Mountains

The period in which a mountain build is defined as **orogeny**. Orogenesis is the process of mountain building. It occurs when two tectonic plates collide with each other. They either force material upwards to form mountain belts such as the Alps and Himalayas or they cause one plate to be subducted below the other, resulting in volcanic mountain chains such as the Andes.

Types of Mountains

On the basis of their mode of formation, mountain can be classified into fold mountains, block mountains and residual mountains.

Fold Mountains

Fold mountains are mountains whose rocks are predominantly folded. These mountains are formed by many forces like lateral compression of the Earth's crust and the movements caused by stresses in the Earth's crust.

These stresses are the result of weight of the overlying rocks, movement in the mantle, expansion and contraction of some part of the Earth, etc. Due to these stresses and compressive forces, wrinkles or folds occur along the lines of weakness which form fold mountains.

Besides this, when an area of sea separates two plates, sediments settle on the sea floor in depressions called **geosynclines**. These sediments gradually become compressed into sedimentary rock. When the two plates move towards each other again, the layers of sedimentary rock on the sea floor become **crumpled**[1] and folded. This result in appearing of the sedimentary rock above sea level as a range of fold mountains.

Upward folds in rocks are called **anticlines** or crest and downward folds in rocks are called **synclines** or troughs. Severely folded and faulted rocks are called **nappes**.

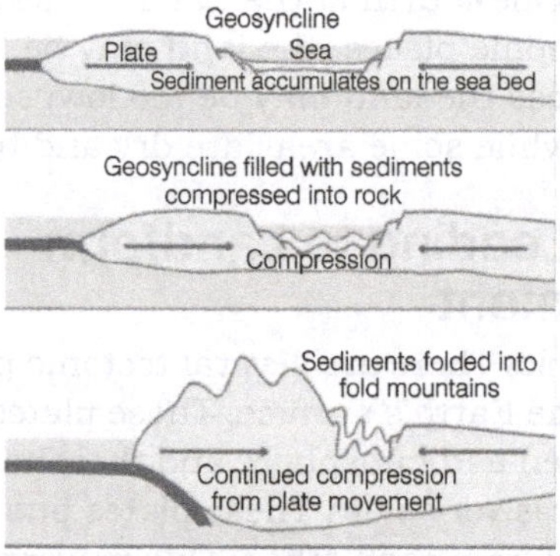

Fold Mountains

Characteristics of Fold Mountains

- Fold mountains are mainly composed of sedimentary rocks. These rocks were formed due to the deposition and consolidation of sediments in shallow oceans like Tethys Sea (e.g. the Himalayas).
- These mountains are highest and most extensive mountains of the world. These are greater in length, but smaller in width, e.g. the Himalayas (2400 km in length). These are associated with volcanic activity.

1 **Crumple** It refers to the compression or pressing together of rocks.

- These mountains are generally formed on the margins of continents (the Himalayas is the exception). They are located in two directions, e.g. the Rockies and Andes mouintains are in North-South direction and the Himalayas are in West-East direction. Due to these evidences, it is clear that all these mountains face the oceans.
- These mountains have parallel ranges and between these ranges, high plateaus known as intermontane plateaus are found, e.g. the Tibetan Plateau and Anatolian Plateau.
- Some fold mountains lie beneath the sea and their tops look like islands, e.g. in the West Indies.
- The fold mountains that generate forces along with volcanic mountain systems lead to the formation of ridges. For example, the Mid-Atlantic Ridge, which rises 3 km above the floor of the Atlantic Ocean and joins the Indian Ocean Ridge.

Types of Fold Mountains

The fold mountains are of two types

(i) **New or Young Fold Mountains** The main characteristics of these mountains are the complex folding of the rocks, faulting, volcanic activities, **cordillera**[2] formation, the erosion and weathering caused by running water, ice, winds and the existence of glacier-capped high peaks, etc. The Rockies, the Alps, the Himalayas, the Circum-Pacific oceanic mountains, etc are the examples of new or young fold mountains.

(ii) **Old Fold Mountains** These mountains were formed in **proterozoic era**[3] and subjected to denudation and uplift. During this peiod, many folds were formed and layers of rocks were wrapped. These mountains still have traces of volcanic activities.

The presence of **monadnocks**[4], **accordant summits**[5], sculptured domes, the irregular forms of peaks, relics plateaus, etc are some of the important characteristics of these mountains.

The examples of old mountains are Urals, the Nanshan, Caledonian and Hercynian mountains of Central Europe, the high-lands of Scotland, etc.

Block Mountains

These mountains are smooth sloped structures of large rocks. These mountains are formed by faults due to vertical tensional forces or epeirogenic forces. Block mountains are characterised by massiveness, steep slopes and comparatively smooth topography.

They usually arise in folded zones that once had a mountain relief, but have lost their plasticity and been smoothed by **denudation**[6]. Due to repeated tectonic action, these sections of the Earth's core do not form folds, but break into separate blocks.

If there are two parallel faults, the crustal block between them may either rise as horst block mountain and begin to form ranges and others sink as grabens or a rift valley and form depressions.

These mountains occur along the plate boundary and especially fault-block mountains are found where plates are moving apart. The Rhine Rift Valley and Vosges, Black forest mountains in Europe, Vindhayas and Satpura ranges between which Narmada river flows, Salt range of Pakistan, Siera Nevada mountains of California, the Great Rift Valley running from East Africa to Syria through the Red Sea, etc are examples of block mountains.

Residual Mountains

These are already existing mountains which have changed their shape due to changed climatic conditions. They are also called **relict mountains.** These mountains are formed due to denudation and **erosion**[7] by which high mountains are gradually shaped into hills and ridges. Denudation and erosion are caused by natural agents such as wind, water, snow, etc.

2 **Cordillera** It is an extensive chain of mountains or mountain ranges.

3 **Proterozoic Era** It is a geological eon (extramely long perid of time) spanning the time interval from 2500 to 538.8 million years ago.

4 **Monadnock** It is an isolated or rigid or erosion-resistant rock rising above a plane.

5 **Accordant Summits** It indicates a denudated surface that become dissected by rivers.

6 **Denudation** It is the long-term process that cause the wearing away of the Earth's surface leading to a reduction in elevation and relief of landforms and landscapes.

7 **Erosion** It is the action of exogenic processes (such as water flow or wind) which remove soil and rock from one location on the Earth's crust and transport it to another location where it is deposited.

These mountains are also formed on plateaus due to down cutting action of rivers, e.g. the Deccan Plateau.

These are also known as mountains of denudation which are characterised by low elevations. Some of these mountains have gentle or precipitous relief, depending on the degree of erosion.

The Catskill range in the Southern New York, the Grand Canyon in Arizona, USA and the mountains of the Western Ghats, the Rajmahal Hills and the Parasnath mountain of Jharkhand are some examples of residual mountains.

Check Your LEARNING...

1. What do you mean by landforms?
2. Mention any one feature of mountains.
3. Give one example of young fold mountains.
4. How are residual mountains formed?

(ii) Plateaus

A plateau is a flat topped tableland that is elevated 500 feet above the mean sea level. Plateaus can be formed by a number of processes, including upwelling of volcanic magma, extrusion of lava, plate tectonic movements and erosion by water and glaciers. Plateaus occupy a large portion on the surface of the Earth. They are known as one of the oldest land forms.

The major characteristic features of the plateaus are

- They have a flat and rough top surface with extensive size.
- The rocks of the plateaus are layered with sandstone, shales and limestone.
- They rise abruptly from the surrounding regions.
- Usually, the plateaus possess a tabular shape.
- Rivers and streams cut deep valleys in the plateau region and change its smooth topography into a dissected plateau.
- The great Deccan Plateau of India is known to be a Tectonic plateau.

Types of Plateaus

On the basis of the locations, the plateaus can be classified into intermontane plateaus and volcanic plateaus.

Intermontane Plateaus

These plateaus are the largest and the tallest known plateaus in the world. They lie between the mountain ranges i.e. they are partly or wholly covered by the mountains.

The **Tibetan Plateau** in Asia is called the roof of the world, as it is the largest and the tallest known plateau of the world. Some other plateaus are Plateau of Bolivia, the Mexican Plateau, North American Cordillera Plateau, etc.

Volcanic Plateaus

These plateaus are formed due to the cooling down of volcanic lava by enormous accumulation of basaltic rock. Volcanic eruptions give rise to lava accumulations that cools and solidifies into rocks. This results in the formation of plateau. These are also known as **basalt plateaus.**

The Peninsular Plateau of India is formed by enormous accumulation of basalt rock. The Deccan Plateau of Peninsular India, Plateau of South Africa, Columbian Plateau and Ethiopian Plateau are some other examples of volcanic plateaus.

(iii) Plains

A plain is a large area of flat land at low elevation. Most of the plains are generally formed by action of rivers like deposition of sediments in a depression or erosion of a high landform into level land.

The height of plains is very close to the mean sea level and generally not more than 200 m above the mean sea level. The Great Plains of India are only 6-10 m high near the mouth of Ganges, while it is 200 m high in Punjab and Haryana. On the other hand, the Kashmir lake plain has an average height of 1700 m above mean sea level.

The characteristics of plains are

- The plains have a very gradual slope of land.
- They are usually flat and have a very slow rolling movement.
- They can even be slightly hilly.
- They are formed by both the internal and the external forces of the Earth.
- They can range from a very small size to very large extents.
- They can be found in every latitude. They are found on the sea coast as well as inside the continents.
- They are highly populated as compared to the mountains and plateaus.

Types of Plains

On the basis of their mode of formation, the plains are classified into structural plains and depositional plains.

Structural Plains

These are the structurally depressed areas of the world that make up some of the most extensive natural lowlands on the Earth's surface. They have been formed due to the upliftment (emergence) or subsidence of continental shelf. They are also formed by horizontally bedded rocks, relatively disturbed by the internal movements (endogenic forces) of the Earth.

Some of the significant structural plains are

- The Great plains of USA between Applachian Mountains and Atlantic Ocean were formed due to the upliftment of the land submerged under water.
- Gulf Coast is another example of emerged coastal plain.
- The Coromandel Plain in India was formed as a result of mild subsidence followed by sedimentation.
- Plains of Russia and Central lowlands of Australia are another examples of subsidence of the Continental shelf.

Depositional Plains

These plains are formed as a result of deposition of the sediments in lowlands, by the rivers, glaciers, wind, sea and volcanic eruptions. Majority of the plains of the world have been formed by deposition.

The depositional plain can be classified as

- **Alluvial Plains** When plains are formed by the river deposits (like silt, clay, alluvium, etc), they are called as riverine or alluvial plains. For example, the Northern Plains of India (the Ganga-Brahmaputra Plains) and Hwang-Ho Plains of China.
- **Drift Plains** These plains are formed as a result of the deposition by the glaciers. These are further classified as
  - **Till Plains** They are formed by the deposition below the ice.
  - **Marginal Moraines** They are formed due to deposition at the edge of the glaciers.
  - **Outwash Plains** These are formed due to the deposition of the fluvo-glacial deposits, e.g. Plains of West Germany.
  - **Loess Plains** They are formed as a result of the deposition by the winds. These are generally sandy deserts which have irregular and undulating surface made by existence of sand dunes and hollows. For example, Plains of Western Rajasthan, Plains of Kansas, Sahara in Africa, Loess Plains in China, etc.
- **Lacustrine Plains** These plains are formed as a result of the sediments in the lake basins. The Kashmir Valley in India is a notable example of the lacustrine plain. The soil that is found in these areas is very fertile which makes these areas suitable for the agricultural activities. Great Lake region of North America are also lacustrine plains.
- **Lava Plains** These plains are formed by the deposition of thin layers of lava. Plains of New Zealand and Central India are lava plains. These have black soil and are good for cotton cultivation.
- **Coastal Plains** These plains are formed by deposition by sea waves. The East Coast of India, the Coast of Germany and Denmark and the estuarine banks in the Netherlands are coastal plains.

Importance of Landforms

- Landforms are important as they give shape and structure to the Earth.
- They act as a geographical boundary and barrier between two locations.
- They provide space where humans can reside.
- They provide opportunity for agriculture and industrial practices.
- They represent the relief features of the Earth which directly have an effect on the environment and climatic conditions of various places. For example, the Himalayas shape the distinctive climate of the Indian subcontinent.

- The mountain ranges of the world become the source of **perennial rivers**[8] due to the presence of excessive snow on them.
- The forests are the habitats for the various plant and animal species. These forests are found on the mountains, hills and plateaus. Thus, forming biodiversity on Earth.
- Due to constant change in landforms, many minerals and fossil fuels come near the surface of Earth which makes their extraction easy.

Check Your LEARNING...

1. Give an example of volcanic plateau.
2. Mention any two features of plains.
3. How are coastal plains formed?
4. State any one importance of landforms for human beings.

QUiCK Revision

- Landforms are natural physical features of the Earth's surface, for example, valleys, plateaus, mountain, plains, etc.
- The landforms can be broadly classified into mountains, plateaus and plains on the basis of their relief features.
- A mountain is a landform that has some kind of significant prominence compared to the surrounding land, usually in the shape of a peak.
- Types of mountains are fold mountains, block mountains and residual mountains.
- Fold mountains are formed by the effects of foldings on layers within the upper part of the Earth's crust.
- Block mountains are formed due to vertical tensional forces or epeirogenic forces.
- Residual mountains are formed due to denudation and erosion.
- Examples of mountains are Himalaya as (Fold mountains), Vindhayas and Satpura range (Block mountains), Mountains of Western Ghats (Residual mountains).
- A plateau is a flat topped table land that is elevated above mean sea level. They occupy a large portion on the surface of the Earth.
- There are two types of plateaus i.e. intermontane plateaus and volcanic plateaus.
- Intermontane plateaus lie between the mountain ranges. Volcanic plateaus are formed due to the cooling down of the volcanic lava by enormous accumulation of basaltic rock.
- Example of pleatues are Deccan plateau, Mexican plateau, Columbian plateau, Ethiopian plateau, etc.
- A plain is a large area of flat land at low elevation.
- Examples of plains are Gangatic planes, Indus plains, Great plains of Nile, Brahmaputra plains, etc.
- Landforms are important for the Earth as they give shape and structure to the Earth.

8 **Perennial River** It is a stream or river (channel) that has continuous flow in parts of its stream bed all year round during years of normal rainfall.

Chapter Practice

Section-I

Multiple Choice Questions

1. External process leads to which of the following?
   (a) Sinking of the Earth surface
   (b) Upliftment of Earth's surface
   (c) Continuous wearing of the internal surface areas
   (d) Continuous wearing down of the land surface

Ans. (d) Continuous wearing down of the land surface

2. Mountains may be arranged in a line known by which name?
   (a) Horsts (b) Range
   (c) Glacier (d) All of these

Ans. (b) Range

3. Which of the following is an example of the fold mountain?
   (a) The Himalayas (b) The Alps
   (c) The Aravallis (d) All of these

Ans. (d) All of these

4. Which is the important mountain range of Europe?
   (a) Alps (b) Rockies
   (c) Andes (d) All of these

Ans. (a) Alps

5. Which of the following is the Peninsular plateau?
   (a) Deccan (b) Sahara
   (c) Chota Nagpur (d) None of these

Ans. (a) Deccan

6. The wearing away of the Earth's surface is called
   (a) mountains (b) plateau
   (c) erosion (d) deposition

Ans. (c) erosion

7. Which area is the most useful for human habitation?
   (a) Plain (b) Mountain
   (c) River (d) Glacier

Ans. (a) Plain

8. Tibet is a ....
   (a) plateau (b) mountain range
   (c) Both (a) and (b) (d) None of these

Ans. (a) plateau

9. Give reason for the following.
   Mountains are also known as storehouse of water.
   (a) Many mountains have glaciers in them.
   (b) Mountains are source region of many rivers.
   (c) Mountains receive highest rainfall.
   (d) Both (a) and (b)

Ans. (d) Both (a) and (b)

10. Give reason for the following.
    Plateaus are economically important.
    (a) These are rich in mineral resources.
    (b) Many plateaus have several waterfalls which help in the generation of hydroelectric power.
    (c) These are suitable for cultivation of crops like cotton.
    (d) All of the above

Ans. (d) All of the above

11. Give reason for the following.
    Plains are suitable for almost all human activities.
    (a) Most of these have fertile soils.
    (b) Most of these have level land.
    (c) These are agriculturally rich regions.
    (d) All of the above

Ans. (a) All of the above

12. Give reason for the following.
    The Mountains are not highly populated as compared to plains.
    (a) These are storehouse of rivers.
    (b) These have undulating topography.
    (c) The climate of mountains is very harsh.
    (d) Both (b) and (c)

Ans. (d) Both (b) and (c)

13. Which of the following statements is correct?
    (i) Tibet is the highest plateau in the world.
    (ii) Fold mountains are formed by the horizontal movements which are known as orogenic movements.
    (iii) Catskill range lies in the Southern New York.

    Codes
    (a) Only (i) (b) Only (ii)
    (c) (ii) and (iii) (d) All of these

Ans. (d) All of these

14. Which of the following statements is incorrect?
    (i) Plains have steep slopes.
    (ii) Usually plateaus posses a tabular shape.
    (iii) Deccan plateau is a tectonic plateau.

    Codes
    (a) Only (i)
    (b) Only (ii)
    (c) (i) and (ii)
    (d) All of the above

Ans. (a) Only (i)

15. Match the following.

	List-I		List-II
A.	Endogenic forces	1.	A raised fault block bounded by normal faults
B.	Exogenic forces	2.	A depressed block of the crust bounded by parallel normal faults
C.	Horst	3.	Inside the Earth
D.	Graben	4.	Outside the Earth

Codes

	A	B	C	D		A	B	C	D
(a)	1	2	3	4	(b)	2	1	4	3
(c)	3	4	1	2	(d)	4	3	2	1

Ans. (c)

16. Match the following.

	List-I		List-II
A.	Storehouse of Minerals	1.	Block mountains
B.	Lowland with gradual slope	2.	Tectonic plates
C.	Elevated tableland	3.	Plain
D.	Graben and Horst	4.	Plateaus

Codes

	A	B	C	D		A	B	C	D
(a)	1	2	3	4	(b)	2	1	4	3
(c)	3	4	1	2	(d)	4	3	2	1

Ans. (d)

Section-II

Short Questions

1. What do you mean by landforms?

Ans. Landforms are natural features of the Earth's surface, e.g. valleys, plateaus, mountains, plains, hills, loess or glaciers.

2. Name the types of mountains.

Ans. The types of mountains are fold mountains, block mountains and residual mountains.

3. How are fold mountains formed?

Ans. Fold mountains are formed by the horizontal compressional forces that crumple the top layer of the surface into arches and troughs when two tectonic plates move towards each other (a convergent plate boundary).

4. Answer the following question.

(i) State any one characteristic of intermontane plateau.

(ii) Where do the intermontane plateau lie?

Ans. (i) The main characteristics of intermontane plateaus is that these are the largest and the tallest known plateaus in the world.

(ii) These plateaus lie between the mountain ranges, i.e. they are partly or wholly covered by the mountains.

5. Differentiate between new or young fold mountains and old fold mountains.

Ans. Differences between new or young and old fold mountains are

New or Young Fold Mountains	Old Fold Mountains
These mountains are characterised by complex folding of the rocks, faulting, volcanic activities, cordillera formation, the erosion and weathering caused by running water, ice, winds, etc. and the existence of glacier-capped high peaks.	These mountains are characterised by presence of monadnocks, accordant summits, sculptured domes, the irregular forms of peaks, relics plateaus, etc.
For example, the Rockies, the Alps, the Himalayas, the Circum-Pacific Oceanic mountains, etc.	For example, the Urals, the Nanshan, etc.

6. Answer the following questions.

(i) How are residual mountains formed?

(ii) State examples of these mountains.

Ans. (i) Residual mountains are formed due to denudation and erosion by which high plateaus are gradually shaped into peaks and ridges. Denudation and erosion are caused by natural agents such as wind, water, snow, etc.

(ii) The mountains of the Western Ghats, the Aravalli mountain and the Parasnath mountain of Jharkhand are examples of residual mountains.

7. What are the key characteristics of the block mountains?

Ans. The characteristics of block mountains are

- They are characterised by massiveness, steep slopes and comparatively smooth topography.
- These mountains occur along the plate boundary.

8. Name any two structural plains with their cause of formation.

Ans. Some of the significant structural plains are the Great Plains of USA, which were formed due to the upliftment of the submerged underwater and the Coromandel Plain in India which was formed as a result of mild subsidence followed by sedimentation.

9. How are erosional plains formed?

Ans. The erosional plains are formed when a landform like a mountain or a plateau is eroded and it lowers down to the surface of the Earth.

10. Answer the following questions.
(i) Which valley in India is the example of lacustrine plain?
(ii) How this plain is formed?

Ans. (i) The Kashmir Valley in India is a notable example of the Lacustrine plain.
(ii) This plain is formed as a result of the depressions in the lake basins.

11. Give two importance of landforms.

Ans. Importance of land forms are
(i) Landforms give shape and structure to the Earth.
(ii) They provide relief features of the Earth which directly have an effect on the environment and climatic conditions of various places.

Long Questions

1. Explain the formation and features of the mountains in detail.

Ans. Refer to chapter theory on page no. 42.

2. Briefly describe the formation of fold mountains.

Ans. Refer to chapter theory on page no 42.

3. What is block mountain? Explain in brief the formation of this mountain.

Ans. Refer to chapter theory on page no. 43.

4. Plateaus are known to be one of the oldest landforms. In this context, answer the following
(i) What are plateaus?
(ii) What are the features of plateaus?

Ans. (i) Refer to chapter theory on page no. 44.
(ii) Refer to chapter theory on page no. 44.

5. Answer the following questions.
(i) Define the term plain.
(ii) Also give the significance of the plains.

Ans. (i) A plain is a landmass that is flat or gently rolling and it extends upto many miles on the surface of the Earth. There are certain lowland areas on the surface of the Earth which are known as plains.
(ii) Significance of the plains is
- They are useful to man as they are fertile and have water tables.
- Construction of the roads, building, railways, etc. is easy in the plains.
- Development of industries is easy in the plains due to high concentration of population.

6. Briefly describe the structural plains.

Ans. Refer to chapter theory on page no. 45.

7. Define the following terms.
(i) Drift plains (ii) Lacustrine plains
(iii) Coastal plains

Ans. (i) **Drift Plains** They are formed as a result of the deposition by the depositional work of the glaciers. These are classified as:
- **Till Plains** They are formed by the deposition below the ice.
- **Marginal Moraines** They are formed due to deposition at the edge of the glaciers.
- **Outwash Plains** These are formed due to the deposition of the fluvo-glacial deposits.
- **Loess Plains** They are formed as a result of the deposition by the winds.

(ii) **Lacustrine Plains** They are formed as a result of the depositions in the lake basins. The Kashmir valley in India is a notable example of the lacustrine plain. The soil that is found in these areas is very fertile, which makes these area suitable for the agricultural activities.

8. Classify the depositional plains.

Ans. Refer to chapter theory on page no. 45.

9. Differentiate between mountains and plains.

Ans. Differences between mountains and plains are

Mountains	Plains
Mountains are the landmasses that rises approx 900 m above mean sea level.	A plain is a landmass that is flat or gently rolling and covers many miles.
Some mountains have extensive chain of mountains that form mountain ranges, like the Andes in South Africa.	Plains can range from a very small size to very large extent.
Mountains occur when two tectonic plates collide with each other either forcing material upwards to form mountains.	The plains are formed by both the internal and the external forces of the Earth.

10. Distinguish between plateaus and plains.

Ans. Differences between plateaus and plains are

Plateaus	Plains
A plateau is a flat topped table land that is elevated above mean sea level.	A plain is a landmass that is flat or gently rolling and covers many miles.
These are less populated area as compared to plains.	The plain regions are highly populated as compared to the mountains and plateaus.
They rise abruptly from the surrounding regions.	The plains have a very gradual slope of land and not abrupt.
These are not much fertile as compared to plains.	These are fertile regions where agricultural practices done extensively.

11. Write a short note on the importance of landforms.

Ans. Refer to chapter theory on page no. 45 and 46.

Map Questions

1. On the map of world, mark the following.

(i) Rockies	(ii) Andes
(iii) Appalachian	(iv) Alps
(v) Himalayas	(vi) Scandinavian highlands
(vii) Pyrenees	(viii) Urals
(ix) Khingan Range	(x) Zagras mountain
(xi) Great Dividing Range	(xii) Drakensberg
(xiii) Atlas Mountains	(xiv) Caucasus

Ans.

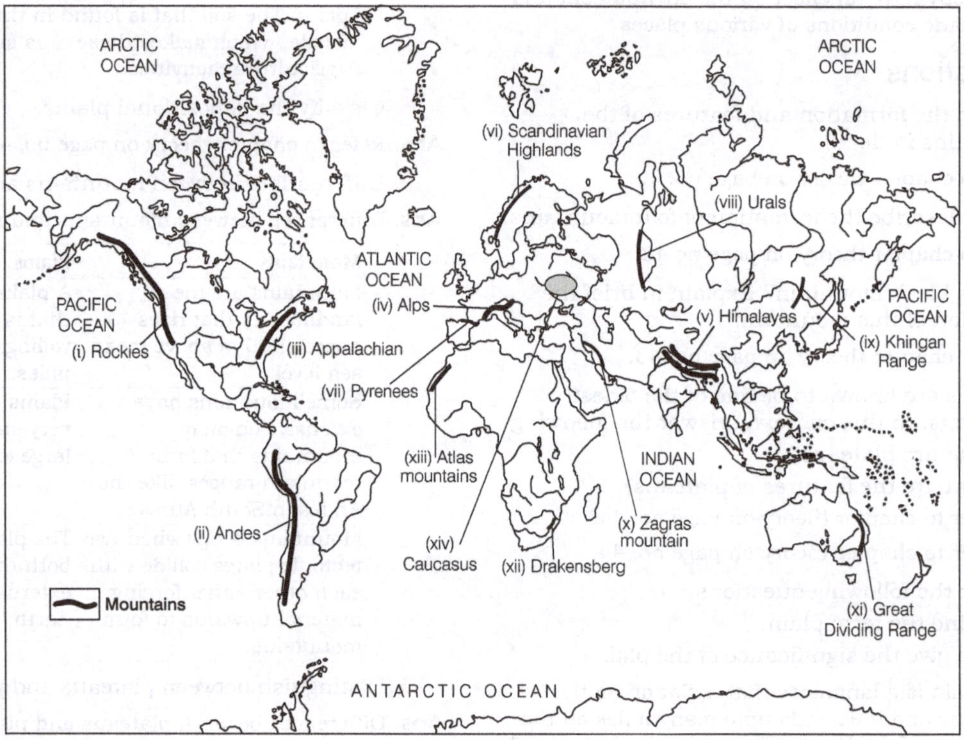

2. On the map of world, mark the following.

(i) Canadian Shield	(ii) Tibetan Plateau
(iii) Brazilian Highlands	(iv) Patagonian Plateau
(v) Iranian Plateau	(vi) Mongolian Plateau

Ans.

Chapter Assessment

Section-I

Multiple Choice Questions

1. The landforms on Earth are formed by
   (a) gradual forces
   (b) tectonic forces
   (c) volcanic forces
   (d) Earth forces
2. The mountains differ from the hills in terms of
   (a) elevation (b) slope
   (c) aspect (d) slant
3. Which of the following is not a volcanic plateau?
   (a) Deccan Plateau
   (b) Rockies
   (c) Columbian Plateau
   (d) Ethiopian Plateau
4. Which of the following is not an agent of erosion and deposition?
   (a) Running water (b) Glaciers
   (c) Earthquake (d) Wind

Section-II

Short Questions

1. What are plains?
2. What are plateaus?
3. Mention any two types of depositional plains.
4. Give examples of any two plateaus.
5. Define the following
   (i) Landform (ii) Mountain
   (iii) Plains (iv) Plateau
6. State any two characteristics of young fold mountains.
7. What are inter montane plateaus?

Long Questions

1. How are plateaus classified? Explain in detail.
2. How are the fold mountains formed?
3. How are landforms important for us?
4. Briefly explain the different types of landforms.

CHAPTER 06

Rocks

SYLLABUS

Rocks Difference between minerals and rocks, types of rocks : igneous, sedimentary, metamorphic, their characteristics and formation; rock cycle.

The Earth is composed of various kinds of elements. These elements are in solid form in the outermost layer of the Earth i.e. crust and in molten form in the interior of the Earth. All such elements combine to form different kinds of rocks and minerals.

Minerals

Minerals are naturally occurring organic and inorganic substances found on the Earth. The Earth as a whole, has a number of minerals, but the most commonly found minerals elements are iron, silicon, magnesium, nickel, sulphur and calcium.

Silicon and aluminium are major minerals of the Earth's crust, while the Earth as a whole contains more iron, silica and magnesium. Only a few of minerals are important as a constituent of rocks, e.g. feldspar, quartz, pyroxene, amphibole, mica and olivine. These are known as major rock forming minerals.

Rocks

A rock is naturally occuring solid mass or aggregate of minerals. Earth's outer solid layer is made up of rocks. Rocks do not have a definite composition of mineral constituents and may vary in terms of colour, texture, hardness, origin and degree of resistance to denudation.

Rocks are both hard and solid matter like granite and soft and loose particles like sand, silt and clay. When a rock has a large proportion of a single mineral, it is called as **ore** of that mineral, e.g. magnetite is an ore of iron.

Types of Rocks

There are different kinds of rocks which are categorised under three groups on the basis of the mode of formation. These three groups are

(i) Igneous Rocks
(ii) Sedimentary Rocks
(iii) Metamorphic Rocks

(i) Igneous Rocks

The word 'Igneous' is derived from the Latin word 'ignis' means 'fire'. Igneous rocks are formed through the cooling and solidification of magma or lava when it rises to the surface of the Earth.

Molten material or rocks under the Earth's layer is known as **magma**, while the molten material that come out to the surface of the Earth in liquid state is known as **lava**. Some examples of igneous rocks are granite, gabbro, basalt, **tuff**[1] pegmatite, volcanic breccia, etc.

Igneous rocks have different chemical compositions like alumino-silicate minerals (quartz, feldspar) and sialic rocks (granite, rhyolite). These rocks form basis for other types of rocks.

1 **Tuff** It is a porous rock made of volcanic ash ejected from a vent during a volcanic eruption.

Characteristics of Igneous Rocks

- These are primary rocks as it is first to be formed in the process of rock formation.
- These rocks are crystalline and compact which are used for building material and sculptures.
- They are harder and granular having many small and distinct parts.
- They do not contain fossils and have no layers.
- They are impervious i.e. fluid cannot be passed through them. They are resistant to erosion, but weathered by mechanical weathering.
- These rocks are associated with volcanic activity and are found mostly in volcanic regions.
- Most of them consists of silicates.
- The size of their crystals depends upon the molten material.

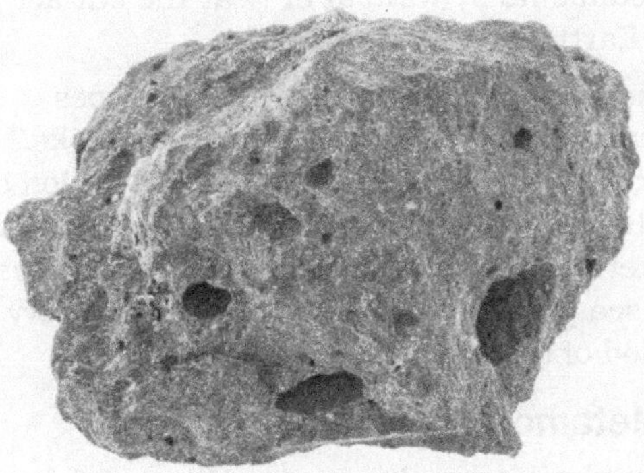

Igneous Rocks

Classification of Igneous Rocks on the Basis of Origin

- **Extrusive Igneous Rocks** The molten magma or lava that solidifies on the Earth's surface forms extrusive rocks. Such rocks are also called **volcanic rocks**. These rocks are smooth, crystalline and fine grained. Basalt is an example of these rocks which forms lava sheets, lava flows and lava plateaus, e.g. the Deccan trap region of Peninsular India. When basalt solidifies, it also forms long polygonal columns, e.g. Giant Causeway in Northern Ireland.
- **Intrusive Igneous Rocks** The molten magma or lava that solidifies within the Earth's crust forms intrusive rocks, e.g. granite. These rocks are also known as **Plutonic rocks**. These are hard rocks with large crystals and coarse texture. Some types of intrusive rocks are
  - **Batholiths** These are formed by intrusion and solidification of magma. They are generally **dome-shaped** rocks with no definite floor. They are mainly composed of coarse-grained rocks such as granite, e.g. Ranchi Batholiths.
  - **Laccoliths** They are formed below the Earth's crust. The upper surface of these rocks is dome-shaped, but the bottom is flat.
  - **Sills** When magma flows horizontally between layers of rocks and harden after cooling, this layer of intrusive rock is called Sill.
  - **Dykes** They are formed when magma forced upwards and fills vertical cracks or fissures in existing rocks and hardens after cooling.
  - **Necks** They are formed when the passage of an extinct volcano is filled with magma and then solidifies there.

Classification of Igneous Rocks on the Basis of Chemical Composition

- **Acid Igneous Rocks** Silica content is an important feature of igneous rocks. Acid igneous rocks contain between 65 to 85 per cent of silica, but they are deficient in iron and magnesium. They are made up of large crystals of quartz, feldspar and mica and are commonly used as building material.
- **Basic Igneous Rocks** These rocks have high percentage of oxides of denser elements. They contain silica between 40 to 60 per cent. These rocks are heavy and dark in colour. Basalt, dolerite and gabbro are examples of these rocks.

(ii) Sedimentary Rocks

These rocks are formed by evaporation, compaction, deposition and subsequent cementation of the **sediments**[2]. These are formed when the rocks are weathered and their weathered material (or sediments) are transported and deposited as sediments by the agents of gradation such as water, wind, waves and glaciers.

These sediments are deposited, layer after layer in seas, lakes, streams, etc that may further turn into rocks. This process is known as **lithification**.

2 **Sediment** It is a naturally occurring material i.e. sand, silt, clay, gravel, etc. which is broken down by processes of weathering and erosion.

The sediments are deposited in layers, therefore these rocks have layers. Sandstone, shale, gypsum, rock salt, etc are examples of these rocks.

These rocks are known by different names. As these rocks are formed through sedimentation process, these are known as sedimentary rocks. These are also known as **secondary rocks** as they are formed from materials derived from other rocks like igneous and metamorphic rocks. When these rocks are deposited into water bodies, these are known as **argillaceous rocks**. As these rocks have layers of various sediments, they are also known as **layered** or **stratified rocks**.

Sedimentary Rocks

Characteristics of Sedimentary Rocks

- These are fossiliferous in nature i.e. fossils are found in them which also help in determining age of these rocks.
- These are most widespread on the Earth's surface i.e around 75%.
- They are permeable and porous in nature which means water can easily go through these rocks.
- These rocks contain important minerals like coal, petroleum, etc.
- These rocks do not have crystals and are prone to weathering due to their softness as compared to other rocks.
- These rocks form extensive landforms. They do not make massive rock forms like batholith and locoliths.

Classification of Sedimentary Rocks on the Basis of Formation

- **Mechanical Sedimentary Rocks** These rocks are formed by the fragments of rocks which are produced by mechanical weathering, e.g. sandstone, shale, siltstone, etc.
- **Chemical Sedimentary Rocks** These rocks are formed by direct precipitation of mineral matter from solution, e.g. limestone, chert, dolomite, ironstone, etc.
- **Organic Sedimentary Rocks** These rocks are formed from the remains of plants and animals, e.g. peat, lignite, chalk, etc.

Classification of Sedimentary Rocks on the Basis of Formation Agents

- **Riverine Rocks** These rocks are formed by alluvial deposits brought by the flowing rivers.
- **Lacustrine Rocks** These rocks are formed at the bottom of lakes by incoming water from rivers or streams.
- **Glacial Rocks** These rocks are formed by the glacial deposits in the form of debris.
- **Aeolian Rocks** These rocks are formed by deposition of sediments by wind at or near the surface of the Earth.
- **Marine Rocks** These rocks are of two types, calcareous rocks and carbonaceous rocks. Calcareous rocks are formed by deposition of shells and skeletons of sea organisms like corals, oysters, etc. Carbonaceous rocks are formed by the sea plants that remain buried for a very long period of time.

(iii) Metamorphic Rocks

The word metamorphic means 'change of form'. Metamorphic rocks are formed through the process of metamorphism which takes place under the influence of extreme pressure, volume and temperature. This process alters the composition or structure of a rock.

In this process, the rocks are forced down to lower level by tectonic processes. When underlying rocks are subjected to great pressure by overlying rocks, then the rocks lying in the lowest layer undergoes chemical changes.

There are different types of metamorphism process depending on their causes such as

- **Thermal Metamorphism** It takes place when high temperature or heat coming from hot magma or from friction of moving rock layers, changes the original rocks into another rocks. For example, clay changes into slate, coal changes into graphite, etc.

- **Dynamic Metamorphism** Rocks in this process change due to high pressure found at a great depth beneath the Earth's surface. When chemically active hot gases pass through the rocks, chemical composition of the rocks gets changed. Due to this effect, minerals get arranged in a series of bands which is known as **foliation**. For example, dolomites changes into marble rock which is used in the Taj Mahal and Dilwara Temple at Mount Abu.
- **Regional Metamorphism** It takes place when both intense pressure of overlying rocks and extensive heat caused by large Earth movement deep inside the Earth, change the form of rocks. This process influences rocks of larger regions, thus it is called regional metamorphism. When this process affects a small area it is known as **local** or **contact metamorphism.**

Metamorphic Rocks

Characteristics of Metamorphic Rocks

- Metamorphic rocks are harder and more compact than their original forms. For example, sandstone (soft rock) changes into quartzite (hard rock), limestone (soft) changes into marble (hard), shale changes into slate, granite into gneiss, basalt into schist, coal into graphite.
- They do not contain fossils due to extreme heat and pressure conditions.
- Most of the metamorphic rocks are impervious.
- Metamorphic rocks have the tendency of splitting along the bedding planes.
- Different metallic minerals are found in these rocks like gold and silver.

Rock Cycle

Rock cycle is a continuous process of transformation of old rocks into new ones. In this process, igneous rocks are the primary and first type of rocks which are formed on the Earth. Sedimentary rocks are formed by the eroded material which is produced by igneous rocks when they get eroded by various agents of denudation.

Metamorphic rocks are formed when both igneous and sedimentary rocks are subjected to pressure and heat. Sedimentary rocks can also be formed again when agents of denudation erode metamorphic rocks.

Further in this process, the igneous, sedimentary and metamorphic rocks may get buried deep inside the Earth due to the influence of various Earth movements. Then, they melt by the heat of the interior to form magma. The magma may be forced to the Earth's surface and when it gets solidified, new igneous rocks are formed.

In the process of rock cycle, any rock (igneous, sedimentary or metamorphic) can transform into any other rock by passing through one or more processes (crystallisation, lithification, sedimentation and metamorphism).

This cycle keeps the Earth young and dynamic and it takes hundreds or thousands of years to complete this process.

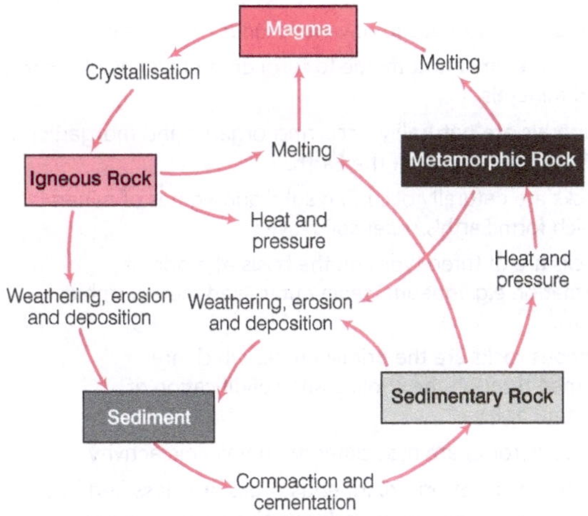

Rock Cycle

Difference between Minerals and Rocks

Points of Difference	Minerals	Rocks
Definition	Minerals are substances that are naturally occurring, stable at room temperature, represented by a definite chemical composition.	Rocks are naturally occurring, solid combination formed from one or many minerals of **mineraloids**[3].
Composition	They have a stable chemical composition, definite atomic arrangement including both organic and inorganic compounds.	They are composed by combination of many minerals.
Characteristics	They are characterised by hardness, luster, colour, streak, tenacity, cleavage, fracture, parting and specific gravity.	They are characterised by mineral and chemical composition, texture and permeability.
Classification	They are classified into silicates, non-silicates, carbonate, sulphides and metallic minerals.	They are classified into igneous, sedimentary and metamorphic rocks.
Colour	They are found in various colours depending on composition.	They are also found in various colours (red, grey, brown, steel) depending on composition.
Uses	They have many industrial applications like silica in window glass, gypsum in plaster, etc. They also assists in bodily functions, like they help in bone and tooth formation, muscle contraction, etc.	They are used in various construction applications, weapons (ancient times) and are mined for their minerals.
Examples	Gold, silver, fluoride, quartz, mica, feldspar, etc are examples of minerals.	Granite, limestone, conglomerate, sandstone, etc are examples of rocks.

Check Your LEARNING...

1. What are minerals?
2. Name any two types of rocks.
3. What is the meaning of the word 'ignis'?
4. State an example of sedimentary rocks.

QUiCK Revision

- The Earth is composed of various kinds of elements.
- All such elements combine to form different kinds of rocks and minerals.
- Minerals are naturallly occurring organic and inorganic substances found on the Earth.
- Rocks are naturally occurring solid aggregates of minerals which form Earth's outer solid layer.
- Rocks are of three types on the basis of mode of formation e.g. igneous, sedimentary and metamorphic rocks.
- Igneous rocks are the primary rocks which are formed through the cooling and solidification of magma or lava.
- Igneous rocks are associated with volcanic activity.
- On the basis of origin, igneous rocks are classified into two types i.e. extrusive and intrusive igneous rocks.
- On the basis of chemical composition, igneous rocks are classified into two types i.e. acid igneous rocks and basic igneous rocks.
- Sedimentary rocks are formed by the evaporation, compaction deposition and subsequent cementation of the sediments.
- Sedimentary rocks contain important minerals like coal, petroleum, etc.
- On the basis of formation, sedimentary rocks are classified into three types i.e. mechanical, chemical and organic.
- On the basis of formation agent, sedimentary rocks are classified into five types i.e. riverine, lacustrine, glacial, aecolian and marine.
- Organic sedimentary rocks are formed from the remains of plants and animals.
- Metamorphic rocks are formed under the influence of pressure, volume and temperature.
- In Dynamic metamophism rock changes due to high pressure inside the Earth's surface.
- Metamorphism rocks contaikn different metallic minerals like gold and silver.
- Rock cycle is important for the formation of different types of rocks. It is a continuous process of transformation of old rocks into new ones.

3 **Mineraloid** It is a mineral-like substance that does not demonstrate crystallinity.

Chapter Practice

Section-I

Multiple Choice Questions

1. Which of the following is the major rock forming minerals?
(a) Quartz (b) Feldspar
(c) Pyroxene (d) All of these

Ans. (d) All of these

2. Igneous, sedimentary, and metamorphic rocks are usually composed of ....
(a) inter-grown crystals (b) minerals
(c) fossil (d) sediments

Ans. (b) minerals

3. Which of these is not responsible for the formation of igneous rock?
(a) Sediments (b) Liquid rock
(c) Magma (d) Lava

Ans. (a) Sediments

4. Granite is an example of ....
(a) intrusive igneous rock (b) extrusive igneous rock
(c) sedimentary rock (d) metamorphic rock

Ans. (a) intrusive igneous rock

5. Which of the following rocks have layered like structure?
(a) Igneous rocks (b) Metamorphic rocks
(c) Sedimentary rocks (d) Extrusive igneous rocks

Ans. (c) Sedimentary rocks

6. Which one among the following rocks does not belong to the same group?
(a) Shale (b) Limestone (c) Slate (d) Sandstone

Ans. (c) Slate

7. Give reason for the following.
Silicates are the most common rock forming minerals.
(a) Only this has the ability to form rocks.
(b) They are most common minerals in the Earth's crust.
(c) No other elements are found on the Earth's surface.
(d) None of the above

Ans. (b) They are most common minerals in the Earth's crust.

8. Give reason for the following.
Rocks are of great economic significance.
(a) After disintegration rocks turn into valuable soils.
(b) Rocks are the store-houses of a large number of minerals.
(c) Rocks are the source of precious metals like gold, silver, platinum, etc.
(d) All of the above

Ans. (d) All of the above

9. Give reason for the following.
Pyroxene is a major mineral.
(a) Pyroxene consists of calcium, aluminium, magnesium, iron and silica.
(b) Pyroxene forms 10 per cent of the Earth's crust.
(c) It is commonly found in meteorites.
(d) Both (a) and (b)

Ans. (d) Both (a) and (b)

10. Give reason for the following.
Feldspar is one of the major rock forming minerals.
(a) Silicon and oxygen are common elements in all types of feldspar.
(b) Half of the earth's crust is composed of feldspar.
(c) Nothing is more important than this mineral.
(d) Both (a) and (b)

Ans. (d) Both (a) and (b)

11. Give reason for the following.
Sedimentary rocks are important rocks.
(a) These are formed beneath the Earth's surface.
(b) These rocks have large size crystals due to slow cooling.
(c) These are a type of metamorphic rocks.
(d) These have large reserves of fossil fuels.

Ans. (d) These have large reserves of fossil fuels.

12. Which of the following statements is correct?
(i) Minerals are only organic in nature.
(ii) Rocks do not have a definite composition of minerals.
(iii) Mineral come in various colour.
Codes
(a) Only (i) (b) Only (ii) (c) Only (iii) (d) (ii) and (iii)

Ans. (d) (ii) and (iii)

13. Which of the following statements is incorrect?
(i) The word 'Ignis' means Magma.
(ii) Igneous rocks are used as building materials.
(iii) Quartzite and gneiss are examples of sedimentary rocks.
Codes
(a) Only (i) (b) Only (ii) (c) Only (iii) (d) (i) and (iii)

Ans. (d) (i) and (iii)

14. Match the following.

List-I	List-II
A. Feldspar	1. It consists of calcium, aluminum
B. Pyroxene	2. It consists of silicon and oxygen
C. Amphibole	3. It consists of potassium, aluminium
D. Mica	4. It consists of aluminium, calcium, silica

Codes

	A	B	C	D		A	B	C	D
(a)	1	2	3	4	(b)	2	1	4	3
(c)	3	4	1	2	(d)	4	3	2	1

Ans. (b)

15. Match the following.

List-I	List-II
A. Plates inside the Earth	1. Responsible for sedimentary rock formation
B. Intensive heat and pressure inside the Earth surface which form metamorphic rocks	2. Water, wind, ocean waves
C. Agents of gradation	3. Metamorphism
D. Lithification	4. Tectonic plates

Codes

	A	B	C	D		A	B	C	D
(a)	1	2	3	4	(b)	2	1	4	3
(c)	3	4	1	2	(d)	4	3	2	1

Ans. (d)

Section-II

Short Questions

1. Define the following.
   (i) Minerals (ii) Ores

Ans. (i) Minerals are naturally occurring organic and inorganic substances found in the Earth. They have a definite chemical composition and physical properties.
(ii) When a rock has a large proportion of a single mineral it is called as 'ore' of that mineral.

2. What are rocks?

Ans. Rocks are the naturally occurring solid aggregates of minerals. They do not have a definite composition of mineral constituents and may vary in terms of colour, texture, origin, hardness, etc.

3. What are the different kinds of rocks? Mention.

Ans. Geologists have classified rocks into three main categories. These are
(i) Igneous rocks (ii) Sedimentary rocks
(iii) Metamorphic rocks

4. How igneous rocks are formed?

Ans. Igneous rocks are formed through the cooling and solidification of magma or lava that comes from the Earth during volcanic eruptions.

5. Give three examples of igneous rocks.

Ans. Examples of igneous rocks are granite, basalt and gabbro.

6. Answer the following questions.
   (i) What are the sedimentary rocks?
   (ii) How they are formed?

Ans. (i) The rocks made up of sediments accumulating in layers are called sedimentary rocks.
(ii) Sedimentary rocks are formed through the deposition and solidification of sediments especially sediments transported by water, ice (glacier) and wind.

7. How the process of rock formation is different in sedimentary rocks and metamorphic rocks?

Ans. Sedimentary rocks are formed through the process of sedimentation of the loosen granular particles, whereas metamorphic rocks are formed under the influence of extreme pressure, temperature and volume.

8. Name different types of metamorphism.

Ans. Different types of metamorphism are
(i) Thermal metamorphism
(ii) Regional metamorphism
(iii) Dynamic metamorphism

9. State two causes which lead to formation of metamorphic rocks.

Ans. Two causes which lead to formation of metamorphic rocks are
(i) Tectonic processes.
(ii) When molten magma rising through the crust comes in contact with the crustal rocks

10. Answer the following questions.
    (i) Give the examples of metamorphic rocks.
    (ii) Give an example of ore.

Ans. (i) The examples of metamorphic rocks are quartzite, marble, slate, gneiss, etc.
(ii) Magnetite is an ore of iron.

11. What is a rock cycle?

Ans. It is a continuous process of transformation of old rocks into new ones. In this process any rock can transform into any other rocks by process of weathering or by presure and heat inside the Earth surface.

Long Questions

1. What are the important characteristics of the igneous rocks?

Ans. Important characteristics of igneous rocks are
- They are formed through the process of solidification of molten magma.
- They are crystalline.
- They are harder and granular.

- They are unfossiliferous (i.e. they do not contain fossils).
- They are impervious and resistant to erosion.
- They are primary rocks, as they are formed first in the process of rock formation.

2. Answer the following questions.
(i) Name the processes which are involved in the formation of sedimentary rocks.
(ii) State two examples of sedimentary rocks.

Ans. (i) The processes which are involved in the formation of Sedimentary rocks are lithification (which involves evaporation, compaction and cementation) and sedimentation.
(ii) The examples of sedimentary rocks are sandstone, limestone, shale, etc.

3. What are the characteristics features of sedimentary rocks?

Ans. The characteristic features of sedimentary rocks are
- They are fossiliferous in nature i.e. fossils are found in it.
- They are formed on the Earth's surface as well as within the water body.
- They are not crystalline.
- They are marked by permeability and are porous in nature.
- They contain layers or strata.

4. Explain the characteristic of the metamorphic rocks.

Ans. The characteristic of the metamorphic rocks are
- Metamorphic rocks are harder and more compact than their original forms. For example, Sand stone (soft rock) changes into quartzite (hard rock), limestone (soft) changes into marble (hard), shale changes into slate, granite into gneiss, basalt into schist, coal into graphite.
- They do not contain fossils due to extreme heat and pressure conditions.
- Metamorphic rocks have the tendency of splitting along the bedding planes.
- Different metallic minerals are found in these rocks like gold and silver.

5. Give reasons for the following.
(i) Igneous rocks are also known as primary rocks.
(ii) Sedimentary rocks have layers.
(iii) Metamorphic rocks do not contain fossils.

Ans. (i) The igneous rocks are called primary rocks because they are formed from magma. They are the first type of rocks formed on the Earth. The rock cycle begins with the formation of igneous rocks.
(ii) Sedimentary rocks form when mud, sand and sediments are deposited in layers on the Earth's surface.
The layers are deposited in many environments including oceans, rivers and deserts. These layers of sand and mud are later buried. The weight of overlying layers compresses the mud and sand to form solid rock.
(iii) Metamorphic rocks are created under great pressure and heat. Fossils do not usually survive in these extreme conditions. Generally, it is only sedimentary rocks that contain fossils.

6. Explain the following terms.
(i) Weathering (ii) Subduction
(iii) Sediments

Ans. (i) Weathering is the breaking down or dissolving of rocks and minerals on the Earth's surface. Water, ice, acids, salt, plants, animals and changes in temperature are all agents of weathering.
(ii) Subduction is a geological process that takes place at convergent boundaries of tectonic plates where plate moves under one another and is forced or sinks due to gravity into the mantle. Regions where this process occurs are known as subduction zone.
(iii) Sediments are naturally occurring eroded particles of rocks that are broken down by processes of weathering and erosion and are subsequently transported by the action of wind, water or ice and/or by the force of gravity acting on the particles, e.g. sand and silt.

7. Explain the entire process involved in rock cycle.

Ans. Refer to chapter theory page no. 55.

8. What are the differences between rocks and minerals? Explain with the help of any three points.

Ans. Differences between rocks and minerals are

Rocks	Minerals
Rocks are naturally occurring, solid combination formed from one or many minerals.	Minerals are naturally occurring organic and inorganic substances, usually have ordered atomic arrangement.
Rocks can be classified into igneous, sedimentary and metamorphic rocks.	Minerals can be classified as silicates and non-silicates.
Rocks are used in various construction applications, weapons (older times) and are mined for their minerals.	Minerals have many industrial application (silica in window glass, gypsum in plaster) as well as assist in bodily functions (bone and tooth formation).

Chapter Assessment

Section-I

Multiple Choice Questions

1. Which type of rocks are found extensively on the Earth's surface?
   (a) Igneous rocks
   (b) Sedimentary rocks
   (c) Metamorphic rocks
   (d) Extrusive rocks
2. What the molten rock is known when it stays under the surface of the Earth?
   (a) Lava
   (b) Magma
   (c) Basalt
   (d) Ignite
3. When molten rock comes out of the Earth's surface, it is known as ....
   (a) lava
   (b) magma
   (c) laccoliths
   (d) metamorphic
4. In which type of rock would you expect to find fossils ?
   (a) Granite (b) Obsidian
   (c) Shale (d) Marble

Section-II

Short Questions

1. What do you understand by minerals?
2. State any three examples of metamorphic rocks.
3. Name different types of rocks.
4. How sedimentary rocks are formed?
5. Mention any two characteristics of igneous rocks.
6. What do you mean by lithification?
7. Define rocks.
8. How metamorphic rocks are formed?

Long Questions

1. Write any three characteristics of sedimentary rocks.
2. Define the following.
   (i) Fossils (ii) Weathering
   (iii) Sediments
3. What is rock cycle? Discuss with suitable diagram.
4. State any three characteristics of igneous rocks.

CHAPTER

07

Volcanoes

SYLLABUS

Volcanoes Meaning, Types-active, dormant and extinct. •Effects-constructive and destuctive. • Important volcanic zones of the world.

Volcanoes are natural phenomena that takes place due to internal forces of the Earth. When pressure builds up inside the Earth, gases and rocks comes out through the opening and spill over the air with **lava**[1] fragments.

Meaning of Volcano

The term volcano comes from the Roman God of Fire, 'Vulcan'. A volcano is an opening or a vent in the Earth's crust that allows hot lava, volcanic ashes and gases (like steam, sulphur dioxide, hydrogen sulphide, hydrogen, carbon dioxide, argon, nitrogen compounds, etc) to escape from the hot interior of the Earth to its surface.

The volcano was earlier known as a **mountain of fire** as it emitted red hot lava. However, a volcano is not a mountain, it is in the shape of a cone or a dome based on the material that is ejected. The study of volcanoes, lava, magma and related geological, geophysical and geochemical phenomena is called **volcanology**.

The forces arising from the interior of the Earth give rise to sudden movements which cause volcanicity. It refers to the process by which **magma**[2] and volatiles are transferred from the interior of the Earth to its surface. Such processes happening in the Earth's interior gives rise to volcanic eruptions.

After volcanic eruption, the ejected materials cool down and solidify on the surface and close the opening in the crust. Generally, volcanic eruption happens violently or quietly at irregular intervals and lasts for few days.

Causes of Volcanic Eruptions

- **Presssure and Heat inside the Earth** Temperature and pressure increases from the surface towards the centre of the Earth. As rocks are bad conductors of heat, they obstruct the path of Earth's heat. As a result, this heat melts the rocks and builds up great pressure. Thus, the pressure forces the heat to find an escape route through fissures and cracks or fault lines in the rocks.
- **Tectonic Plates** The margins of tectonic plates are the source regions of most volcanic eruptions. Due to intense heat inside the Earth's core, these plates move towards each other or slide away from each other and their edges create faults along the lines of weakness. It is along these plate boundaries, that the hot magma comes out leading to volcanic eruption.

1 **Lava** When the magma come out on the surface of the Earth, it is known as lava.

2 **Magma** It is a molten and semi-molten rock mixture found in the surface of the Earth.

- **Magma Chamber** It is a reservoir of molten material which lies deep inside the Earth's crust. Magma tends to melt weak rocks and creates a huge chamber for itself. As magma contains different materials like silicate material, gases and water vapours, the pressure always acts vertically upwards and when it found a passage, it rises to the surface.

Generally, major volcanoes have a huge magma chamber beneath them which is linked to the Earth's surface by a conduit known as **volcanic vent**.

Structure of Volcano

- **Vent** It is a narrow opening in the volcano that allows hot magma, gases and ashes to escape. It is usually pipe shaped. Generally there may be one opening at the summit, but due to repeated eruptions, subsidiary vents are formed.
- **Crater** The upper part of the vent that is a bowl shaped depression is known as the crater of the volcano. It is the highest point of the volcano.
- **Cinder** The solid rocks that are ejected from the volcanoes are known as cinders. These are extrusive igneous rocks.
- **Caldera** It forms when a volcano gets hollow and then collapses on itself. A caldera could look like a large depression on the side of the volcano or it could happen at the very top.
- **Volcanic Cone** When the volcanic fluid material collects around the vent, it cools down, solidifies and gives a typical cone-like shape to the volcano. It is known as the volcanic cone.

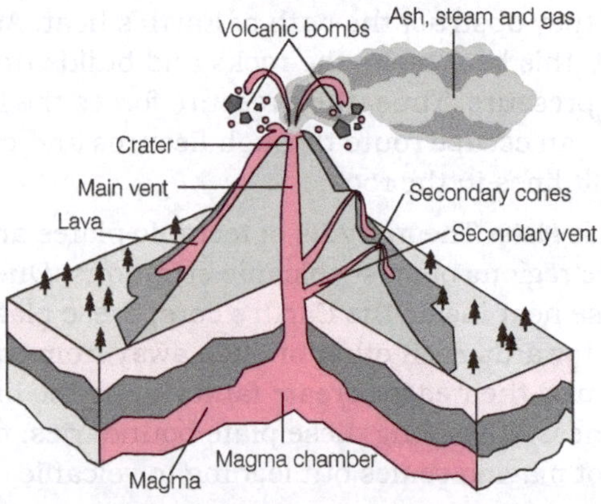

Structure of Volcano

Types of Volcanoes

On the Basis of Frequency of Eruption

On the basis of their frequency of eruption, volcanoes can be classified into three categories

(i) **Active Volcano** It is the one that is in active state and has erupted in the recent past. About 500 active volcanoes on land are known in the world. Out of these volcanoes 20 are expected to erupt any time. For example, **Mt. Etna** and **Mt. Stromboli** (Light house of the Mediterranean) in Italy, **Pinatubo** in Philippines, **Mauna Loa** in Hawaii and **Baren Island** in Andaman and Nicobar Islands in India.

(ii) **Dormant Volcano** It is the one that hasn't erupted in the past 10,000 years, but which is expected to erupt again. It is also known as **sleeping volcano**. For example, **Mt. Vesuvius** near Naples in Southern Italy, which experienced violent eruptions after centuries of inactivity in 1944. Since then, there is no major eruption. **Mt. Kilimanjaro** (Japan) is also an example of this volcano.

(iii) **Extinct Volcano** It is the one that has not erupted in the recent geological period and it is not expected to ever erupt again. For example, **Lassen Park** in Northern California, **Mt. Aconcagua** in South America and **Mt. Kenya** in Africa.

On the Basis of Mode of Eruption

On the basis of mode of eruption, volcanoes can be classified into two types

(i) **Central Volcanoes** In these volcanoes, the volcanic eruption led from a central point and magma rise to the surface of the Earth through the narrow opening which gets accumulated around the point of eruption. This leads to the formation of an almost symmetrical volcano having a conical hill. For example, Vesuvius and Fujiyama in Italy.

(ii) **Fissure Volcanoes** These volcanoes are narrow openings or fractures on the Earth's surface through which lava, **pyroclastics**[3] and gases are erupted and **effused**[4]. Here, the magma spreads over a large area leading to the formation of plateaus of volcanic rock. For example, the Deccan trap of India, Columbia Plateau in USA, etc are formed this way.

3 **Pyroclastic** It is the flow of hot gases and rocks erupted out of volcano.
4 **Effused** It means the solidification of the magma.

On the Basis of Shape of the Volcano

On the basis of shape of the volcano, volcanoes can classified into four types

(i) **Shield Volcano** It is a type of volcano usually built almost entirely of fluid magma flows i.e. basalt. It is named so for its large size and low profile, resembling like a shield lying on the ground. Mauna Kea and Mauna Loa in Hawaii Island are shield volcanoes. They are the world's largest active volcanoes, rising nearly 9 km above the sea floor around the island of Hawaii.

(ii) **Conical Volcano** It is a volcano having a conical shape. Such a volcano is characterised by steep slopes, e.g. Mount Taranaki in New Zealand.

(iii) **Cinder Cones** Those cones that are circular in shape and are made up of small fragments of lava and erupt from a single vent are called cinder cones. For example, Hawaiian Island of Maui and Paricutin, Mexico.

(iv) **Composite Cones** These are formed as a result of multiple eruptions that occurs after hundreds or thousands of years. These are also known as **strato volcanoes.** The composite cone can expand to a height that its slope become unstable and can collapse due to the gravitational pull of the Earth. For example, Mount Fuji in Japan, Mount Rainier in USA, Mount Pelee in Martinique, etc. There are chains of numerous composite volcanoes around the **Pacific Rim**[5] of the Earth.

Check Your LEARNING...

1 When is a caldera formed?
2 State one example of active volcano.
3 What is meant by Shield volcano?
4 What is the other name of dormant volcano?

Effects of Volcanoes

The volcanoes produce both constructive and destructive effects.

Constructive Effects

- **Formation of Black Soil** Lava deposits on weathering becomes black soil that is good for cotton, groundnut, sugarcane, banana and production of other crops. The lava obtained from the plains are most fertile, e.g. lava from the parts of Brazil, Java in Indonesia, black soil region of Peninsular India i.e. Deccan Trap, etc.
- **Hot Springs** These are also known as thermal springs. They are made when magma inside the Earth heats up the underground water especially around magma chambers. After getting sufficient heat, water turns into steam and moves up to the surface.

  These springs contain many dissolved minerals and are a rich source of sulphur which has medicinal value to cure many skin diseases. For example, sulphur hot springs at Manikaran in Kullu Valley of Himachal Pradesh. Heat energy of hot springs can also be used to generate power.
- **Geysers** A geyser acts like a fountain of hot water and steam. It escapes when underground water comes into contact with hot volcanic rocks, e.g. the 'Old Faithful' Geyser in Yellowstone National Park in Wyoming, USA. It erupts every 50-100 minutes and has a temperature around 95°C - 95.6°C.
- **Caldera Lake** Caldera is formed when the magma chamber is unable to emit sufficient magma which results in the collapse of a cone. This depression eventually gets filled with water and forms a lake. For example, Crater Lake in the USA is 10 km wide and the deepest lake in the USA.
- **Landforms** Volcanic activities also form different types of landforms which are created due to cooling and solidification of magma below the Earth's surface and lava on the Earth's surface. The landforms created on Earth's surface are called extrusive landforms. These include

  (i) **Volcanic Plains** These types of plains are formed when lava flows and covers extensive area. These are vast and smooth. For example, the Western Victorian Plains in Victoria, Australia were formed by volcanoes over the last six million years with most recent eruption being at Mount Napier, 7200 years ago.

  (ii) **Volcanic Plateaus** These are also a result of lava flow from volcanic eruptions. When the lava on the surface of the Earth or of the ocean cools down, the agents of weathering with time, transforms it into a plateau. For example, the Peninsular Plateau of India, (North-Western Deccan), South African Plateau, Columbian Plateau, Ethiopian Plateau, etc.

5 **Pacific Rim** A geographic area surrounding the edges of the Pacific Ocean.

(iii) **Volcanic Mountains** These mountains are the result of ejected materials which come out from the fissures in the Earth's crust. Volcanic mountains are of diverse nature depending upon the different volcanic eruptions and various ejected materials. For example, Mauna Loa in Hawaii is a volcanic mountain (rises 9 km from the ocean floor). The Circum-Pacific Belt has many volcanic mountains and volcanic peaks such as Mt. Fuji (Japan), Mt. Mayon (Philippines), Mt. Merapi (Sumatra), Mt. Agung (Bali) and Mt. Cotopaxi (Ecuador).

- **Precious Minerals** Many of the precious stones and useful minerals are found in the volcanic eruptions, e.g. diamond mines in South America, Kimberley in South Africa and Sudbury in Canada.
- **Volcanic Spots** The volcanic spots on the Earth are a source of scenic beauty for the humans, e.g. Lake Volcanic in South America.
- **Evidence of Civilisation** Volcanic eruptions at times play an important role in the preservation of the old civilisation as lots of information about Earth can be collected from it.

Destructive Effects

- Ash and mud can mix with rain and melting snow, forming **lahars**. Lahars are mudflows flowing at very fast pace.
- Volcanic eruption leads to formation huge clouds which give heavy rain and become a cause of floods and landslide.
- Many poisonous gases are released during volcanic activities which pollute environment and cause health problems.
- Landscapes and natural sceneries can be destroyed due to volcanic eruptions.
- The volcanic areas become inhabitable for man as no human activity is possible in such areas.
- A number of cities, forests and local economies have been destroyed due to volcanic activity.
- Volcanic activities under the sea may give rise to tsunamis causing large scale destruction on land. For example, in 1883 the explosive eruption of Mt. Karakatoa lying between Sumatra and Java in Indonesia destroyed the entire island.
- Ash discharged by volcanic eruption, which rise very high into the stratosphere, can have negative consequences on the ozone layer. It also destroys agricultural fields.
- Eruptions occurring close to human settlements may spill and destroy lives and property.

Volcanic Zones of the World

Most of the world's volcanoes are associated with the plate boundaries and occur near earthquake belts around the young fold mountains. About 15% of the volcanoes are associated with the **divergent plate**[6] and 80% are associated with the **convergent plate**[7]. The major belts or zones of the volcanic eruptions are

Circum-Pacific Belt

This is the most important belt of volcanoes which lies in Pacific Ocean. This belt is also known as the **Pacific Ring of Fire**. It includes the volcanoes of Eastern and Western coastal area of the Pacific Ocean.

This belt covers areas of Erebus mountains of Antarctica, Andes of South America, Central America, Mexico, the Rocky mountains of North America, the Aleutian Islands, Kamchatka, the Kuril Island, Sakhalin, Japan, Philippines, Celebes, New Guinea, the Soloman Island, Indonesian Islands, Hawaii Islands, New Caledonia and New Zealand.

This belt is nearly 3200 km in length. It has 80% of the total active volcanoes. This belt meets the mid-continental belt in the East Indies. This belt is characterised by high volcanic cones and volcanic mountains.

In this belt, **Cotopaxi** which is one of the highest volcanic mountains (5,911 m) in the world is found. Other important volcanoes found in this belt are Chimborazo, Mt. Mayon (Philippines), Karakatoa (Indonesia), Fujiyama, Shasta, Rainier and Hood. Alaska, there is a valley of ten thousand smokes.

Mid-Continental Belt

This belt extends along the fold mountain zone of Alpine-Himalayan region. It is also known as Mid-World Mountain Belt. From East side of the Himalayas, this belt goes South towards the Andaman and Nicobar Islands group where Barren Island, the only active volcano of India is found.

6 **Divergent Plate** Plates below the Earth's surface pulling apart from each other.
7 **Convergent Plate** Plates below the Earth's surface coming towards each other.

This belt merges with the Circum-Pacific belt in Indonesia. The Alpine and Himalayas are the Young Fold Mountain systems in this belt.

This belt has various volcanoes of the Alpine mountain chain, Mediterranean Sea (Stromboli, Vesuvius, Etna, etc.) and stretches towards Himalayas. Volcanoes of the Aegean Sea, Mt. Ararat, Elburz and Hindukush are also included in this belt. The important active volcanoes in this belt are Mt Vesuvius, Mt Etna and Mt Stramboli.

Mid-Atlantic Belt

This belt includes the volcanoes of the mid-Atlantic ridge. The volcanoes associated with the Atlantic Ocean are located either on swells or ridges rising from the sea floor or on near the edge of the continent where it slopes abruptly into the deep oceanic basins. These volcanoes are associated with zones of crustal movement.

The volcanoes formed along the mid-Atlantic ridge actually represent the splitting zone of the American plate moving towards the West and the Eurasian plate moving towards the East. In the splitting zone, there is constant **upwelling**[8] of magma.

Thus, it is a zone of crustal weakness. Volcanoes in this belt are generally of fissure eruption type. Volcanoes of Lesser Antilles, Azores, St. Helens, etc are included in this belt.

Check Your LEARNING...

1. What are lahars?
2. Which natural disaster may occur due to volcanic activity?
3. Name any two volcanoes which are found in the Circum-Pacific belt.
4. St. Helens volcano is found in which belt of volcanoes?

QUiCK Revision

- Volcano is an opening or a vent in the Earth's crust that allows hot lava, volcanic ashes and gases to escape from the hot interior of the Earth to its surface.
- The study of volcanoes, lava, magma and related geological, geophysical and geochemical phenomena is called volcanology.
- Volcanoes can be classified on the basis of frequency of eruption as
  - An active volcano is the one that is in active state and has erupted atleast once since the past 10000 years.
  - A dormant volcano is the one that hasn't erupted in the past 10000 years, but which is expected to erupt again.
  - An extinct volcano is the one that nobody expects to ever erupt again.
- Volcanoes can be classified on the basis of mode of eruption as
  - **Central Volcano** The volcanic eruption is from a central point and the magma and the solid matter rise to the surface of the Earth through the narrow opening which gets accumulated around the point of eruption.
  - **Fissure Volcano** A narrow opening on the Earth's surface through which lava, pyroclastics and gas are erupted and effused.
- Volcanoes are classified on the basis of the shape of the volcano as
  - A shield volcano is a type of volcano usually built almost entirely of fluid magma flows. They are named for their large size and low profile, resembling a warrior's shield lying on the ground.
  - A conical volcano is characterised by steep slopes as the lava is thick and do not flows for long distances. Rather it keeps accumulating around vent giving rise to conical shaped volcanic mountains.
- Volcanic activity has both constructive and destructive impacts on the environment and human activity.
- The major belts of the volcanic eruptions are Circum-Pacific belt, Mid-Continental belt and Mid-Atlantic belt.
  - Circum-Pacific Belt is also known as the Ring of Fire of the Pacific Ocean. It includes the volcanoes of Eastern and Western coastal areas of the Pacific Ocean.
  - Mid-Continental Belt has various volcanoes of the Alpine mountain chain, Mediterranean Sea (Stromboli, Vesuvius, Etna, etc.). Volcanoes of the Aegean sea, Mt Ararat, Elburz and Hindukush are also included in this belt.
  - Mid-Atlantic Belt includes the volcanoes of the mid-Atlantic ridge.

8 **Upwelling** It is an oceanographic phenomenon that involves wind driven motion of dense, cooler and usually nutrient rich water towards the ocean surface, replacing the warmer and usually nutrient depleted surface water.

Chapter Practice

Section-I

Multiple Choice Questions

1. The magma which is forced onto the Earth's surface is known by which name?
   (a) Vent (b) Cone
   (c) Lava (d) Magma chamber

Ans. (c) Lava

2. Which of the following is an example of composite volcano?
   (a) Mount Everest (b) Puy de Dome
   (c) Mauna Loa (d) Mount Merapi

Ans. (d) Mount Merapi

3. Volcanoes are usually located on
   (a) divergent plate boundaries
   (b) convergent plate boundaries
   (c) hotspot
   (d) All of the above

Ans. (d) All of the above

4. Which one has examples of volcanoes caused by convergent tectonic plate, coming together?
   (a) Mid-Atlantic Ridge
   (b) Pacific Ring of Fire
   (c) Both (a) and (b)
   (d) None of the above

Ans. (b) Pacific Ring of Fire

5. Which ridge has examples of volcanoes caused by divergent tectonic plates, pulling apart?
   (a) Pacific Ring of Fire
   (b) Mid-Atlantic Ridge
   (c) Both (a) and (b)
   (d) None of the above

Ans. (b) Mid-Atlantic Ridge

6. Volcanoes are generally found where .... pull apart or are coming together.
   (a) altra-plates (b) tectonic plates
   (c) Earth's crust (d) None of these

Ans. (b) tectonic plates

7. Give reason for the following.
   Volcano was earlier known as mountain of fire.
   (a) It emits red hot lava.
   (b) It emits poisonous gases.
   (c) It constructs many landforms.
   (d) All of the above

Ans. (a) It emits red hot lava.

8. Give reason for the following.
   Volcanology is useful for geologists.
   (a) It is the study of volcanoes, lava, and magma.
   (b) It is the study of geological and geophysical phenomena of the Earth.
   (c) It provides information of minerals.
   (d) All of the above

Ans. (d) All of the above

9. Give reason for the following.
   In volcanic eruption, the pressure always acts vertically upwards.
   (a) Magma contains different materials like silicate material, gases and water vapours.
   (b) Tectonic plates release pressure from inside the Earth.
   (c) Melting of rocks forms magma.
   (d) Both (a) and (b)

Ans. (d) Both (a) and (b)

10. Give reason for the following.
    The Circum-Pacific Belt is also known as 'The Ring of Fire'.
    (a) It is region of transform plate boundary.
    (b) 80% active volcanoes erupting fire are located in this belt.
    (c) It has natural gas reserves which explode frequently.
    (d) All of the above

Ans. (b) 80% active volcanoes erupting fire are located in this belt.

11. Which of the following statements is correct?
    (i) Erebus Mountain is located in Antarctica.
    (ii) Aleutian Island is located in the Circum- Pacific Belt.
    (iii) Volcanoes of Mid-Atlantic Belt are associated with zone of crustal movement.

    Codes
    (a) Only (i) (b) Only (ii)
    (c) Only (iii) (d) All of these

Ans. (d) All of these

12. Which of the following statements is incorrect?
    (i) Magma is found on the surface of the Earth.
    (ii) American Plate is moving towards West.
    (iii) Fujiyama is an example of central volcano.

    Codes
    (a) Only (i) (b) Only (ii)
    (c) Only (iii) (d) (i) and (iii)

Ans. (a) Only (i)

13. Match the following.

	List-I		List-II
A.	Vent	1.	Extrusive igneous rock
B.	Crater	2.	When a volcano gets hollow and collapses on itself
C.	Caldera	3.	Upper part of vent
D.	Cinder	4.	A narrow opening in volcano

Codes

	A	B	C	D		A	B	C	D
(a)	1	2	3	4	(b)	2	1	4	3
(c)	3	4	1	2	(d)	4	3	2	1

Ans. (d)

14. Match the following.

	List-I		List-II
A.	Molten rock material on the surface	1.	Constructive effect of volcanoes
B.	Ring of Fire	2.	Destructive effect of volcanoes
C.	Geyser	3.	Lava
D.	Lahars	4.	Pacific Rim

Codes

	A	B	C	D		A	B	C	D
(a)	1	2	3	4	(b)	2	1	4	3
(c)	3	4	1	2	(d)	4	3	2	1

Ans. (c)

Section-II

Short Questions

1. Describe the shape of a volcano.

Ans. A volcano is an opening or a vent in the Earth's crust that allows hot lava, volcanic ashes and gases to escape from the hot interior of the Earth to its surface.

2. Define the process of volcanicity.

Ans. Volcanicity refers to the process by which magma and volatiles are transferred from the interior of the Earth to its surface.

3. What are the effects of volcanic eruptions?

Ans. Volcanic eruptions lead to the various changes on the Earth's surface, starting from the formation of new landforms to effecting the lives and property of people.

4. Why rainfall takes place after volcanic eruption?

Ans. Rainfall takes place after volcanic eruption because all the ash particles that are thrown up into the atmosphere are good at attracting/collecting water droplets. Water vapour along with other gases comes out from volcanic vent. It rises high in the air and after cooling, it causes rainfall.

5. Mount Stromboli is an example of which type of volcano?

Ans. Mount Stromboli is one of the most active volcanoes on Earth and has been erupting almost continuously since 1932.

6. Which type of volcanoes are known as sleeping volcanoes?

Ans. Dormant volcanoes are known as sleeping volcanoes. These type of volcanoes have not been erupted since past 10,000 years, but are expected to erupt again.

7. Give two examples of fissure volcanoes.

Ans. Two examples of fissure volcanoes are
(i) The Deccan trap of India.
(ii) Columbia Plateau in USA.

8. State any two types of volcanoes which are classified on the basis of shape.

Ans. Two types of volcanoes on the basis of shape are
(i) **Shield Volcano** It is a type of volcano built almost entirely the flows of fluid magma.
(ii) **Conical Volcano** A volcano having a conical shape is called a conical volcano. Such volcano is characterised by steep slopes.

9. What do you understand by Lahar?

Ans. Lahar is a type of mud flow or debris flow composed of a slurry of pyroclastic material, rocky debris and water.

10. What is the percentage of volcanoes associated with the divergent and convergent plate boundaries?

Ans. About 15% of the volcanoes are associated with the divergent plate and 80% are associated with the convergent plate.

11. Answer the following questions.
(i) Cotopaxi is located in which belt of volcanic eruption in the world?
(ii) What is the height of Cotopaxi?

Ans. (i) Cotopaxi is one of the highest volcanic mountains in the world. It is located in Circum-Pacific Belt.
(ii) The height of Cotopaxi is 5,911 m.

12. Why is Mid-Atlantic Belt a zone of crustal weakness?

Ans. The volcanoes formed along the Mid-Atlantic Ridge actually represent the splitting zone of the American plate moving towards West and the Eurasian plate moving towards East. In the splitting zone stated above, there is constant upwelling of magma. Thus, it is a zone of crustal weakness.

Long Questions

1. Answer the following questions.
(i) Describe the structure of a volcano.
(ii) What happens when the pressure builds up inside the Earth?

Ans. (i) The structure of a volcano can be described as
- **Vent** It is a narrow opening in the volcano that allows hot magma, gases and ashes to escape. It is usually pipe shaped.

- **Crater** The upper part of the vent that is a bowl shaped depression is known as the crater of the volcano. It is the highest point of the volcano.
- **Cinder** The solid rocks that are ejected from the volcanoes are known as cinder.
- **Caldera** It forms when a volcano gets hollow and then collapses on itself. A caldera could look like a large indentation on the side of the volcano or it could happen at the very top.
- **Magma Chamber** The large underground pool of molten rocks found beneath the surface of the Earth is called the magma chamber.

(ii) When pressure builds up inside the Earth, gases and rock comes out through the opening and spill over or fill the air with lava fragments.

2. Give reasons, why?

(i) Volcanic eruption is associated with water.

(ii) Volcanic activity leads to earthquakes.

Ans. (i) Volcanic eruption is associated with water because when water comes in contact with magma, it dissolves and crystallises which makes the dissolved water free. At high temperature and pressure, this water escapes out through many holes and thus causes explosion.

(ii) Volcanic activity leads to earthquake as during this activity, the magma exerts pressure on the rocks until it cracks the rock. Then the magma squirts into the crack and starts building pressure again. Every time the rock cracks, it makes a small earthquake.

3. Explain the following

(i) Active Volcano

(ii) Dormant Volcano

(iii) Extinct Volcano

Ans. (i) **Active Volcano** It is the one that is in active state and has erupted in the recent past. At present about 500 active volcanoes on land are known in the world. Out of these volcanoes 20 are expected to erupt any time. For example, Mt Etna and Mt Stromboli (Light house of the Mediterranean) in Italy, Pinatubo in Philippines, Mauna Loa in Hawaii and Baren Island in Andaman and Nicobar Islands in India.

(ii) **Dormant Volcano** It is the one that hasn't erupted in the past 10,000 years, but which is expected to erupt again. It is also known as sleeping volcano. For example, Mt. Vesuvius near Naples in Southern Italy, which experienced violent eruptions after centuries of inactivity in 1944. Since then there is no major eruption. Mt Kilimanjaro (Japan) is also an example of this volcano.

(iii) **Extinct Volcano** It is the one that nobody expects to ever erupt again. Examples of extinct volcanoes are Lassen Park in Northern California and Mt. Kenya in Africa.

4. What are the products of a volcano? Discuss.

Ans. Volcanoes erupt a large variety of materials ranging from gases to the solid matter. These include

- **Gases** The gases ejecting from the volcanoes largely contain water vapour with varying amounts of carbon dioxide, hydrogen sulphide and chlorine. Often these gases get mixed with each other resulting in the dark clouds that can be seen from a distance of a few miles.
- **Liquids** The liquid matter produced by volcanoes is the lava, great quantities of hot molten rock. The crater of the volcano usually erupts the lava, but in some cases it also erupts from the sides of the volcano by the means of fissures developed around the zones of weakness.
- **Solid Matter** The solid matter that erupts from the volcanoes varies in size from finer dust to huge rocks that weighs several tons. These solid products from the volcano are known as pyroclasts. The large fragments of rocks erupted from the volcanoes are known as blocks. The smaller stone sized particles are called lapilli.

5. Define the following.

(i) Magma (ii) Dome

(iii) Convergent plate boundary

Ans. (i) **Magma** It is a molten and semi-molten rock mixture found under the Earth's surface. It is extremely hot between 700° to 1300° Celsius.

(ii) **Dome** It is a rounded vault forming the roof of a building or structure, typically with a circular base.

(iii) **Convergent Plate Boundary** It is a tectonic boundary where two plates are moving towards each other.

6. 'Volcanoes have a number of impacts on people.' Discuss in brief.

Ans. Refer to chapter theory on page no. 63 and 64.

7. What are the constructive effects of volcanic eruptions?

Ans. Volcanic eruptions are often seen as distructive for environment and human life, but it too has constructive effects. Some of the constructive effects of volcanoes are

- **Formation of Black Soil** Lava becomes black soil when weathered by agents of weathering. It is very useful for cultivation of cotton, sugarcane banana, etc. Lava obtained from plains is much fertile, for example, the land masses like Deccan Traps, parts of Brazil and Indonesia are very fertile.
- **Landforms** Various landforms are created by the solidification of magma on the surface of the Earth. The landforms are called extrusive landforms.
- **Caldera Lake** These lakes are formed when the cone of volcano collapses during eruption. This depression eventually gets filled with water and form a lake.

- **Geysers** They act like fountain of hot water and steam. It escapes when underground water comes in contact with hot volcanic rocks.

8. How are the volcanoes distributed along the various belts?

Ans. Volcanoes are not randomly distributed on the surface of the Earth, rather they are found in certain well defined belts.

The major belts of the volcanic eruptions are

- **Circum-Pacific Belt** This belt is also known as the 'Ring of Fire' of the Pacific Ocean. It includes the volcanoes of Eastern and Western coastal areas of the Pacific Ocean. It extends from the Erebus mountains of Antarctica to Alaska through the Andes of South America and Rockies of North America. It is nearly 3200 kms length.
- **Mid-Continental Belt** This belt extends along the fold mountain zone of Alpine-Himalayan region. It is also known as Mid-World Mountain Belt. From East side of the Himalayas, this belt goes South towards the Andaman and Nicobar Islands group where Barren Island, the only active volcano of India is found. This belt merges with the Circum-Pacific belt in Indonesia. The Alpine and Himalayas are the Young Fold Mountain systems in this belt. The important active volcanoes in this belt are Mt. Vesuvius, Mt. Etna and Mt. Stramboli.
- **Mid-Atlantic Belt** This belt includes the volcanoes of the Mid-Atlantic Ridge. The volcanoes associated with the Atlantic Ocean are located either on swells or ridges rising from the sea floor or on or near the edge of the continent where it slopes abruptly into the deep oceanic basins. These volcanoes are associated with zones of crustal movement.

Chapter Assessment

Section-I

Multiple Choice Questions

1. Magma contains the contents of
   (a) silica
   (b) aluminium
   (c) magnesium
   (d) none of the above
2. The volcanoes formed by the alternating layers of lava and rock fragments are called ....
   (a) cinder cones
   (b) spatter cones
   (c) composite volcanoes
   (d) shields
3. Composite volcanoes are also known as
   (a) strato volcanoes
   (b) shields
   (c) compound volcanoes
   (d) none of the above
4. Shield volcanoes are .... in size.
   (a) small (b) medium
   (c) long (d) huge

Section-II

Short Questions

1. How many active volcanoes are known in the world?
2. Give two examples of sleeping volcanoes.
3. What do you understand by divergent plate boundary?
4. What is known as the Ring of Fire?
5. Write two advantages of volcanoes.
6. Write two negative effects of volcanoes.
7. What do you mean by calderas?
8. Give the meaning of magma chamber.

Long Questions

1. Classify the volcanoes based on the frequency of distribution.
2. Why volcanic eruptions may lead to ejection of materials in all forms?
3. Describe the distribution of volcanoes around the world.

CHAPTER 08

Earthquakes

SYLLABUS

Earthquakes ●Meaning, causes and Measurement. ● Effects : destructive and constructive. ● Earthquake zones of the world.

Meaning of Earthquake

Earthquake is a natural phenomenon which is caused by internal forces of the Earth. It can be defined as the shaking of the Earth's crust due to the powerful movement below the surface of the Earth. This is not a normal movement inside the Earth, rather it is caused due to the movement of the Plate Tectonics, which has devastating effects on both human life and property. This movement occurs in the crust or upper mantle, which ranges to the depth of about 800 kms from the Earth's surface.

The point where the earthquake originates in the interior of the Earth is known as **seismic focus**. The point vertically (directly) above the focus on the surface of the Earth is called **epicenter**. During earthquake, the epicenter faces the maximum lose of life and property.

Causes of Earthquakes

The strain in the Earth's crust is the reason responsible which gives rise to earthquakes. Strain is caused by number of factors. When the tectonic movement is near the Earth's crust, then these strains suddenly release tremendous energy in the form of a sudden violent shock on the surface of the Earth. A series of shocks that result from sudden Earth's movement are known as **earthquake waves** or **seismic waves**. These waves spread out from the seismic focus and become a cause of widespread destruction.

The major causes of the earthquakes are

Volcanic Eruptions

Volcanic eruptions are mostly accompanied by an earthquake. Volcanic eruption and earthquakes are interrelated i.e. one leads to the other. Volcanic earthquakes are caused by gas explosions and may also happen after the volcanic eruptions. For example, eruption of Krakatoa volcano between the Java and Sumatra islands in 1883 led to a violent earthquake which caused tsunami in Java and Sumatra.

Hot gases, erupted by the volcanic eruptions, violently push the surface of the Earth's crust upward causing earthquakes. The intensity of the volcanic earthquakes is highest near the volcano and they merely, exceed only a few hundred square kms. Such earthquakes of volcanic origin are generally less violent and more limited in extent than tectonic earthquakes.

Tectonic Plates

The crust of the Earth consists of different tectonic plates. These plates move slightly due to the movement of magma in the interiors of the Earth.

Sometimes the intensity of the movement increases, due to which the balance and position of all the plates disturb, thus leading to earthquake. These type of earthquake are most frequent and powerful and are destructive in nature.

Three types of stresses led to the plate movements

(i) **Compressional Stress** It occurs at convergent plate boundaries where two plates are pushed into one another due to collision.

(ii) **Tensional Stress** It occurs at divergent plate boundaries where two plates are pulled apart from each other.

(iii) **Sheer Stress** It occurs at transform boundaries where two plates slide pass each other in opposite directions.

Convergent or transform plate movements are more prone to earthquakes because their edges produce faults along the lines of weakness. This is happened because of the **subduction**[1] and collision of the heavy oceanic plates below the continental plates.

Tectonic earthquakes occur mostly in 'Ring of Fire' of South-East Asia (Philippines and Indonesia) and Northern India. In India, the earthquake of Bhuj in Gujarat in 2001 occurred due to the lowering of the Indian plate below the Eurasian plate.

Faulting and Folding

They occur due to the horizontal and vertical movements of the Earth due to compressional and tensional forces. These movements cause rocks to bend, buckle and fracture or crumple into folds. This is called folding.

Extreme stress and pressure due to these movements can sometimes cause the rocks to tear along a plane of weakness, creating a fault. This is called faulting.

Any such dislocation (fold and fault) beneath the Earth's surface causes earthquakes, e.g. the continental transform fault in San Andreas in California led to an earthquake in 1906. This earthquake was recorded 8.3 on the Richter scale.

Human Activities

The interaction of the humans with nature has been a major cause of a number of earthquakes. Certain human activities such as underground mining, pumping of groundwater and oil, nuclear explosions, construction of dams and big reservoirs and the deposition of a large amount of eroded material in a lowland area, disturbs the equilibrium of underlying layer of rocks (crustal balance), which can lead to some major earthquakes.

For example, Koyana earthquake of 1967 was caused due to construction of Koyanar dam in Maharashtra. Another example of earthquake cause by human activities was seen in Colorado (USA) in 1960s, where chemical waste dump into the ground and underground explosions triggered a number of earthquakes.

Earthquake Waves

Earthquake waves are basically of two types i.e. body waves and surface waves.

(i) **Body Waves** These waves are generated due to the release of energy at the focus and move in all directions travelling through the body of the Earth. Due to this reason, they are known as body waves. There are two types of body waves which are

(a) **Primary waves (P-waves)** These waves move faster and are the first to arrive at the surface. They are first to be recorded by the seismograph. The P-waves are similar to sound waves. They travel through gaseous, liquid and solid materials.

(b) **Secondary waves (S-waves)** These waves arrive at the surface after P-waves and are recorded to be second on the seismograph. These waves can travel only through solid materials.

(ii) **Surface Waves** These waves move along the surface. The surface waves are the last to report on seismograph. These are long waves which are more destructive. They cause displacement of rocks and hence, collapsing of structures occur. These are further divided into two parts i.e. Love waves and Rayleigh waves.

Measurement of Earthquakes

The direction and intensity of earthquakes can be measured through Richter Scale, Mercalli Scale and Seismograph.

1 **Subduction** It is the process that takes place at convergent boundaries by which one tectonic plate moves under another tectonic plate and sinks into the mantle as the plates converge.

Richter Scale

The most common standard for the measurement of an earthquake is the Richter Scale. It was developed in 1935 by **Charles F Richter** of the California Institute of Technology. It is used to rate the magnitude of an earthquake and the amount of energy it released. This is calculated using information gathered by a seismograph. The Richter Scale measures the intensity of earthquakes on a scale of 1 to 9.

Mercalli Scale

It is a seismic scale used for measuring the intensity of an earthquake. It measures the effects of an earthquake. It is distinct from the moment magnitude (M_W) usually reported for an earthquake, which measure the release of energy. It measures the intensity on a scale of 1 to 12.

Seismograph

It is an instrument that measures and record details of earthquakes, such as direction of movement of waves, their passage and duration. Seismographs are equipped with electromagnetic sensors that translate ground motions into electrical changes, which are processed and recorded by the instruments' analogue or digital circuits.

There is a pen attached to the seismograph which vibrates with the earthquake waves and records their movements on a strip of paper. It also calculates the difference in the arrival of primary and secondary waves and the distance between the recording station and the epicenter.

The terms seismograph and seismometer are often used interchangeably. Both the devices may detect and measure seismic waves, but only a seismograph possesses the capacity to record the phenomena. A record produced by a seismograph on a display screen or paper printout is called a **seismogram.**

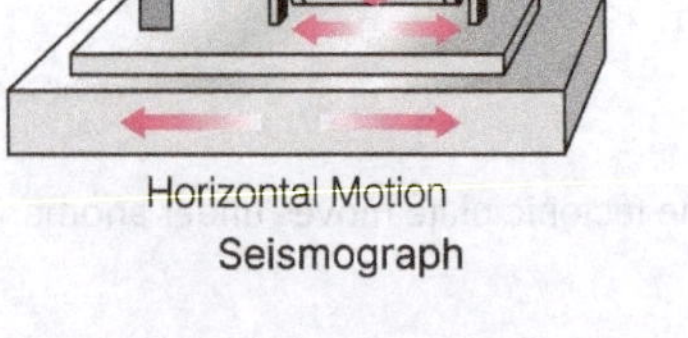

Seismograph

Check Your LEARNING...

1. Why do earthquakes occur?
2. Why tectonic plates always move?
3. Mention two human causes of earthquake.
4. What are secondary waves?
5. Who discovered Richter scale?

Effects of Earthquakes

Generally, earthquake is seen as a destructive phenomenon as it causes destruction of human life. However, it is sometimes also considered as constructive phenomenon. Its destructive and constructive effects are

Destructive Effects

- **Collapse of Buildings** Earthquake causes destruction of buildings, bridge and other structures at or near epicenter. Many men and animals are killed or buried under collapsed houses. This is the type of damage that leads to the worst casualties. Groundwater pipes also get damaged, affecting the supply of water.
- **Loss of Life** The cities and towns are worst affected due to high density of buildings and population, the mortality is high. As large building collapse, humans get buried under debris. Thus, leading to the loss of lives.
- **Damage of Dams, Power Plants, etc** The earthquakes may damage large dams, power installations and nuclear power plants.
- **Fire** Fire breaks out inevitably in large towns due to earthquakes which leads to major casualties. Fire can be caused due to high vibrations inside the houses, mines and factories, inflammable materials, leakage of gases, etc.
- **Tsunamis** Earthquakes originating in the sea cause very high sea waves that are called tsunamis. These waves cause major losses in the coastal areas.
- Tsunami can also be caused by landslide, volcanic eruption, meteoritic effects and so on. It is a common phenomenon in the Pacific Ocean and other large water bodies like lakes (due to landslides).

  For example, on December, 2004 the Indian Ocean earthquake led a series of tsunamis which caused a number of casualties in the surrounding coastal regions like Indonesia (most affected country which lies on the Pacific Ring of Fire), Sri Lanka, India, Maldives, and Thailand.

- **Cracks and Fissures** Earthquakes result in the formation of cracks and fissures on the ground formation. For example, the Koyna earthquake in 1967 in Maharashtra created a 10–15 cm fissure in the ground which spread over a length of 25 km. The fissures or cracks lead to change in sea level or land.
- **Landslides** The earthquakes in the hilly and mountainous regions, e.g. the Himalayas, Andes, Alps, etc can cause landslides and disturb the **isostatic equilibrium**[2]. The landslides affect the various settlements and the transport systems. Landslide due to earthquake may block valleys to form lakes.
- **Flash Floods** Very strong earthquakes result in the collapse of dams and cause severe flash floods. It blocks the flow of water in the river and may change the main course of river.
- **Submergence of Coastal Areas** Earthquakes also lead to submergence of coastal areas due to uplift and subsidence forces of the Earth, e.g. Dwarka in Gujarat is now a submerged city under the Arabian Sea.

Constructive Effects

- **Formation of Hot Springs and Lakes** Sometimes, the earthquake cause formation of hot springs as the heat energy of the earth comes to the surface. The hot springs have medicinal value. Many natural lakes have been formed in the Himalayas due to landslides triggered by earthquakes.
- **Formation of Inlets, Bays and Gulfs** The earthquake sometimes cause submergence in coastal land and result in formation of inlets (estuary), bays and gulfs which help to develop fishing, shipping, etc.
- **Bring Fertile Shore** Sometimes, the earthquake cause emergence of coasts and bring fertile shore out of water to develop crop production. Some mineral rich rocks may also be uplifted to the surface which provide valuable minerals.
- **Release of Energy** Due to earthquakes, the stored energy inside the Earth is released especially along the plate margins which keeps the Earth in good condition, as well as in good shape.

Earthquake Zones of the World

Earthquakes can strike any location at any time. But according to history, they occur in the same general patterns year after year, principally in three large zones or belts of the Earth.

These zones are

(i) The Circum-Pacific Belt

It is the world's biggest earthquake belt, found along the rim of the Pacific Ocean. In this belt, about 90% of the world's earthquake and 81 per cent of the world's largest earthquakes occur. This seismic belt in the West Coast covers areas from Alaska to Kurlie, Japan, Mariana and Philippines trenches, Indonesian Archipelago and Andes Mountains.

On the Eastern side, this belt covers West Coast of North America and continues Southward along Peru and Chile trench on the West Coast of South America. This belt also has a part of San Andreas Fault (in USA). Due to this fault-line, California is highly prone to earthquakes.

This belt forms an arc like shape and due to having around 75 per cent of the world's active and dormant volcanoes, it is also known as the **Ring of Fire**. Thus, most of the earthquakes here are of volcanic origin. This belt was responsible for Japan's mega earthquake on 11th March, 2011 with a magnitude of 9.0–9.1.

(ii) The Mid-Atlantic Belt

This earthquake belt runs along the mid-oceanic ridges and several islands near the ridges in the Atlantic Ocean. About 10 per cent of the world's earthquakes occur in this belt. Sea floor spreading is the characteristic of this belt which is the main cause of the occurrence of earthquake in it.

Since the divergent plates in this belt move in opposite directions and there is splitting as well, transform faults and fractures are created. All this becomes the causative factor for the occurrence of shallow focus earthquakes of moderate intensity.

(iii) The Mid-Continental Belt

This belt covers the Alpine mountain system of Europe, North America, Asia Minor, Caucasia, Iran, Afghanistan, Pakistan, Himalayan mountain systems including Tibet, Pamir, Tien-Shan, Altai and the mountains of China, Myanmar and Eastern Siberia regions.

2 **Isostatic Equilibrium** When a certain area of the Earth's crust reaches the state of isostasy (equilibrium), it is said to be in isostatic equilibrium.

This belt does not have any deep focus earthquakes. About 20 per cent of the total earthquakes of the world occur in this belt. This belt is also known as **Mid World Mountain Belt.**

Major Earthquakes of the World

Location of Earthquake	Year
Indonesia (Sulawesi Province)	2018
Nepal	2015
Near the East Coast of Honshu, Japan	2011
China	2008
Pakistan	2005
Off West Coast of Northern Sumatra	2004
Gujarat, India	2001
Tapei, Taiwan	1999
Izmit, Turkey	1999
Rostaq, Afghanistan	1998
Takhar, Afghanistan	1998
North-East Iran	1997
Tangshan, China	1976
Near Xining, China	1927
Kwanto, Japan	1923
Gansu, China	1920
Kolkata, India	1737
Shansi, China	1556

Check Your LEARNING...

1. What are constructive effects of Earthquake ?
2. What do you understand by the term 'Ring of Fire'?
3. Mention any one characteristic of mid-Atlantic belt.
4. Name the mountain systems included in the Mid-Continental Belt.

QUiCK Revision

- Earthquake can be defined as the shaking of the Earth's crust due to the tremors below the surface of the Earth.
- Earthquake waves and seismic waves are the series of shocks that results from sudden Earth's movement.
- Major causes of earthquake are volcanic eruption, movement of tectonic plates, folding, faulting and different human activities.
- Earthquake waves are basically of two types i.e. body waves and surface waves.
- The earthquakes are measured using Richter scale, Mercalli scale and seismograph.
- Richter scale was developed in 1935 by Charles F Richter of the California Institute of Technology.
- Mercalli scale is used for measuring the intensity of an earthquake.
- Seismograph is an instrument which measures and record details of earthquakes.
- The major effects of the earthquake includes collapse of buildings, floods, landslides, loss of population, fires, cracks and fissures, soil liquefaction and ground deformation.
- Sometimes the earthquakes cause formation of hot springs, lakes, which are very useful to people.
- The major earthquake distribution belts are Circum-Pacific belt, Mid-Atlantic belt and the Mid-Continental belt.
- Circum-Pacific belt is the world's biggest earthquake belt. It is found along the rim of the Pacific Ocean, where about 90% of the world's earthquake and 81 per cent of the world's largest earthquake occur.
- Mid-Atlantic belt runs along the mid-oceanic ridges and several islands, where about 10 per cent of the world's earthquake occur.
- Mid-Continental belt is known as Mid-World Mountain belt, where about 20 per cent of the world's earthquake occur.

Chapter Practice

Section-I

Multiple Choice Questions

1. Earthquakes occur when there is a sudden release of stored up energy in the Earth's
   (a) inner core (b) outer core
   (c) upper mantle (d) lower crust

Ans. (c) upper mantle

2. Tremors that have occurred in Earth's crust are known as
   (a) earthquakes (b) volcanic eruptions
   (c) bed eruptions (d) volcano-earthquake

Ans. (a) earthquakes

3. Where do most earthquakes occur?
   (a) Along dikes (b) Along faults
   (c) Along folds (d) Along joints

Ans. (b) Along faults

4. Which waves cause the greatest amount of damage?
   (a) All equal (b) P-waves
   (c) S-waves (d) Surface waves

Ans. (d) Surface waves

5. The greater the magnitude, the
   (a) lesser the amount of energy released.
   (b) greater the amount of energy released.
   (c) lesser the amount of energy absorbed.
   (d) greater the amount of energy absorbed.

Ans. (b) greater the amount of energy released.

6. Instrument used to measure the earthquake is known as ....
   (a) quake meter
   (b) quake graph
   (c) seismograph
   (d) typanicgraph

Ans. (c) seismograph

7. The intensity scale of the earthquake is called
   (a) Mercalli scale (b) Richter scale
   (c) Number scale (d) None of these

Ans. (a) Mercalli scale

8. Give reason for the following.
   Tremors occur inside the Earth.
   (a) Movements of the Earth's crust along lines of weakness produces great tremors.
   (b) During volcanic activity movement of lava beneath the crust causes tremors inside the Earth.
   (c) Both (a) and (b)
   (d) None of the above

Ans. (c) Both (a) and (b)

9. Give reason for the following.
   Seismology is useful for geologists.
   (a) It is the study of earthquakes, seismic waves and related phenomena.
   (b) It is the study of geological and geophysical phenomena of the Earth.
   (c) It provides information of minerals.
   (d) All of the above

Ans. (a) It is the study of earthquakes, seismic waves and related phenomena.

10. Give reason for the following.
    The Circum-Pacific Belt is also known as 'The Ring of Fire'.
    (a) It is region of transform plate boundary.
    (b) It has natural gas reserves which explode frequently.
    (c) 90 per cent world's earthquakes occur in this belt.
    (d) All of the above

Ans. (c) 90 per cent world's earthquakes occur in this belt.

11. Give reason for the following.
    Volcanic activity and earthquakes occur in the same belt.
    (a) Earthquakes and volcanoes are formed along faults between tectonic plates, where the crust is weakest.
    (b) Volcanoes have power to lead earthquakes.
    (c) Each tectonic plate in the Earth's crust has volcanic belt.
    (d) None of the above

Ans. (a) Earthquakes and volcanoes are formed along faults between tectonic plates, where the crust is weakest.

12. Give reason for the following.
    The destructive effects of an earthquake are far more than its constructive effects.
    (a) It causes large scale destruction of life and property.
    (b) It changes course of rivers which triggers flash floods.
    (c) It caused land to collapse and creates faults in lands.
    (d) All of the above

Ans. (d) All of the above

13. Which of the following statements is/are correct?
    (i) Earthquakes occur due to internal forces of the Earth.
    (ii) Aleutian Island is located in the Circum-Pacific Belt.
    (iii) San Andreas Fault is a continental transform fault.

Codes

(a) Only (i) (b) Only (ii)
(c) Only (iii) (d) All of these

Ans. (d) All of these

14. Which of the following statements is/are incorrect?

(i) Most of the earthquakes occur at transform fault-line.
(ii) Magma is found on the surface of the Earth.
(iii) South American plate is moving towards West.

Codes

(a) Only (i) (b) (i) and (ii)
(c) Only (iii) (d) All of these

Ans. (b) (i) and (ii)

15. Match the following.

List-I	List-II
A. Volcanic gas	1. Magma
B. Molten rocks beneath the Earth's surface	2. Sulphur dioxide
C. Plates inside the Earth	3. To measure magnitude of earthquake
D. Richter scale	4. Tectonic

Codes

	A	B	C	D
(a)	1	2	3	4
(b)	2	1	4	3
(c)	3	4	1	2
(d)	4	3	2	1

Ans. (b)

16. Match the following.

List-I	List-II
A. Focus	1. Seismic waves
B. Epicenter	2. Where one tectonic plate slides down the other plate
C. Primary and secondary	3. Origin place of earthquake below the Earth crust
D. Subduction zone	4. A place on Earth surface just above the origin point of earthquake

Codes

	A	B	C	D		A	B	C	D
(a)	1	2	3	4	(b)	2	1	4	3
(c)	3	4	1	2	(d)	4	3	2	1

Ans. (c)

17. Match the following.

List-I	List-II
A. Molten rock material on the surface	1. Destructive effect of earthquake
B. Ring of Fire	2. Constructive effect of earthquake
C. Hot spring	3. Pacific Rim
D. Tsunami	4. Lava

Codes

	A	B	C	D
(a)	1	2	3	4
(b)	2	1	4	3
(c)	3	4	1	2
(d)	4	3	2	1

Ans. (d)

Section-II

Short Questions

1. Answer the following questions.

(i) Define earthquake.
(ii) Is the earthquake a movement of the Earth?

Ans. (i) Earthquake can be defined as the shaking of the Earth's crust due to the movement of plates below the surface of the Earth.

(ii) An earthquake is not a movement of the Earth, rather it is caused due to the movement of the Earth.

2. Answer the following questions.

(i) Why do earthquake occurs?
(ii) Which type of stress causes a fault?

Ans. (i) Earthquake is caused by the movement of Earth's outer layer which is split into tectonic plates. These plates move slightly due to the movement of magma in the layer below.

(ii) Tensional and compressional stress causes fault on the surface of the Earth.

3. What was the effect of the violent eruption of Krakatoa volcano?

Ans. The violent eruption of Krakatoa volcano between the Java and Sumatra islands, caused a severe earthquake. The explosions were so violent that they were heard 3,110 km away in Perth, Western Australia and islands near Mauritius, 4800 km away. This led to Tsunami waves of height 30 to 40 metres which killed many people in the coastal areas of Java and Sumatra islands.

4. Why are moderate earthquakes caused near the divergent plates?

Ans. Moderate earthquakes are usually caused on the divergent plate boundaries because the rupture rate of the crust from the consequent movement of the plates away from the oceanic region is slower than other areas.

5. What is plate tectonic theory?

Ans. The theory of plate tectonics deals with mobility of crustal blocks of the Earth relative to each other and the resultant structural changes. When any two plates collide with each other, faults are produced at their edges, which ultimately lead to earthquakes.

6. Answer the following questions.
(i) What are folds?
(ii) Where are they more visible?

Ans. (i) A fold can be defined as a bend in rock that is the response to compressional forces.
(ii) Folds are most visible in rocks that contain layering.

7. Define
(i) Seismology
(ii) Seismometer and Seismograph

Ans. (i) The science of study of earthquake is known as seismology.
(ii) The instrument used to detect and record earthquake is known as seismometer and seismograph.

8. What is the meaning of M_w?

Ans. M_w stands for moment magnitude. It is a scale which is used by seismologists to measure the size of earthquakes.

9. How seismograph is different from seismometer?

Ans. The terms seismograph and seismometer are often used interchangeably. However, both devices may detect and measure seismic waves, but only a seismograph possesses the capacity to record phenomena.

10. (i) What is the function of electromagnetic sensors in a seismograph?
(ii) What is meant by intensity of the earthquake?

Ans. (i) Electromagnetic sensors in seismograph translate ground motions into electrical changes.
(ii) The intensity is a number describing the severity of an earthquake in terms of its effects on the Earth's surface and on humans and their structures.

11. Answer the following questions.
(i) When is effect of earthquake felt more?
(ii) What is the other name given to the shock waves?

Ans. (i) The effect of an earthquake is felt more if the shockwave epicenter is near the surface of the Earth.
(ii) The shock waves are also known as the seismic waves which emits energy of different magnitude and meets at the epicenter where the earthquake originated near the surface of the Earth.

12. What causes the deformation of the ground surface?

Ans. Severe tremors and resultant vibrations caused by earthquakes result in the deformation of ground surface because of rise and subsidence of ground surface and faulting activity (formation of faults).

Long Questions

1. Briefly explain the causes of earthquake.

Ans. Refer to chapter theory page no. 70 and 71.

2. Differentiate between convergent plate boundary and divergent plate boundary.

Ans. Differences between convergent and divergent plate boundaries are

Convergent Plate Boundary	Divergent Plate Boundary
In this boundary, two plates move towards each other.	In this boundary, two plates move away from each other.
This result in mountains and subduction zones.	This results in plate margin ridges and ocean floor spreading.
For example, Ocean trenches and chains of volcanoes. The Andes mountain chain and off-shore ocean trench.	For example, the Mid-Atlantic ridge.

3. Describe about the instruments that are used for measuring earthquakes.

Ans. Refer to chapter theory on page no. 71 and 72.

4. Describe any three destructive effects of earthquake.

Ans. Destructive effects of earthquake are

- **Collapse of Buildings** Earthquake causes dismantling of buildings, bridges and other structures at or near epicenter. Groundwater pipes get damaged, affecting the supply of water.
- **Loss of Population** The cities and towns are worst effected due to major loss by the high density of buildings and population. As large buildings collapse, humans and animals get buried under the debris. Thus, leading to the loss of lives.
- **Fire** Electric poles and underground wires gets broken due to earthquakes. Fire breaks out inevitably in large towns leading to major casualties. Fire can be caused due to high vibrations inside the houses, mines and factories.

5. Describe how earthquakes can be beneficial?

Ans. Earthquakes can be beneficial through the following points

- Sometimes, the earthquake cause formation of hot springs which are very useful to people.
- The earthquake sometimes cause submergence in coastal land and result in formation of inlets, bays and gulfs which help to develop fishing and shipping, etc.
- Sometimes, the earthquake cause emergence of coasts and bring fertile shore out of water to give chance to develop crop production.

6. Briefly describe the three belts of earthquake.

Ans. Refer to chapter theory on page no. 73 and 74.

7. (i) Give reasons, why
   (a) Circum-Pacific belt is known as Ring of Fire.
   (b) Transform faults and fractures found in Mid-Atlantic Belt.
   (ii) What is subduction zone found at convergent plate boundaries?

Ans. (i) (a) The Ring of Fire is a major area in the basin of the Pacific Ocean. It has around 75 per cent of the world's active and dormant volcanoes, thus it is known as 'Ring of Fire'. About 90 per cent of the world's earthquakes and 81 per cent of the world's largest earthquakes occur along the Ring of Fire.

(b) The belt of earthquakes extends along the mid-oceanic ridges and several islands near the ridges of the Atlantic Ocean. The presence of divergent tectonic plates in Mid-Atlantic Belt move in opposite directions and there is splitting as well, thus transform faults and fractures are created here.

(ii) At convergent plate boundaries, two plates collide. The thinner and more dense oceanic plate is overridden by the thicker and less dense continental plate. The oceanic plate is forced down into the mantle. This process is known as subduction and this zone is known as 'subduction zone'.

Chapter Assessment

Section-I

Multiple Choice Questions

1. Waves produced due to the earthquake are known as ....
   (a) seismic waves
   (b) shock waves
   (c) infrasonic waves
   (d) None of the above
2. Which instrument(s) record the direction of movement of earthquake waves?
   (a) Richter scale
   (b) Seismograph
   (c) Mercalli scale
   (d) All of the above
3. Which of the following is/are the measuring instrument of earthquake?
   (a) Seismograph
   (b) Richter scale
   (c) Mercalli scale
   (d) All of the above
4. Earthquakes usually occur at the boundary of
   (a) crustal plates
   (b) mantle plates
   (c) coral plate
   (d) volcanic beds

Section-II

Short Questions

1. What is the meaning of an earthquake?
2. Which belt is known as the 'Ring of Fire'?
3. Write two man-made causes of earthquakes.
4. What is meant by Richter scale?
5. Write two uses of seismograph.
6. Define the following
   (i) Subduction
   (ii) Isostatic equilibrium
   (iii) Flash floods
7. Give reasons, why?
   (i) Collision of plates causes earthquakes.
   (ii) Seismic waves effect the water bodies on Earth.

Long Questions

1. Describe
   (i) The destructive effects of earthquakes.
   (ii) The constructive effects of earthquakes.
2. Classify the belts of earthquake.
3. Describe the instruments used for measuring an earthquake.

CHAPTER

09

Weathering and Denudation

SYLLABUS

Weathering and Denudation Meaning types and effects of weathering. •Types : Physical Weathering-block and granular disintegration, exfoliation; Chemical Weathering- oxidation, carbonation, hydration and solution; Biological weathering - caused by humans, plants and animals. • Meaning and agents of denudation, work of river and wind. •Stages of river course and associated land forms - V-shaped valley, waterfall, meander and delta. •Wind - deflation hollows and sand dunes.

Weathering

It is defined as the mechanical disintegration and chemical decomposition of rocks through the actions of various elements of weather and climate. A very little or no motion of material takes place in weathering. It is an **in situ**[1] or on-site process. It is the process of breaking down of rocks, but not its removal.

Features of Weathering

- It involves disintegration or decay of solid rocks.
- It depends characteristics of rocks and on climatic elements.
- It affects the surface of the Earth.
- It causes soil formation.
- It transforms hard massive rocks into finer materials.
- By agents of gradation, it prepares rock materials for transportation.

Types of Weathering

There are three types of weathering i.e. physical, chemical and biological.

(i) Physical Weathering

Physical or mechanical weathering is the disintegration of a rock by the natural or physical agents. Physical weathering does not change the chemical composition of rocks.

Most of the physical weathering processes are caused by thermal expansion, pressure release forest action and wind action. These processes are slow, but in long-term, they weaken the rocks by repetition of expansion and contraction.

The major processes of physical weathering are

- **Block Disintegration** The repeated expansion and contraction of rocks due to change in temperature causes the weakening and breaking down of the rocks into rectangular blocks. This is known as block disintegration. For example, in desert regions, the high diurnal range of temperature (10°C to 15°C or more) causes the splitting of rocks.

1 **In Situ** When weathering take place on the same place where the material is present.

- **Granular Disintegration** It is a form of weathering where the grains of rocks becomes loosened and breakdown into pieces and fragments. It may happen due to the **frost action**[2], temperature change or the biotic factors.
- **Exfoliation** It is a form of mechanical weathering in which the curved plates of rocks are stripped off from the rocks below. This process is common in the desert and the tropical region, exfoliation is also known as onion weathering.

(ii) Chemical Weathering

It is extremely slow and gradual decomposition of rocks due to exposure to the chemical elements contained in air and water. It leads to decomposition of rocks and minerals, as chemical reaction transform them into different chemical combinations. The rate of chemical weathering is higher in tropical areas with high temperatures.

The major chemical weathering processes are

- **Oxidation** In weathering, oxidation means a combination of minerals with oxygen to form oxides (like rusting in case of iron) or hydroxides. For example, when the rocks containing iron comes in contact with air, they get oxidised and weaken the overall rock structure, resulting in the breaking down of the rocks.
- **Carbonation** It is the reaction of carbonates and bicarbonates with the minerals. For example, carbon dioxide from the atmosphere and soil is absorbed by water to form carbonic acid. It then converts calcium carbonate into the much more soluble calcium bicarbonate. Thus, rainwater as a result erodes limestone and other calcareous rocks easily.
- **Hydration** Under this process, the mineral takes up the water and expand. This expansion causes an increase in volume of the rock itself. Continuous repetition of this process causes fatigue in the rocks and may lead to their disintegration.
- **Solution** In this process, when the rocks and soluble minerals come in contact with water, they undergo chemical change and dissolve. Reaction of solution varies from mineral to mineral. For example, sedimentary rocks like limestone are more prone to chemical weathering than the other rocks. When rainwater penetrate down the surface in the rocks through cracks and joints, it also dissolves soluble minerals present there such as rock salt and gypsum. The rate of solution is affected by both mineral composition and structure of the rock.

(iii) Biological Weathering

It is the weakening and subsequent disintegration of rocks by plants, animals, humans and microbes. It is also known as **organic weathering**.

The main agents of biological weathering are

- **Plants** Plant roots exert a tremendous pressure on the Earth materials. This pressure results in widening of the cracks and splitting apart of the rocks.
- **Animals and Other Organisms** Animals and organisms like earthworms, rodents, etc, through the process of burrowing and wedging, make holes in the ground or rocks which expose them to more intense chemical, physical and biological processes. The process of burrowing by animals loose the surface material around the rocks that led to their physical disintegration. After death, decaying animals also provide many chemicals for rock disintegration.
- **Humans** Humans contribute to the weathering of rocks through their activities like mining, deforestation, quarrying, etc. These activities make the rocks more vulnerable to the agents of denudation.

Effects of Weathering

The effects of weathering can be categorised into two broad categories i.e. positive and negative.

(i) Positive Effects

- Weathering of rocks helps in the formation of soil, which is an essential component for the existence of human life.
- Weathered rock material is used by the people for construction purposes.
- The process of weathering also results in the formation of new landscape.
- New minerals get exposed during the process of weathering.

2 **Frost Action** Freezing of water in the cracks of rocks, disintegrate them.

(ii) Negative Effects

- Mechanical weathering may cause extensive soil erosion.
- Loosening of rock material through weathering can result in landslides and mudslides.
- Humans avoid settlements in those regions which are more prone to weathering like Karst region (limestone region).
- Chemical weathering may cause the soil to become infertile.

Check Your LEARNING...

1. Give an example of block disintegration.
2. Which organisms help in biological weathering?
3. Mention any one negative effect of weathering.
4. What is carbonation?

Denudation

Denudation involves the processes that causes the erosion of the Earth's surface by moving water, ice, wind, leading to the reduction in elevation and in relief of landforms. It is the process of breaking and removing the rocks from surface of the Earth.

Denudation is carried out in following four stages

(i) **Weathering** The gradual disintegration of rocks by atmosphere and weather forces.

(ii) **Erosion** The active wearing away of the Earth's surface by moving agents like running water, wind, etc.

(iii) **Transportation** The removal of the eroded debris to new location.

(iv) **Deposition** The dumping of debris in certain parts of the Earth, where it may accumulate to form new rocks.

All these processes work simultaneously in different parts of the world at different rates.

Agents of Denudation

The main agents of denudation involves running water, wind, waves and ice. The action of running water is considered to be the most important agent of denudation.

Work of Rivers

The river water is one of the most important sources of denudation. It shapes landforms over a large part of the Earth's surface. In rivers, erosions and transportation go on simultaneously through certain interaction processes, like **corrosion**[3] or **abrasion**[4], **attrition**[5], etc.

Stages of the River

The course of the river can be divided into three distinct stages. These are

(i) **Upper Course** It is also known as mountain course. It begins at the source of the river near the watershed, generally at the crest of the mountain range. Vertical erosion is predominant action here.

Landforms Associated with Upper Course of River
The river in this course develops various landforms like v-shaped valley, waterfall, rapids, cataract, etc.

V-shaped Valley It is formed by erosion from a river or stream over time. It is called a V-shaped valley as the shape of the valley is the same as the letter 'V'. During the upper stage of the river, the valley developed is deep, narrow V-shaped because the river performs the task of downcutting. These valleys are formed in the initial stages of the river and have steep slopes. In a region of hard rocks, it develops I-shape. These valleys are abundantly found in the region which have sufficient rainfall.

Waterfall A river that falls vertically down from a cliff, rock, etc is known as a waterfall. A waterfall is generally formed due to large differences in the rate of erosion. Step-like features known as **rapids** are formed due to smaller differences. The water that falls down the edge of hard resistant rock may have a soft rock at the bottom. This soft rock gets eroded fast and creates a hollow basin called **plunge pool**.

(ii) **Middle Course** In this course, lateral erosion tends to replace vertical erosion (i.e. active corrosion of the river banks, thus widening the V-shaped valley). The gradient decreases as the river enters the plains. Volume of water increases with the confluence of many

3 **Corrosion** The mechanical erosion of soil and rock by the coarse action of particles set in motion by running water, wind, etc.
4 **Abrasion** The process of scraping or wearing something away.
5 **Attrition** It means the wear and tear of the transported materials when they roll and collide with one another.

tributaries, which increases river load. The work of the river is predominantly transportation with some deposition in clear manner, although the velocity does not decrease.

Landforms Associated with Middle Course of River The river in this course develops many landforms e.g. alluvial fan, flood plain, meanders, oxbow lake, braided river, etc.

Meander is a winding curve or bend in a river. It is formed by both erosion and deposition work of rivers. Meanders generally form under conditions of a gentle slope and sufficient water in rivers. S-shaped meanders are most commonly form in rivers when a channel-forms a curved path. When the curvature of meander become more circular, then the river breaks through the meander and form an oxbow lake.

(iii) **Lower Course** In lower course, the river flows slowly as the gradient is almost flat. It also flows slowly as it is full of debris brought down from the upper course. In lower course, vertical erosion almost ceased, though lateral erosion still goes on to erode its banks further. In this course, the river is also divided into many distributaries.

Landforms Associated with Lower Course of River The river in this course develops many landforms e.g. delta, distributary and estuary, etc.

Delta When the river reaches the sea, the fine material that has been carried out with it is deposited at the mouth, in the front part as well as in the bed of the river. This deposition over a large area led to a triangular-shaped formation known as **delta**. The formation of delta depends on conditions like amount of sediment and size of the river. Thus, not all the rivers form deltas.

Work of Wind

The wind is not the most effective agent of erosion, but it is a great agent of transportation. Wind may transport large quantities of fine particles of sand and dust, even against the general slope of land, over hundreds of kilometer. This action is dominant in the arid and semi-arid regions. It causes erosion through many ways such as deflation, abrasion and attrition.

Landforms Associated with Wind

Strong wind occasionally blows across the desert surfaces and creates variety of landforms. Some of them are

Deflation Hollows

The process of deflation involves lifting and blowing away of loose material from the ground. When the loose material like sand and dust is blown away during deflation, it forms large depressions on the surface of the land or lowering of the surface, which are called deflation hollows.

Sand Dunes

Dunes are the hills of sand, formed by the accumulation of sand and shaped by the movement of winds. They may be active dunes (constantly moving) or inactive dunes (rooted with vegetation).

When the desert winds blow, they carry a lot of sand all around. When the wind stops blowing, the sand falls and gets deposited. These deposits look like little hills or mounds.

These little hills are sand dunes. Sand dunes are usually temporary structures as the next **gust**[6] of wind can shift them to another place.

The conditions required for sand dune formation are

- A large supply of sand.
- A large flat beach.
- Time for the sand to dry, so an extensive tidal range is needed.
- An onshore wind (wind blowing from the sea to the land) for sand to be transported to the back of the beach.
- An obstacle is required for the dune to form against, for example pebble or driftwood.

Dunes that are found in tropical areas of Asia and Africa are of two types

(i) **Barchan** It is a crescent-shaped (moon-shaped) sand dune produced by the action of wind predominately from one direction. It commonly occurs in sandy deserts all over the world. It consists of horns or tips that point downwind or against the wind. The face of a barchan is very steep.

6 **Gust** A sudden strong rush of wind.

(ii) **Seif or Longitudinal Dune** A seif is a long, narrow sand dune or chain of dunes, generally placed in a direction parallel to the prevailing wind or in a direction resulting from two or more winds blowing at sharp angles to each other.

Check Your LEARNING...

1. Mention the chief agents of denudation.
2. Name the stages of rivers?
3. Which natural force is responsible for the formation of sand dunes?
4. What are Sand Dunes?

QUiCK Revision

- Weathering is a process which can be defined as the mechanical disintegration and chemical decomposition of rocks by various agents of weathering.
- Weathering transforms hard massive rocks into finer materials.
- There are three types of weathering i.e. physical, chemical and biological weathering.
- Physical weathering categorises into three types i.e. block disintegration, granular disintegration and exfoliation.
- There are four types of chemical weathering i.e. oxidation, carbonation, hydration and solution.
- Biological weathering is the weakening and subsequent disintegration of rocks by plants, animals, microbes and human actions.
- The effects of weathering can be categorised into two types, namely positive and negative effects.
- Denudation involves the processes that causes the wearing away of the Earth's surface by various agents.
- Denudation is carried out in four different stages i.e. weathering, erosion, transportation and deposition.
- The main agents of denudation involves running water, wind, waves and ice.
- One of the most important sources of denudation is river water.
- The course of river may be divided into three distinct stages i.e. upper course, middle course and lower course.
- Landforms which are associated with the upper course of rivers are v-shaped valleys, and waterfalls.
- Landform which is associated with middle course of rivers is meander.
- Landform which is associated with lower course of river is delta.
- Landforms associated with the winds are deflation hollows and sand dunes.
- Dunes that are found in tropical areas of Asia and Africa are of two types i.e. Barchan and Seif.

Chapter Practice

Section-I

Multiple Choice Questions

1. .... is defined as mechanical disintegration and chemical decomposition of rocks through the action of various elements of weather and climate.
(a) Delta (b) Weathering
(c) Erosion (d) Soil formation

Ans. (b) Weathering

2. .... is the disintegration of rocks by natural or physical agents.
(a) Mechanical weathering
(b) Exfoliation
(c) Block disintegration
(d) Chemical weathering

Ans. (a) Mechanical weathering

3. What is the reason behind breaking up of bedded rocks into rectangular blocks?
(a) Mechanical weathering
(b) Soil condition
(c) Exfoliation
(d) Block disintegration

Ans. (d) Block disintegration

4. Which of the following process of weathering is most common in the regions of deserts?
(a) Granular disintegration (b) Exfoliation
(c) Block disintegration (d) Hydration

Ans. (b) Exfoliation

5. Which of the following process of weathering can't be considered as chemical weathering?
(a) Hydration (b) Oxidation
(c) Solution (d) Exfoliation

Ans. (d) Exfoliation

6. "When the rocks containing iron, comes in contact with air, they get break." What is the reason behind this?
(a) Increase in rock volume by iron.
(b) Oxidation in rocks.
(c) Dissolution of soluble iron in rock.
(d) Both (a) and (c)

Ans. (b) Oxidation in rocks

7. Under which process of weathering, the minerals takes up the water and expand and this expansion causes an increase in volume of rock which may further lead to their disintegration?
(a) Solution (b) Carbonation
(c) Oxidation (d) Hydration

Ans. (d) Hydration

8. .... is the weakening and disintegration of rocks by plants, animals, humans and microbes.
(a) Chemical weathering
(b) Physical weathering
(c) Biological weathering
(d) Denudation

Ans. (c) Biological weathering

9. Which of the following weathering can cause extensive soil erosion?
(a) Chemical weathering
(b) Mechanical weathering
(c) Rock weathering
(d) Biological weathering

Ans. (b) Mechanical weathering

10. .... involves the processes that cause the erosion.
(a) Denudation (b) Chemical weathering
(c) Biological weathering (d) Mechanical weathering

Ans. (a) Denudation

11. Which is one of the most important sources of denudation?
(a) Pond (b) Lake
(c) Streams (d) Rivers

Ans. (d) Rivers

12. Which of the following course of river is known as mountain course?
(a) Upper course (b) Middle course
(c) Upper left course (d) Lower course

Ans. (a) Upper course

13. Give reason for the following.
Reason behind V shape of V-shaped valley.
(a) Falling of water on the landform suddenly.
(b) River performing the task of downcutting.
(c) Falling of water under gravity.
(d) All of the above

Ans. (b) River performing the task of downcutting.

14. Give reason for the following.
Reason behind formation of waterfall.
(a) Formation of fan shaped alluvial area around river.
(b) Sudden fall and plunging down of speedy moving water.
(c) Deposition of alluvial soil on river mouth.
(d) Both (a) and (b)

Ans. (b) Sudden fall and plunging down of speedy moving water.

15. Which of the following landforms are created by river in lower course?
(a) Delta (b) V-shaped valley
(c) Meander (d) Waterfall

Ans. (a) Delta

16. The erosion of soil by wind is most common in the areas of ....
(a) tropical (b) sub-tropical
(c) arid region (d) Northern plains

Ans. (c) arid region

17. Which of the following sand dunes are rooted with vegetation?
(a) Inactive sand dunes (b) Active sand dunes
(c) Linear sand dunes (d) Star sand dunes

Ans. (a) Inactive sand dunes

18. Consider the following statements regarding weathering and choose the correct options.
(i) Weathering depends on climatic elements and on the nature of rocks.
(ii) Weathering prepares rock materials for transportation by agents of gradiation.
(iii) Weathering are used to eliminate soil erosion.

Codes
(a) (i) and (iii) (b) Only (iii)
(c) (i) and (ii) (d) (ii) and (iii)

Ans. (c) (i) and (ii)

19. Consider the following statement regarding sand dunes and choose the correct option.
(i) Sand dunes are usually permanant structure as the next gust of wind cannot shift them to another place.
(ii) The conditions required for sand dune formation are large supply of land and a large flat beach.
(iii) Sand dune has a rough slope on the side the wind blows against.

Codes
(a) (i) and (iii) (b) Only (ii)
(c) (i) and (ii) (d) (ii) and (iii)

Ans. (d) (ii) and (iii)

20. Match the following.

List-I	List-II
A. Hydration	1. Minerals react with dissolved chemicals.
B. Carbonation	2. Minerals react with oxygen to form oxides.
C. Solution	3. Minerals takes up water and expand.
D. Oxidation	4. Minerals react with bicarbonates and carbonates.

Codes

	A	B	C	D		A	B	C	D
(a)	1	3	4	2	(b)	3	4	1	2
(c)	4	2	3	1	(d)	2	4	3	1

Ans. (b)

21. Match the following.

List-I	List-II
A. Weathering	1. Removal of eroded debris
B. Erosion	2. Accumulated debris from rocks
C. Transportation	3. Breaking down of rocks
D. Deposition	4. Weathering away the Earth's surface

Codes

	A	B	C	D		A	B	C	D
(a)	3	4	1	2	(b)	4	3	1	2
(c)	2	4	3	1	(d)	1	2	4	3

Ans. (a)

Section-II

Short Questions

1. What do you understand by weathering?

Ans. Weathering is defined as mechanical disintegration and chemical decomposition of rocks through the actions of various elements of weather and climate.

2. Name the major types of weathering processes.

Ans. The major types of weathering processes are
- **Physical Weathering** It is the physical disintegration of rocks by the natural or physical agents. In physical weathering, chemical composition of rocks does not change.
- **Chemical Weathering** It is the decomposition of rocks due to exposure to the chemical elements contained in air and water.
- **Biological Weathering** It is the weathering caused by humans, plants and animals.

3. What is block disintegration?

Ans. Block disintegration is the repeated expansion and contraction of rocks due to changes in temperature causes the weakening and breaking down of the rocks. For example, in desert regions, the high range of temperature causes the splitting of rocks into rectangular blocks.

4. What do you mean by the term exfoliation?

Ans. Exfoliation is a form of mechanical weathering in which the curved plates of rocks are stripped off from the rocks below. This process is also known as onion weathering because the various layers look like the layers of the onion peeled off after one another. This process is common in the desert and the tropical region.

5. How does the rocks get weakened by the process of oxidation?

Ans. Under oxidation process, the minerals present in the rocks gets oxidised by coming in contact with the oxygen (present in air and water). This weakens the rocks and results in its disintegration.

6. (i) What is carbonation?
(ii) What are the various agents involved in biological weathering?

Ans. (i) Carbonation is the process of reaction of carbonate and bicarbonate with minerals. This causes the weakening of minerals of the rocks.
(ii) The process of biological weathering involves plants, animals and humans as agents.

7. How the humans are involved in the weathering of rocks?

Ans. Humans contribute to the weathering of rocks through their activities like mining, deforestation, quarrying, etc., These activities make the rocks more vulnerable to the agents of denudation.

8. Explain any two positive effects of weathering.

Ans. Two positive effects of weathering are
(i) It helps in the formation of new landscape.
(ii) Weathered materials are used for construction works.

9. What are the negative effects of weathering? Give any two.

Ans. Following are the negative effects of weathering
(i) Mechanical weathering may cause extensive soil erosion.
(ii) Loosening of rock material through weathering can result in landslides and mudslides.

10. What do you mean by denudation?

Ans. Denudation involves the processes that causes the wearing away of the Earth's surface by moving water, ice, wind, leading to the reduction in elevation and in relief of landforms and of landscape.

11. Name the three stages, through which the river passes during its course.

Ans. Three stages of the river course are
(i) Upper course or mountain course.
(ii) Middle course or valley course.
(iii) Lower course or plain course.

12. What is delta?

Ans. When the river reaches the sea, the fine material that has been carried out with it is deposited at the mouth, in the front part as well as in the bed of the river. This deposition over a large area led to a triangular-shaped formation known as delta.

13. (i) What is deflation?
(ii) How deflation hollows are formed?

Ans. (i) The process of deflation involves lifting and blowing away of loose material from the ground.
(ii) Deflation results in the lowering of the land surface to form depressions called deflation hollows.

Long Questions

1. Explain any two types of physical weathering process.

Ans. Two types of physical weathering process are
(i) **Granular Disintegration** It is a form of weathering, where the grains of the rocks becomes loosened and fallout, to leave a pitted, uneven surface.
(ii) **Exfoliation** It is a form of weathering in which the curved plates of rocks are stripped off from the rock below. It is also known as onion peeling.

2. Define the following
(i) Hydration (ii) Solution

Ans. (i) **Hydration** Under this process, the mineral takes up the water and expand. This expansion causes an increase in volume of the rock itself. Continuous repetition of this process causes fatigue in the rocks and may lead to their disintegration.
(ii) **Solution** In this process, when the rocks and soluble minerals come in contact with water, they undergo chemical change and dissolve. Reaction of solution varies from mineral to mineral.

3. Give any three features of biological weathering.

Ans. The three features of biological weathering are
(i) Biological is the weakening and subsequent disintegration of rocks by plants, animals, humans and microbes.
(ii) Plant cause biological weathering as their roots exert a tremendous pressure on the Earth materials. This pressure results in widening of the cracks and splitting apart of the rocks.
(iii) Animals and other organisms also cause biological weathering as through the process of burrowing and wedging, they make holes in the ground or rocks which expose them to more intense chemical, physical and biological processes.

4. How does the wind and river acts as the agents of denudation?

Ans. The chief agents of denudation involves the running water, wind and ice. The action of running water is considered to be the most important agent of denudation. Through interaction processes like corrasion, attrition, solution, river water involves itself in the process of denudation.

The wind though not the most effective agent of erosion, but is a great agent of transportation. Winds may transport the large quantities of fine particles of sand and dust, as it is very dominant in the arid and semi-arid regions. Through the processes of abrasion, deflation and attrition, wind engages itself in the process of denudation.

5. Explain the characteristic features of the following.
(i) Upper course (ii) Lower course
(iii) Middle course

Ans. (i) **Upper Course** It is also known as mountain course. It begins at the source of the river near the watershed, generally at the crest of the mountain range. Vertical erosion is predominant action here.

(ii) **Lower Course** In the lower course of the river, the river water moves downstream across a broad level plain which is full of debris brought down from the upper course.

(iii) **Middle Course** In this river course, lateral erosion tends to replace vertical erosion (i.e. active erosion of the river bank which widens the V-shaped valley).

6. Define the following terms.
(i) V-shaped valley
(ii) Meander
(iii) Sand dunes

Ans. (i) **V-shaped Valley** This river valley is a deep and narrow valley that develops during the youthful stage of the river course. It is an important erosional feature.

(ii) **Meander** is a winding curve or bend in a river. It is formed by both errosion and deposition work of rivers. Meanders generally form under conditions of a gentle slope and sufficient water in rivers. S-shaped meanders are most commonly form in rivers when a channel-forms a curved path. When the curvature of meander become more circular, then the river breaks through the meander and form an oxbow lake.

(iii) **Sand dunes** These are the most common depositional landform. Dunes are like hills of sand and are shaped by the movement of winds, e.g. barchans, transverse dunes, etc.

7. Give an example of the landform that is formed through the process of deposition. Explain how it is formed.

Ans. The landform that is formed through the process of deposition is delta. A river delta is formed through the deposition of sediments carried by a river, as it enters slow-moving or standing water. This occurs where a river enters into an ocean, sea, estuary, lake, reservoir, that cannot transport away the supplied sediments.

8. Differentiate between the following pairs.
(i) Deflation and abrasion
(ii) Vertical erosion and lateral erosion

Ans. (i) Differences between deflation and abrasion are

Deflation	Abrasion
It is the process of removal of loose and dry material from the surface by the wind.	It is the process of wearing away of exposed rock surface by the impact of sand particles being carried by wind.
This process is responsible for the formation of deflation hollows.	It leads to the formation of rock pedestals.

(ii) Differences between the vertical erosion and lateral erosion are

Vertical Erosion	Lateral Erosion
It is a geological process of deepening the channels of a stream or valley by removing material from the streams bed.	It refers to the widening of a stream channel or valley.
It is dominant in the upper river course.	It is dominant in the middle and lower river courses.

9. Differentiate between the following.
(i) Meander and delta
(ii) Upper course and lower course
(iii) Oxidation and carbonation

Ans. (i) Differences between the meander and delta are

Meander	Delta
It develops when the water under gravity seldom flows straight for long distance and develops the winding course.	It is formed through the deposition of sediments carried by a river, as it enters the slower moving or standing water.
It develops in the middle course of the rivers.	It develops in the lower course of the river.

(ii) Differences between the upper course and lower course are

Upper Course	Lower Course
It is known as the mountain course.	It is known as the downstream course.
Predominant action here is vertical erosion.	Predominant action in this course is lateral erosion.
Example of this course are waterfalls, gorges.	Example of this course are flood plains, deltas.

(iii) Differences between the oxidation and carbonation are

Oxidation	Carbonation
In this process, there are combination of minerals with oxygen to form oxides and hydroxides.	It is the process of reaction of carbon with other minerals to form carbonates and bicarbonates.
Breaking of rocks takes place after combining of air.	Weakening of rocks takes place after combining with water.

Map Based Question

1. On the map of world, mark the following rivers.

(i) Mississippi (ii) Colorado (iii) Amazon
(iv) Paraguay (v) Nile (vi) Zaire
(vii) Niger (viii) Zambezi (ix) Orange
(x) Rhine (xi) Volga (xii) Danube

Ans.

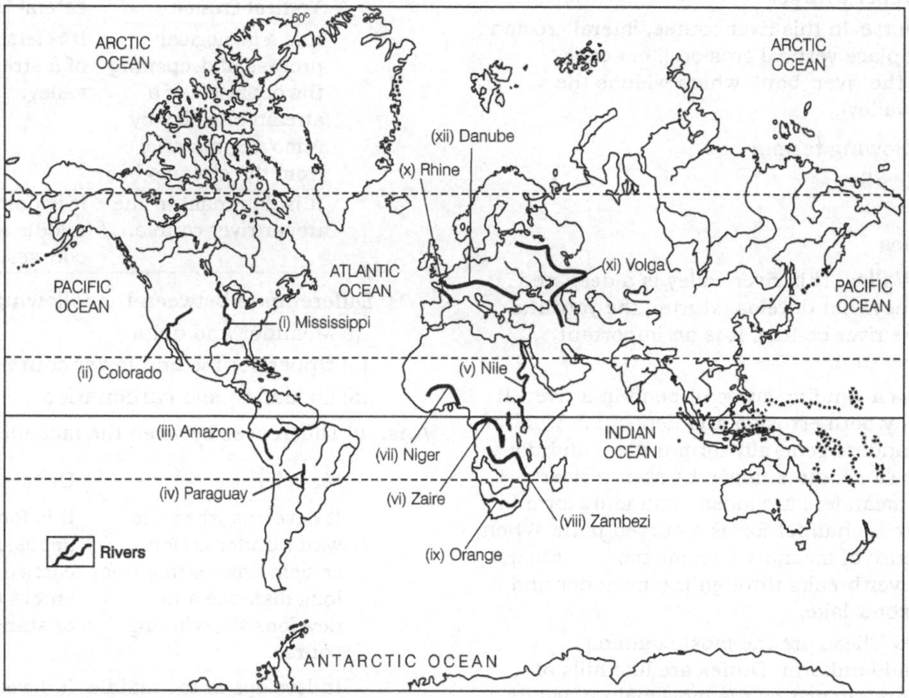

2. On the map of world, mark the following rivers.

(i) Murray (ii) Darling (iii) Hwang Ho
(iv) Yangtse Kiang (v) Ob (vi) Indus
(vii) Ganga (viii) Mekong (ix) Irrawaddy
(x) Tigris (xi) Euphrates

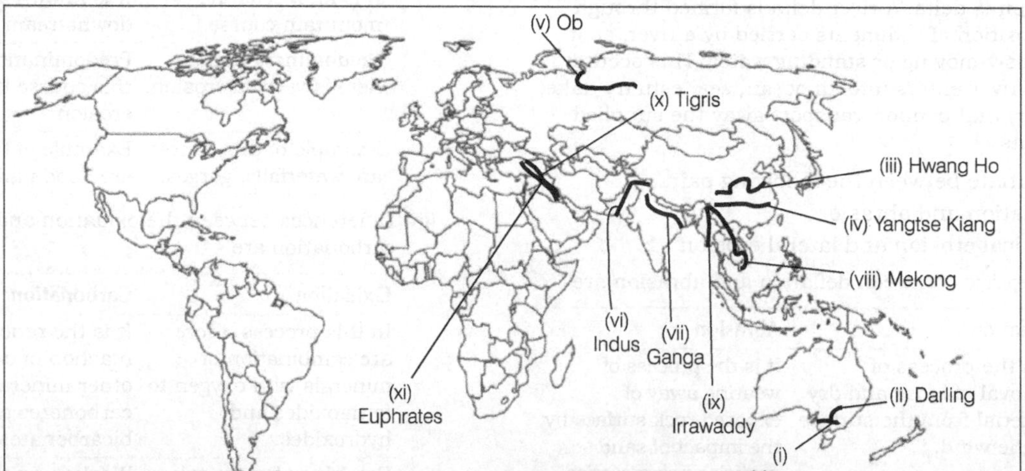

Chapter Assessment

Section-I

Multiple Choice Questions

1. Which of the following process of weathering can't be considered as mechanical weathering?
   (a) Block disintegration
   (b) Oxidation
   (c) Granular disintegration
   (d) Exfoliation
2. When rainwater penetrate down the surface in the rocks through cracks and joints it also dissolves soluble minerals presents there such as salt water and ....
   (a) soil (b) silt
   (c) gypsum (d) saline water
3. Loosing of rock materials through weathering can cause ....
   (a) soil (b) earthquake
   (c) flood (d) landslide
4. "The river in this course develops various landforms such as gorge". Which of the following stage of river has been discussed here?
   (a) Upper course (b) Lower course
   (c) Bottom course (d) Middle course

Section-II

Short Questions

1. What is physical weathering?
2. Explain any two agents of biological weathering with example.
3. Differentiate between positive and negative effects of weathering.
4. How do rivers work as the source of denudation?
5. Explain about the different types of landforms associated with rivers.
6. Explain the work done by the wind.
7. How wind forms different types of landforms?

Long Questions

1. Explain the process of chemical weathering with suitable examples.
2. Discuss the contribution of plants, animals and humans in biological weathering.
3. Explain the different stages of denudation.
4. In what ways landforms associated with rivers are different from landforms associated with winds?

CHAPTER 10

Hydrosphere

SYLLABUS

Hydrosphere Meaning of hydrosphere. •Tides-formation and Pattern.
•Ocean Currents - their circulation pattern and effects. (Specifically of Gulf Stream, North Atlantic Drift, Labrador Current, Kuroshio and Oyashio)

Meaning of Hydrosphere

The term hydrosphere is used to represent the combined mass of water found on the surface and under the surface of the Earth.

Earth's hydrosphere is made up of oceans, lakes, rivers, glaciers, ice caps, ice bergs, groundwater and even the water present in soil, clouds and biosphere. 71 per cent of the Earth's surface is occupied by seas and oceans.

Water is a cyclic resource which can be used and re-used. The continuous circulation of water within the Earth's hydrosphere in different forms, i.e. solid, liquid and gaseous forms is known as **hydrological cycle.** It also refers to the exchange of water between the oceans, atmosphere, land surface, sub-surface and organisms. The movement of water in the oceans takes place majorly through tides and ocean currents.

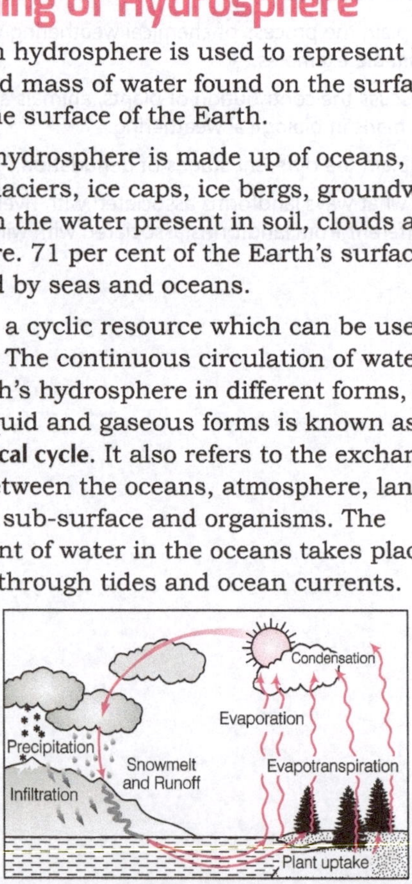

Hydrological Cycle

Tides

Tides are the periodical rise and fall of the sea level, once or twice in a day. These are very long-period waves that move through the ocean in response to the forces exerted by the Moon and Sun. Tides originate in the ocean and progress towards the coastlines where they appear as the regular rise and fall of the sea surface. The sea waves produced by tides are called **tidal waves.**

Formation of Tides

The strong gravitational force exerted by the Sun and the Moon on Earth's surface causes the tides. The Earth orbits the Sun in all elliptical manner and similarly, the Moon orbits the Earth. In this process, when Moon comes close to the Earth, its gravitational forces pulls the oceanic water facing towards the Moon, which causes the tide to occur. On the basis of formation, tides are divided into

- **High tides** High tides are formed when the Sun, Moon and Earth are in the same line. All the forces will be added together and water will reach its maximum height.
- **Low tides** Low tides are formed when all the forces work against one another. It will happen when the Sun, Moon and Earth are perpendicular to each other. Therefore, water will not acquire much height. The difference between high tide and low tide is called **tidal range.**

Patterns of Tides

Tides vary in their frequency, direction and movement from place to place and also from time to time. They are grouped into various categories on the basis of their frequency of occurrence in one day or 24 hours or based on their height. The different patterns of tides are

Tidal Patterns on the Basis of the Frequency of Occurrence

- **Semi-Diurnal Tides** Under this pattern, two high tides and two low tides occur each day. This is the most common tidal pattern.
- **Diurnal Tides** Under this pattern, only one high tide and one low tide occurs each day.
- **Mixed Tides** Tides having variations in height are known as mixed tides.

Tidal Patterns on the Basis of the Positions of the Sun, the Moon and the Earth

- **Spring Tides** When the Sun, the Moon and the Earth are in the straight line, spring tides take place. The gravitational force of the Sun and the Moon work together with combined force and cause a very high tide. The height of such tide is 20% more than that of normal tide. Such tide take place twice in a month (during the full Moon and the new Moon) at fixed time.
- **Neap Tides** It occurs when the Sun and the Moon are at right angle to each other. The tide producing forces of Sun and Moon work in opposite direction and cause a low tide. Neap tides are weaker than spring tides. There is 7 days interval between the formation of neap tides and spring tides. The height of neap tide is 20% lower than that of normal tide.

Effects of Tides

- Tides act as a link between the ports and open sea, e.g. Kolkata port on river Hugli.
- They help in generating **hydroelectricity**[1].
- They also help in removing polluted water from river **estuaries**[2].
- With the high tides, fish move into the **creeks**[3] and this helps in fishing activity.
- Due to tides, sea ports do not get filled with sediments.
- Ships can move upto ports during high tide.
- During high tide, sea water can be stored in salt pans from which water can be obtained.
- Tides helps in maintaining the mangroves and biodiversity.

Check Your LEARNING...

1. What is hydrological cycle?
2. Mention the tidal patterns on the basis of their frequency of occurrence.
3. Which tide takes place when the Sun, Moon and Earth are in the straight line?
4. What is the interval of period between the formation of neap tides and spring tides?

Ocean Currents

An ocean is a body of saline water that forms most of the Earth's hydrosphere. Ocean currents are the movement of large masses of surface water that circulate in regular patterns around the oceans. The speed of a current is called 'drift'. It is measured in terms of knots.

Types of Ocean Currents

On the Basis of Depth

- **Surface Currents** They move on the surface of ocean water upto 400 metres of depth. They constitute about 10% of all the waters in the oceans.
- **Deep Water Currents** These currents move at greater depth i.e. around the ocean basins, due to density and gravity differences. These make upto 90% of the total ocean water.

On the Basis of Temperature

- **Cold Currents** Currents which bring cold waters into warm water areas are known as cold currents. These currents are found on the West coast of continents in the low and middle latitudes (in both hemispheres) and on the East coast in the higher latitudes (only in the Northern hemisphere).
- **Warm Currents** Currents which bring warm water into cold water areas are known as warm currents. They are generally found on the East coasts of continents in the low and middle latitudes (in both hemispheres). In the Northern hemisphere, these are found on the West coasts of continents in high latitudes.

1 **Hydroelectricity** It is the electricity produced from hydropower.
2 **Estuaries** It is a partially enclosed coastal body of brackish water with one or more rivers flowing into it and with a free connection to the open sea.
3 **Creeks** A natural stream of water normally smaller than and often a tributary of a river.

Causes of Ocean Currents

The ocean currents are caused by wind, differences in the density of water masses caused by gravity, salinity variations and temperature and events such as earthquakes.

- **Wind** It is responsible for ocean currents as it blows the water on the surface, causing the currents. The wind is responsible for surface currents where ocean water is divided based on its density and temperature.
- **Gravity** Gravity tends to pull items towards the surface of the Earth. When the wind blows ocean water, the water piles up in the direction of the wind. Gravity, therefore, pulls the water down against the pressure of the flow of water.
- **The Salinity of the Water** When water moves towards the poles, it gets cold and freezes into ice, leaving a share of salt behind. It makes the underlying water saltier, making it denser. The cold, saltier and denser water sinks to the floor of the ocean and is replaced by surface water in the process.
- **Temperature** The water in the oceans near the Tropics and Equator is warm. When the denser, saltier and cold water moves towards the Equator, it warms up and becomes less dense and rise to the surface of the ocean.
- **Underwater Earthquakes** Earthquakes in oceans trigger downslope movements of water, resulting in strong turbidity currents.

Circulation Pattern of Ocean Currents

The circulation pattern of ocean currents is similar to the Earth's atmospheric circulation pattern. It can be explained as

- **Oceanic Circulation in the Mid-Latitudes**
  In mid-latitudes, the air circulation over the oceans is mainly anti-cyclonic i.e. anti-clockwise (more effective in the Southern Hemisphere than in the Northern Hemisphere), thus the oceanic circulation pattern follows the pattern of air circulation.
- **Oceanic Circulation at the Higher Latitudes** At higher latitudes, winds flow in cyclonic way, thus ocean circulation also follows same clockwise pattern (in the Southern hemisphere).
- **Regions of Pronounced Monsoon Flow** In these regions, the monsoon winds influence the current movements. Due to coriolis force, the warm currents from low latitudes tend to move to the right in the Northern Hemisphere and to their left in the Southern Hemisphere.

Ocean Currents of the World

The ocean currents of the world are generally divided into the warm ocean currents like Equatorial current, Gulf Stream current, Kuroshio current and the cold ocean currents like Peruvian current, California current, etc.

Some of the major ocean currents of the world are

Gulf Stream

It is a warm ocean current of the North Atlantic ocean. This current system originates in the Gulf of Mexico around 20°N latitude. It moves in North Easterly direction along the Eastern Coast of North America and reaches the Western Coast of Europe.

It influences the climate of the East Coast of North America Florida to Newfoundland and West Coast of Europe. The convergence of Gulf Stream and Labrador current near the Newfoundland, causes heavy fog. Gulf Stream also led to the development of cyclone both within the atmosphere and within the ocean.

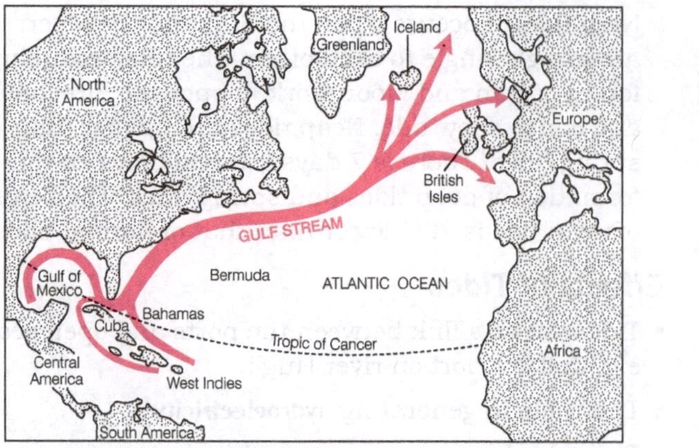

Gulf Stream

North Atlantic Drift

It is a warm ocean current. When the warm Gulf Stream current deflect towards the East under the influence of **Westerlies**[4] and rotation of the Earth and reaches Europe, it becomes the North Atlantic Drift or North Atlantic current.

4 **Westerlies** They are prevailing winds from West towards the East in the middle latitude between 30 and 60 degree latitude.

It runs from the Grand Bank near Newfoundland to Western Europe. It maintain the climate of Western Europe and keep the ports of Europe free from extreme cold in winters. It flows Eastwards to UK, Northwards to the Arctic region and Southwards along the Spanish Coast.

Labrador Current

It is a cold current that originates in the Baffin **Bay**[5] and Davis **Strait**[6] which flows from Arctic Ocean along the Coast of Labrador in the South. It passes around Newfoundland flowing along the East Coast of Nova Scotia. It meets the warm Gulf Stream at the Grand Banks, South-East of Newfoundland and again at the North of the outer Banks of North Carolina. The combination of these two currents produces heavy fog and creates one of the richest fishing grounds in the world.

This current transport icebergs from the glaciers of Greenland into trans-Atlantic shipping lanes during spring and early summers. The waters of the Labrador current have a cooling effect on the Canadian Atlantic provinces and coastal New England.

(iv) Kuroshio and Oyashio Currents

Kuroshio is a warm current that originates from the East Coast of Taiwan and flows in the Northern direction on the West side of the North Pacific Ocean. It flows North-Eastward after passing Japan and merges with the easterly drift of the North Pacific current.

Kuroshio current is similar to the Gulf Stream in the North Atlantic and it is a strong Western boundary current. It is also known as **Black Stream** or **Japan Current**. It is responsible for mild weather around Southern coast of Alaska. It sustain the **coral reefs**[7] of Japan and brings rich fisheries from the East China Sea to the Sea of Japan.

Oyashio current originates in the Arctic Ocean and flows through the Bering Strait in Southern direction and thus, transports cold water of the Arctic Sea into the Pacific Ocean and the Sea of Okhotsk. It impacts the climate of Russian far East, mainly Kamchatka and Chukotka. It has extremely high nutrient content of cold water.

Oyashio current makes the coast of Asian mainland and the West coast of Japan severely cold in winter. The convergence of the Kuroshio and the Oyashio current form the North Pacific current causes dense fog which became potential hazard for navigation.

Effects of Ocean Currents

- Warm ocean currents are responsible for rains. As warm currents migrate from the Equator towards the poles, the warmth causes the water to evaporate. This result in rains around the coastal regions or the ocean.
- Warm ocean currents are responsible for keeping the ports in polar regions operational. It is because they keep the ports ice-free.
- Humans rely on ocean currents to travel by sea vessels, (such as boats) by the oceans. Ocean currents help in docking and undocking boats, speeding up shipping lanes, and keeping the ships safe, primarily in narrow waterways
- Marine wildlife is heavily dependent on the balance created by the ocean and is maintained by the ocean currents. The currents carry nutrients and food organisms, feeding the plants and animals that depend on them.
- Ocean currents are responsible for moving the heat from the Equator towards the poles. As such, they maintain the natural order and balance of the climate.
- When warm ocean currents meet cold ocean currents, they form dense fog over the area and also led to the high growth of planktons.
- Some currents might be too strong and result destroying **planktons**[8]. For instance, EI Nino currently destroys planktons along the Peruvian coasts. It also brings with it several diseases that kill fishes.

Check Your LEARNING...

1. In what terms the speed of ocean current is measured?
2. Mention any one effect of ocean currents.
3. Give two examples of warm ocean current.
4. Give two examples of cold ocean current.

5 **Bay** It is a recessed, coastal body of water that directly connects to a larger main body of water such as an ocean, lake or another bay.

6 **Strait** It is a naturally formed narrow, typically navigable waterway that connects two larger bodies of water.

7 **Coral Reefs** They are under water structures that are formed of coral polyps that are held together by calcium carbonate.

8 **Plankton** They are small micro organisms in water that are unable to move themselves against a current.

QUiCK Revision

- Hydrosphere is the combined masses of water found on the surface and under the surface of the Earth.
- 71 percent of Earth is covered with water.
- The hydrological cycle is the continuous circulation of water within the Earth's hydrosphere in different forms like solid, liquid and gaseous forms.
- Tides are the periodical rise and fall of the sea level, once or twice in a day.
- The Moon's gravitational pull to the greater extent and the gravitational pull of the Sun to the lesser extent are responsible for the occurrence of tides.
- Tidal pattern based on the frequency of occurrence is divided into three types i.e. semi-diurnal tide, diurnal tide and mixed tide.
- Tidal pattern based on the position of the Sun, the Moon and the Earth are of two types i.e. spring tide and neap tide.
- Tides help in maintaining the mangroves and biodiversity.
- Ocean currents is the movement of large surface of water into rectangular pattern with respect to ocean.
- Ocean currents on the basis of depth is divided into two types i.e. surface currents and deep water currents.
- Ocean currents on the basis of temperature is divided into two types i.e. cold currents and warm currents.
- Wind, gravity, salinity of the water, temperature and underwater earthquakes are the main causes of ocean currents.
- There are three oceanic circulation patterns
  - (i) Oceanic circulation in the mid-latitude
  - (ii) Oceanic circulation at the higher altitude
  - (iii) Monsoon wind influences the oceanic current movement.
- Major oceanic current of the world are Gulf Stream, North Atlantic drift, Labrador current, Kuroshio and Oyashio current.
- Warm ocean currents are responsible for rains. As warm currents migrate from Equator toward the poles, the warmth cause water to evaporate.

Chapter Practice

Section-I

Multiple Choice Questions

1. Which of the following element of nature is not a part of hydrosphere?
   (a) Soil (b) Groundwater
   (c) Streams (d) Ice caps

Ans. (a) Soil

2. ....refers to the exchange of water between the ocean, atmosphere, land surface, sub-surface and organism.
   (a) Atmospheric cycle
   (b) Biosphere
   (c) Oceans
   (d) Hydrological cycle

Ans. (d) Hydrological cycle

3. Which of the following tide take place twice in a month at time of the full Moon and the new Moon ?
   (a) Low tide (b) Diurnal tide
   (c) Mixed tide (d) High tide

Ans. (d) High tide

4. Which of the following tides have variation in their height ?
   (a) Diurnal (b) Semi diurnal
   (c) Neap (d) Mixed

Ans. (d) Mixed

5. The height of ....tide is 20 per cent lower than that of normal tide.
   (a) high (b) low
   (c) neap (d) spring

Ans. (c) neap

6. .... is a body of saline water that forms most of the Earth's hydrosphere.
   (a) Sea (b) Ocean
   (c) Lake (d) Groundwater

Ans. (b) Ocean

7. What is the speed of a ocean current is called ?
   (a) Neap (b) Drift
   (c) Spring (d) Currents

Ans. (b) Drift

8. ....are warm ocean currents of North Atlantic ocean.
   (a) Oyashio currents
   (b) Gulf Stream currents
   (c) Labrador currents
   (d) Atlantic Drift currents

Ans. (b) Gulf Stream currents

9. Which of the following current along with Gulf Stream causes heavy fog ?
   (a) Labrador current (b) Kuoshio current
   (c) Oyashio current (d) North Atlantic current

Ans. (a) Labrador current

10. Give reason for the following.
    Reason behind rise and fall of tides.
    (a) Atmospheric pressure
    (b) Temperature of sea shore
    (c) Gravitational pull of the Sun and the Moon
    (d) Gravitational pull of Earth

Ans. (c) Gravitational pull of the Sun and the Moon

11. Give reason for the following.
    Reason behind high tides.
    (a) Strong gravitational pull of the Earth.
    (b) The Sun, the Moon and Earth comes in the same line.
    (c) All focus work against each other and when Sun, Moon and Earth are perpendicular to each other.
    (d) High force at coast line.

Ans. (b) The Sun, the Moon and Earth comes in the same line.

12. Give reason for the following.
    Reason behind neap tides
    (a) The Sun and the Moon are at right angle to each other.
    (b) The Sun and the Moon are in the straight line with Earth.
    (c) Occuring of high and low tides.
    (d) Due to salinity.

Ans. (a) The Sun and the Moon are at right angle to each other.

13. Give reason for the following.
    Reason behind moderate climate of Western Europe.
    (a) Warm waters of North Atlantic drift
    (b) Combination of Gulf current and Labrador current
    (c) Warm currents of North Pacific oceans
    (d) Both (a) and (c)

Ans. (a) Warm waters of North Atlantic drift

14. Give reason for the following.
    Reason behind cooling effect on the Canadian Atlantic Provinces.
    (a) Warm water currents of Gulf Stream.
    (b) Relatively warm waters of North Atlantic drift.
    (c) Transportation of icebergs from the glaciers of Greenland Southwards into trans-Atlantic areas.
    (d) All of the above

Ans. (c) Transportation of icebergs from the glaciers of Greenland Southwards into trans-Atlantic areas.

15. Consider the following statements with reference to tides and choose the correct option
(i) High tides moves the fishes into the creeks and this help fishing activity.
(ii) Due to high tides, sea ports get filled with sediments.
(iii) During high tide, sea water can be stored in salt pans.

Codes
(a) Both (i) and (iii) (b) Only (iii)
(c) (i) and (ii) (d) (i), (ii) and (iii)

Ans. (a) Both (i) and (iii)

16. Consider the following statements regarding Ocean and choose the correct options
(i) Ocean currents are caused by wind, gravity, salinity, temperature, coriolis effect, underwater earthquakes.
(ii) Ocean currents are responsible for rains.
(iii) Warm ocean currents are responsible for keeping the ports in polar regions operational. It is because they keep the port ice free.

Codes
(a) (i) and (ii) (b) (i) and (iii)
(c) (i), (ii) and (iii) (d) (ii) and (iii)

Ans. (c) (i), (ii) and (iii)

17. Match the following.

A	B
A. Greenland Southward	1. Warm ocean current
B. North Atlantic drift	2. One high and one low tide
C. Diurnal tides	3. An iceberg region
D. Neap tides	4. Weaker tides

Codes

	A	B	C	D		A	B	C	D
(a)	1	2	3	4	(b)	4	3	1	2
(c)	3	4	2	1	(d)	3	1	2	4

Ans. (d)

18. ....is a naturally formed narrow waterway that connects two larger body of water.
(a) Strait (b) Delta
(c) Ocean (d) Bay

Ans. (a) Strait

Section-II

Short Questions

1. What is hydrosphere?

Ans. The term 'hydrosphere' is used to represent the combined mass of water found on the surface and under the surface of the Earth. Earth's hydrosphere is made up of oceans, rivers, lakes, groundwater, water in soil, clouds and biosphere.

2. What is tide?

Ans. Tide is the periodic rise and fall of the sea level, once or twice a day, caused by the combined effects of the gravitational pull of the Sun, the Moon and the rotation of the Earth.

3. Name the different forms of tidal patterns on the basis of their frequency of occurrence.

Ans. Tidal patterns based on the frequency are
- Semi-diurnal tides
- Diurnal tides
- Mixed tides

4. What do you mean by 'Spring tide'?

Ans. Spring tides are the high tides. These tides take place when the Sun, the Moon and the Earth are in a straight line.

5. (i) What are ocean currents ?
(ii) What is drift?

Ans. (i) Ocean currents are large masses of surface water that circulate in regular patterns around the oceans.
(ii) The speed of a current is called drift. It is measured in terms of knots.

6. How wind is responsible for causing ocean current ?

Ans. The wind is reponsible for ocean current as it blows the water on the surface, causing the currents. The wind is responsible for surface currents where ocean water is redistributed based on its density and temperature.

7. Mention any two effects of ocean currents.

Ans. Two effects of ocean currents are
(i) Warm ocean currents are responsible for keeping the ports in polar regions operational. It is because they keep the port ice free.
(ii) Ocean currents are responsible for moving the heat from the equator and towards the pole. In this way, it helps in maintaining order and balance of climate.

8. Define the following.
(i) Warm ocean current
(ii) Cold ocean current

Ans. (i) **Warm Ocean Current** Currents which bring warm water into cold water areas are known as warm currents.
(ii) **Cold Ocean Current** Currents which bring cold waters into warm water areas are known as cold currents.

9. Name the current which originates in Gulf of Mexico.

Ans. The ocean current that originates in Gulf of Mexico is the Gulf-stream. It is a warm ocean current that moves along the North Easterly direction along the East coast of North America and reaches the Western coast of Europe.

Long Questions

1. What are the different tidal patterns?

Ans. Refer to chapter theory page no. 91.

2. What are the effects of tides?

Ans. The effects of tides are

- Tides act as a link between the ports and open sea, e.g. Kolkata port on river Hugli.
- The tidal currents clean away the river sediments and slows down the growth of deltas.
- Tides in generating hydroelectricity.
- Tides also help in removing polluted water from river estuaries.

3. What are the factors that affects the ocean currents?

Ans. Factors that affects the ocean currents are

- Heating by solar energy.
- Wind which helps the water to move.
- Gravity which tends to pull water down to pile and create gradient variation.
- Coriolis force which causes the water to move to the right in the Northern hemisphere and to the left in the Southern hemisphere.

4. What are the effects of ocean currents?

Ans. Refer to chapter theory page no. 93.

5. Describe the impact of ocean currents on the following.
   (i) Navigation
   (ii) Fishing

Ans. (i) **Navigation** When the warm and cold ocean currents mix with each other, then dense fog is created. This may pose danger to the navigation, e.g. Hot Kuroshio current meets Cold Kuroshio current.

(ii) **Fishing** The best fishing grounds of the world are located in those regions where there is intermixing of the cold and the warm currents, e.g. Newfoundland.

6. Explain the following.
   (i) Surface ocean current
   (ii) Deep ocean current

Ans. (i) **Surface Currents** They move on the surface of ocean water upto 400 metres of depth. They constitute about 10% of all the waters in the oceans.

(ii) **Deep Water Currents** These currents move at greater depth i.e. around the ocean basins, due to density and gravity differences. These make upto 90% of the total ocean water.

7. Explain any two warm ocean currents.

Ans. Two warm ocean currents are

(i) **Gulf Stream** It is a warm ocean current of the North Atlantic ocean. This current system originates in the Gulf of Mexico around 20°N latitude. It moves in North Easterly direction along the Eastern Coast of North America and reaches the Western Coast of Europe.

(ii) **Kuroshio** It is a warm current that originates from the East coast of Taiwan and flows in the Northern direction on the West side of the North Pacific Ocean. It flows North-Eastward after passing Japan and merges with the easterly drift of the North pacific current.

8. Explain the following terms
   (i) Oceanic circulation in the higher latitudes
   (ii) Newfoundland
   (iii) North Atlantic Drift

Ans. (i) **Oceanic Circulation in the Higher Latitudes** The oceanic circulation pattern roughly corresponds to the Earth's atmospheric circulation pattern. Therefore in the higher latitudes, the oceanic circulation is cyclonic because the air circulation is also cyclonic here.

(ii) **Newfoundland** It is one of the richest fishing ground of the world. In this region, the intermixing of the warm ocean current and the cold ocean current creates sufficient conditions necessary for increasing fish production. Here, the warm ocean current Gulf Stream mixes with the cold ocean current Labrador current.

(iii) **North Atlantic Drift** It is a warm ocean current. When the warm Gulf Stream current deflect towards the East under the influence of Westerlies and rotation of the Earth and reaches Europe, it becomes the North Atlantic Drift or North Atlantic current.

9. Briefly explain the following.
   (i) Labrador current
   (ii) Impact of Perihelion on tide.

Ans. (i) Labrador current is a cold current that originates in the Baffin Bay and Davis Strait which flows from Arctic Ocean along the Coast of Labrador in the South. It passes around Newfoundland flowing along the East Coast of Nova Scotia. It meets the warm Gulf Stream at the Grand Banks, South-East of Newfoundland and again at the North of the outer Banks of North Carolina.

(ii) Perihelion is that time of the year when the Earth is closest to the Sun. The impact of perihelion is that during this period, tidal range is higher than the normal tidal average.

Map Based Questions

1. On the map of the world, mark the following.

(i) Caribbean Sea (ii) North Sea (iii) Black Sea
(iv) Caspian Sea (v) South China Sea (vi) Mediterranean Sea

Ans.

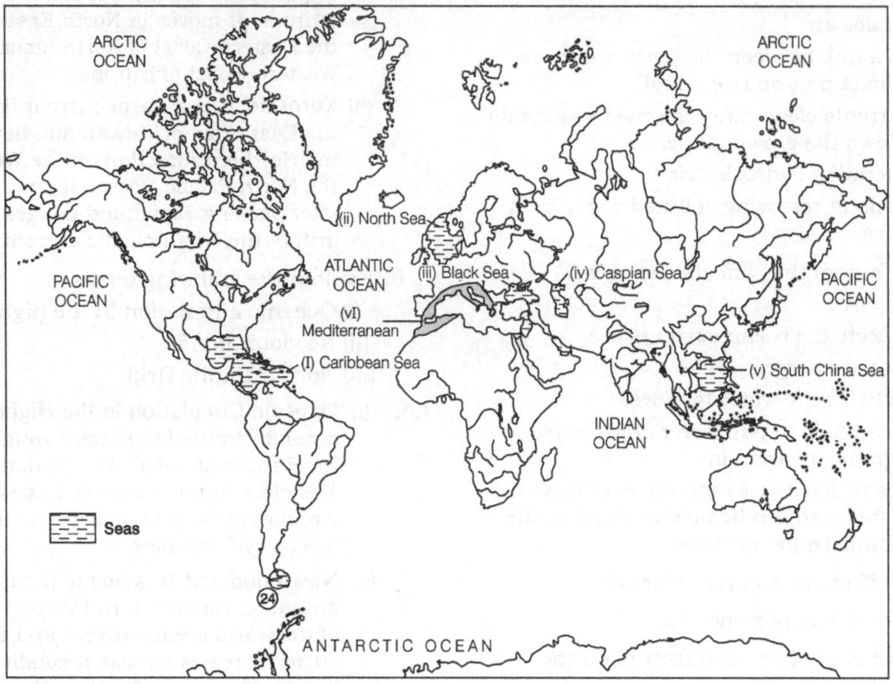

2. On the map of the world, mark the following.

(i) Gulf of Carpenteria (ii) Persian Gulf (iii) Gulf of Guinea
(iv) Gulf of Mexico (v) Hudson Bay

Ans.

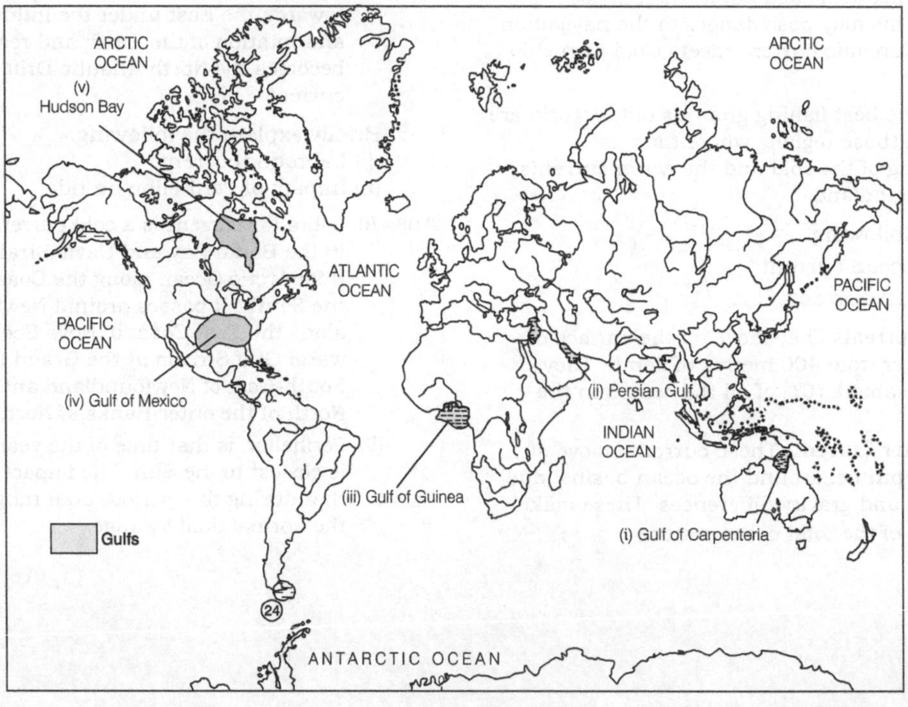

3. On the map of the world, mark the following.
(i) Bering Strait (ii) Strait of Gibraltar (iii) Strait of Malacca

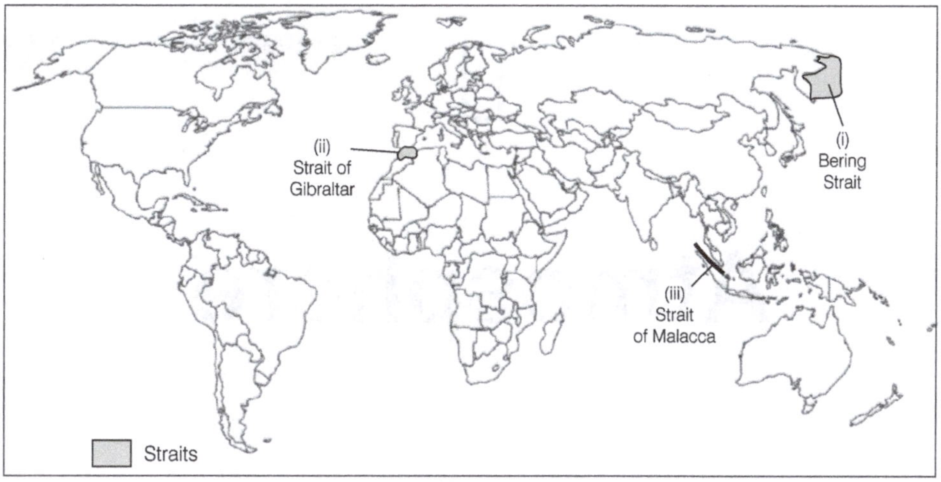

Chapter Assessment

Section-I

Multiple Choice Questions

1. ....is a exchange of water between the oceans, atmosphere, land surface, sub-surface and organism.
(a) Hydrosphere
(b) Hydrological cycle
(c) Biosphere
(d) Atmospheric cycle

2. The height of ....tides is 20 per cent more than that of normal tides.
(a) neap (b) diurnal
(c) spring (d) high

3. ....refers to the rotation of Earth.
(a) Coriolis effect
(b) Rotational effect
(c) Gravity
(d) Ocean currents

4. ....is a warm current that flows in the North direction on West side of North Pacific ocean.
(a) Kuroshio current (b) North Atlantic current
(c) Labrador current (d) Gulf Stream

Section-II

Short Questions

1. Why the Earth is called a 'Blue Planet'? Explain.
2. What is coriolis force?
3. What do you mean by neap tides?
4. What do you mean by hydrological cycle?
5. Mention any two effects of the tides.
6. Mention any two effects of ocean currents.

Long Questions

1. Briefly explain the following.
(i) Features of deep ocean current
(ii) Features of warm ocean current
(iii) Consequences of convergence of warm and cold ocean currents
2. Discuss the patterns of ocean currents.
3. Describe the different patterns of tides.
4. Differentiate between Gulf Stream and North Atlantic Drift current.

CHAPTER

11

Atmosphere

SYLLABUS

Atmosphere Composition and structure of the atmosphere.
• Troposphere, Stratosphere, Ionosphere and Exosphere; Ozone in the stratosphere, its depletion. • Global warming and its impact.

The blanket of air surrounding the Earth is known as atmosphere. The atmosphere is one of the most important components of the Earth. It is a layer of gases which is colourless, tasteless, odourless and formless. It is bounded to the Earth by gravity.

The atmosphere is not only the largest source of oxygen, but it also protects the Earth from the harmful ultraviolet radiation of the Sun. In the absence of atmosphere, life is not possible on the Earth. It is also the source of nitrogen and carbon dioxide which are important for plant nutrients. It also plays a vital role in the circulation of water vapour which is the source of rainfall.

Composition of Atmosphere

The Earth's atmosphere or air consists of a mixture of various gases surrounding the Earth. It varies from one place to another and also varies at height in atmosphere.

The two most abundant gases in the atmosphere are nitrogen and oxygen which constitute about 99% of clean dry air. The remaining gases constitute about 1% of atmosphere. These gases are argon, carbon dioxide, helium, hydrogen, ozone, etc.

In lower layers of the atmosphere, the proportion of gases is constant, so it is called the **fixed components of atmosphere**. There are also some variable components of atmosphere present which vary from place-to-place and time-to-time. These include smoke, water vapour, salt particles from the water bodies, dust, etc.

Main Components of Atmosphere

- **Oxygen** It is very important gas that represents about 21% of the air volume. The photosynthesis process in the green plants is the main source of oxygen gas on the Earth. It is very important gas, which is necessary for the respiration process and burning of the fuel.
- **Nitrogen** It is the most abundant gas in the air. It is about 78% of the volume of the atmosphere. It has no taste or smell. In the combustion process, nitrogen gas reduces the effects of oxygen gas. It keeps temperature lower. It is used in the industries for making chemical fertilisers.
- **Carbon dioxide** It represents about 0.03% of the volume of the atmosphere. It is necessary for photosynthesis process of plants. The green plants take carbon dioxide gas and give out oxygen gas.

- **Water Vapour** It is found in a small ratio in the atmosphere. It is a variable gas which decreases with altitude. It is responsible for all forms of precipitation and circulation of fresh water. Evaporation from oceans, lakes and rivers, transpiration from vegetation and respiration of animals are responsible for addition of water vapour in the air.

Permanent Gases of the Atmosphere

Constituent	Formula	Percentage by Volume
Nitrogen	N_2	78.08
Oxygen	O_2	20.95
Argon	Ar	0.93
Carbon dioxide	CO_2	0.036
Neon	Ne	0.002
Helium	He	0.0005
Krypton	Kr	0.001
Xenon	Xe	0.00009
Hydrogen	H_2	0.00005

Structure of Atmosphere

On the basis of temperature and air pressure, the atmosphere is divided into different layers, which are

Troposphere

The word 'Troposphere' is derived from the Greek word 'tropos' which means 'mixing', i.e. troposphere is region of mixing. It is the lowermost atmospheric layer in which we live. It contains water vapour and dust particles. The degree to which water vapour present in air is called **humidity**.

The height of this layer is maximum at the Equator (18 km), but least at the Poles (8 to 10 km). Thickness of the troposphere is greatest at the equator because heat is transported to great heights by strong convectional currents.

In this layer, temperature decreases as altitude increases. Temperature in this layer decreases at the rate of 1° C for every 165 m of height. The temperature variation within troposphere causes many turbulences.

The upper limit of troposphere is called the **tropopause** where the temperature stops decreasing with height. The air temperature at the tropopause is about minus 80° C over the equator and about minus 45° C over the poles. Temperature in this layer is nearly constant that is why it is known as tropopause.

Troposphere contains 80% of the mass of the Earth's atmosphere. It is the layer where most of the Earth's weather takes place. If condensation of water vapour is excessive in troposphere, then hail, rain, snow or sleet, collectively known as precipitation, takes place.

Stratosphere

It is the second-lowest layer of atmosphere. It lies above the troposphere. The lowermost limit of stratosphere is at tropopause. It extends up to 50 km from the Earth's surface.

This layer is free from water vapour and dust particles. There is no clouds or **turbulence**[1] in the air. Due to the absence of weather disturbances, this layer is considered ideal for flying jet aircraft. This layer contains **ozone layer** between 20-50 km, which absorbs the ultraviolet radiation coming from the Sun.

In stratosphere, the temperature is about minus 55°C. It remains constant, but at higher level, temperature increases with height due to solar heating and absorption of ultraviolet radiation from the Sun.

The temperature begins to fall again at about 50 km and this is the upper limit of stratosphere which is known as **stratopause**.

Ozone Layer

Ozone is a pale, blue gas that consists of oxygen atoms (O_3). Ozone molecules form a gaseous layer in the Earth's upper atmosphere called stratosphere. The lower region of stratosphere containing relatively higher concentration of ozone, is called **ozonosphere**.

Ozone is formed when energetic ultraviolet (UV) radiation dissociates molecules of oxygen (O_2) into separate oxygen atoms. Free oxygen atoms can recombine to form oxygen molecules, but if a free oxygen atom collides with an oxygen molecule, it joins up forming ozone layer.

Oxygen molecules can also be decomposed by ultraviolet radiation into a free oxygen atom and an oxygen molecule. Ozone is thus, continuously created and destroyed in the atmosphere by UV radiation coming from the Sun.

1 **Turbulence** Violent movement of air or water or of some other fluid.

The thickness of ozone layer is between 10 to 50 km above the ground and also differs as per season. It is also present in significant amount in troposphere. The tropospheric ozone is generated by the action of ultraviolet light on the molecules of nitrogen dioxide and became pollutant.

Ozone Layer Depletion

Ozone depletion occurs when the destruction of the ozone in stratosphere is more than the production of the molecules. The major reason of ozone layer depletion is the continuous release of synthetic chemicals primarily chlorofluorocarbons (CFCs) in the atmosphere. These chemicals are used in refrigerators, fire extinguishers, air conditioners, etc.

CFCs molecules are splitted by UV radiations and the chlorine atoms. The chlorine radicals react with ozone molecule and destroy their molecular structure, thus depleting the ozone layer.

The amount of ozone depletion varies with latitude and seasons because of variations in the intensity of sunlight. A hole in ozone layer is noticed by the scientists which was larger in Antarctica.

Causes of Ozone Layer Depletion

There are two causes which are responsible for ozone layer depletion. They are

(i) **Natural Causes** Ozone layer has been affected by certain natural phenomena such as sun-spots and stratospheric winds, but these effects are temporary. It is also believed that major volcanic eruptions are also responsible for ozone depletion.

(ii) **Man-made Causes** Excessive release of chlorine and bromine from man-made compounds such as Chlorofluorocarbons (CFCs), Methyl Chloro form (CH_3CCl_3), Carbon Tetrachloride (CCl_4), Hydro Chlorofluorocarbons (HCFCs) and Methyl bromide are the main causes of ozone layer depletion.

Main Ozone Depleting Substances

- **Chlorofluorocarbons** CFCs are synthetic industrial chemical compounds containing chlorine, fluorine and carbon atoms. These are responsible for more than 80% of ozone depletion. It is used in freezers, air cooling, hospital **sterilants**[2], etc.
- **Methyl Chloroform** It is used for **aerosols**[3] and chemical processing.
- **Hydro Chlorofluorocarbons** It is a substitute for CFCs.
- **Carbon Tetrachloride** It is mainly used in fire extinguishers.

Mesosphere

It lies above the stratosphere which extends up to a height of 80 km. Temperature decreases with increase in altitude and reaches up to minus 100° C at the height of 80 km. The upper limit of mesosphere is known as the **mesopause**.

Thermosphere

It is the second highest atmospheric layer of the Earth. It extends from 50 km to 480 km. In this layer, temperature again increases with height because of the absorption of energetic ultraviolet and X-ray radiation from the Sun. Inosphere is present in this layer.

Ionosphere

It is located between 80 and 400 km above the ground. It contains electrically charged particles known as ions. **Ionisation**[4] occurs in this layer as a result of ultraviolet rays, gamma rays and x-rays.

Ionosphere is known as **Aurora Borealis** in the Northern hemisphere and **Aurora Australis** in the Southern hemisphere. It helps in long distance communication.

Radiowaves are refracted back to the Earth by the electrically charged gas molecules in this layer. This layer is completely cloudless and free of water vapour. It also protects us from meteors and obsolete satellites. The end point of this layer is known as **thermopause**.

Exosphere

It is the topmost layer of the atmosphere or the outermost layer of the Earth's atmosphere. It extends from exobase (lower exosphere) which is located at the top of the thermosphere. It extends between 480 kms and 960 kms above the Earth's surface.

2 **Sterilants** An agent used to destroy micro-organisms.

3 **Aerosols** It is a colloid of fine solid particles or liquid droplets in air or another gas.

4 **Ionisation** It refers to the process by which atoms are changed into ions through removal or addition of electrons, giving them an electrical charge.

The temperature in the atmosphere varies greatly and can range from 0° to over 1700° Celsius. It is colder at night and much hotter during the day. Density becomes extremely low in this layer.

This layer is mainly composed of extremely low densities of hydrogen, helium and several heavier molecules including nitrogen, oxygen and carbon dioxide closer to the exobase. Exosphere is also called the **outermost boundary** of atmosphere. It acts as a transitional zone between the Earth and **inter planetary space**[5].

Global Warming

Global warming is primarily a problem of too much carbon dioxide (CO_2) in the atmosphere which acts as a blanket, trapping heat and warming the planet. The phenomena of global warming is the result of enhanced concentration of **greenhouse effect** which increase the atmospheric temperature that causes melting of glaciers, health disorders and invites so many natural diseases.

Causes of Global Warming

- **Human activities** The main causes of global warming is the careless activities of the human beings. Increasing human population are demanding more resource to live easy and healthy life. In order to make their life easy and luxurious, people are using refrigerator/AC, car/automobiles, electric machines, oven, microwave, washing machine, etc. All such resources ultimately contribute to the global warming.
- **Greenhouse Effect** It is the process by which infrared radiations (reflect from the Earth's surface) are trapped by greenhouse gases which led to heating up of the Earth's atmosphere. The greenhouse gases, are carbon dioxide (CO_2), methane, ozone, nitrous oxide, hydro fluorocarbons, etc.
- Greenhouse gases are important as they make the Earth habitable and save it from extremely freezing temperatures during nights i.e. –153°C and extremely hot conditions during days i.e. 134 °C. But the global warming has increased the amount of greenhouse gases in the atmosphere, leading to increased methane, nitrous oxide, etc.
- **Deforestration** Forest has been cleaned and destroyed for plantation agriculture and industrialisation, which increased global warming.

Impacts of Global Warming

- **Climate Change** Global warming led to climate change which has significant implications on the health of living beings. Rising temperatures will likely to increase air pollution, the spread of insect-borne diseases, heavier rainstorm and flooding, which may pose great threats to living beings.
- **Extreme Weather Events** Global warming will increase certain types of extreme weather events, including heat waves, coastal flooding, precipitation, severe droughts, etc.
- **Heavier Precipitation and Flooding** As temperature increases due to global warming, heavy downpours take place.
- **Melting of Ice/Glaciers** Temperature are rising in the polar regions due to global warming, especially in Arctic, Antarctica, Alaska and Greenland. Scientists expect the rate of melting would accelerate with serious implications for future sea level rise.
- **Destruction of Coral Reefs** As global temperature increases due to global warming, it cause long term damage to coral reefs and make more difficult for corals to build their calcium carbonate skeletons.
- **Plant and Animal Range Shifts** A changing climate due to global warming affects the range of plants and animals, changing their behaviour and causing disruptions in the food chain.
- **Agriculture** Change in climate due to global warming will bring changes in the agriculture production. It will largely impact the coarse grains.

Check Your LEARNING...

1. Name the components of atmosphere.
2. What is the composition of exosphere?
3. State any one harmful effect of ozone depletion.
4. Name any one ozone depleting substances.
5. Define greenhouse effect.

5 **Inter Planetary Space** It is the region between two planets.

QUiCK Revision

- The atmosphere of the Earth is a layer of gases.
- In the absence of atmosphere, life is not possible on the Earth.
- Atmosphere also protects the Earth from harmful ultraviolet radiation from the Sun.
- The two most abundant gases in the air are nitrogen (78%) and oxygen (21%).
- Remaining gases almost constitute about 1% of atmosphere.
- Oxygen, nitrogen, carbon dioxide and water vapour are the main components of atmosphere.
- There are five layers of atmosphere. They are troposphere, stratosphere, mesosphere, ionosphere and exosphere.
- The troposphere is the first layer of atmosphere from the Earth's surface.
- Troposphere contains 80% of the mass of the Earth's atmosphere.
- The stratosphere is the second lowest layer of atmosphere.
- It extends upto 50 km from Earth's surface. It is free from water vapours and dust particles.
- Ozone layer in the stratosphere absorbs the burning ultraviolet radiation from the Sun.
- CFCs, Methyl Chloroform, Hydro CFCs, and Carbon Tetrachloride are the main Ozone depliting substances.
- Mesosphere extends from the stratopause at an altitude of about 80 km.
- Thermosphere is the secoond highest atmospheric layer of the Earth.
- Ionosphere is also called thermosphere.
- Exosphere is the topmost layer of the atmosphere. This layer connects Earth's atmosphere with inter planetary space.
- The phenomena of global warming is the result of enhanced concentration of greenhouse effect.
- Careless activities of the human beings are the main cuases of global warming.
- Greenhouse gases are carbon dioxide (Co_2), methane, nitrous oxide and water vapour.
- Effects of global warming are climate change, extreme weather events, heavier precipitation and flooding, melting ice, destruction of coral reefs and plant and animal habitat loss.

Chapter Practice

Section-I

Multiple Choice Questions

1. The blanket of air surrounding the earth is known as ....
(a) hydrosphere (b) lithosphere
(c) atmosphere (d) biosphere

Ans. (c) atmosphere

2. Which of the following statement is not true regarding oxygen gas?
(a) It constitutes 21% of atmosphere.
(b) It is important in burning fuel.
(c) It helps in respiration.
(d) Photosynthesis is the main source of oxygen.

Ans. (a) It constitutes 21% of atmosphere.

3. Which of the following gases are most abundant in atmosphere?
(a) Carbon dioxide (b) Oxygen
(c) Nitrogen (d) Argon

Ans. (c) Nitrogen

4. What is the percentage of nitrogen in atmosphere?
(a) 21% (b) 76%
(c) 23% (d) 78%

Ans. (d) 78%

5. Which of the following layer of atmosphere contains the water vapour and dust particles?
(a) Ionosphere
(b) Troposphere
(c) Stratosphere
(d) Mesophere

Ans. (b) Troposphere

6. What is the uppermost limit of stratosphere?
(a) 16 km (b) 50 km
(c) 10 km (d) 30 km

Ans. (b) 50 km

7. What is the reason behind increasing temperature at stratosphere?
(a) Absorption of UV rays
(b) Solar heating
(c) Low atmospheric pressure
(d) Both (a) and (b)

Ans. (d) Both (a) and (b)

8. How many atoms of oxygen are there in ozone?
(a) 1 (b) 2
(c) 4 (d) 3

Ans. (d) 3

9. Give reason for the following.
Ozone can be continuously created and destroyed in the atmosphere.
(a) Movement of free oxygen atoms in atmosphere.
(b) UV radiation emitted by Sun.
(c) Pollution in the atmosphere.
(d) All of the above

Ans. (b) UV radiation emitted by Sun.

10. Give reason for the following.
Reason behind ozone depletion.
(a) Damaging of ozone is less than its production.
(b) Damaging of ozone is more than its production.
(c) Reaction of chlorine metals with molecules of ozone.
(d) Both (b) and (c)

Ans. (d) Both (b) and (c)

11. What is the use of carbon tetrachloride?
(a) Refrigerators
(b) Air conditioners
(c) Fire extinguisher
(d) Aerosol

Ans. (c) Fire extinguisher

12. .... is completely cloudless and free of water vapour.
(a) Troposphere (b) Exosphere
(c) Ionosphere (d) Stratosphere

Ans. (c) Ionosphere

13. Which of the following layer of atmosphere is composed of extremely low densities of hydrogen and helium?
(a) Exosphere
(b) Stratosphere
(c) Troposphere
(d) Ionosphere

Ans. (a) Exosphere

14. Consider the following statements regarding atmosphere and choose the correct option
(i) The atmosphere protects the Earth from various ultraviolet rays.
(ii) The two most abundant gases in atmosphere are nitrogen and oxygen.
(iii) Even without atmosphere, life is possible on Earth.

Codes
(a) (i) and (iii) (b) (ii) and (iii)
(c) (i) and (ii) (d) (i), (ii) and (iii)

Ans. (c) (i) and (ii)

15. Consider the following statement regarding global warming and choose the correct option
(i) It is the result of enhanced concentration of greenhouse effect.
(ii) Certain waste management and agricultural practices can eliminate the negative impacts of global warming.
(iii) Global warming decreases global temperature.
Codes
(a) (i) and (iii)
(b) Only (ii)
(c) (i) and (ii)
(d) (i), (ii) and (iii)

Ans. (c) (i) and (ii)

16. Match the following.

List-I	List-II
A. Troposphere	1. 50 km to 480 km
B. Termosphere	2. 480 km to 960 km
C. Exosphere	3. 18 to 50 km
D. Stratosphere	4. 0-18 km

Codes

	A	B	C	D
(a)	3	2	1	4
(b)	1	2	3	4
(c)	4	1	2	3
(d)	3	2	4	1

Ans. (c)

17. Match the following.

List-I	List-II
A. CFC	1. Aerosols
B. Methyl CFC	2. Fire extinguisher
C. Hydro CFC	3. Refrigerator
D. Carbon Tetrachloride	4. Substitute for CFC

Codes

	A	B	C	D
(a)	3	1	4	2
(b)	4	2	3	1
(c)	2	4	1	2
(d)	1	3	2	4

Ans. (a)

Section-II

Short Questions

1. (i) What is atmosphere?
(ii) How atmosphere is important for the Earth?

Ans. (i) The atmosphere is a layer of gases which is colourless, tasteless, odourless and formless.
(ii) The atmosphere is important for the Earth because it is the largest source of oxygen and also protects the Earth from the harmful ultraviolet radiation radiated from the Sun.

2. Name the variable components of atmosphere.

Ans. The variable components of atmosphere are water vapour, dust particles, smoke, salt, pollen grains, etc present in air.

3. Name the various components and layers of the atmosphere.

Ans. Various components of the atmosphere are oxygen, nitrogen, carbon dioxide and water vapour and the various layers of the atmosphere are troposphere, stratosphere, mesosphere, ionosphere and exosphere.

4. Give the importance of carbon dioxide (CO_2) in the atmosphere.

Ans. Carbon dioxide (CO_2) is important for the atmosphere due to its ability to absorb heat radiation from the Earth. It helps in the process of photosynthesis to produce food for the plants.

5. Define the term troposphere.

Ans. It is the lowermost layer of the atmosphere in which all the living beings live. It contains water vapour and dust particles. It extends up to 16 km at the equator and 8 km at the poles.

6. Define stratosphere.

Ans. The stratosphere is the second lowest layer of the atmosphere. It extends up to 50 km from the Earth's surface. This layer is free from water vapour and dust particles. In this layer, there is no formation of clouds or having any turbulence in the air.

7. Which layer of atmosphere provides ideal conditions for jet aircrafts to fly?

Ans. Stratosphere layer of the atmosphere provides ideal conditions for jet aircrafts to fly. It is due to the absence of any weather condition that there is no turbulence in this layer.

8. How tropospheric ozone formation occurs?

Ans. The majority of tropospheric ozone formation occurs when Nitrogen Oxides (NO_x), Carbon Monoxide (CO) and Volatile Organic Compounds (VOCs) such as xylene, react in the atmosphere in the presence of sunlight.

9. Give the natural causes for the depletion of ozone layer.

Ans. The natural causes for the depletion of ozone layer is stratospheric wind, major volcanic eruption and the CFCs gases emitted from the various source like refrigerator, etc.

10. (i) What is ionosphere?
(ii) How is it important for us?

Ans. (i) Ionosphere refers to that process by which atoms are changed into ions through the addition or subtraction of electrons which give them an electrical charge.
(ii) Ionosphere is important as it helps in the long distance communications by refracting back the radiowaves to the Earth.

11. (i) Which layer is called outermost boundary of the atmosphere?
(ii) How is it important?

Ans. (i) Exosphere is the outermost boundary of the atmosphere.
(ii) Exosphere is important as it acts as a transitional zone between the Earth and the inter planetary space.

12. Distinguish between troposphere and exosphere.

Ans. Differences between troposphere and exosphere are

Troposphere	Exosphere
It is the lowest layer of atmosphere.	It is the topmost layer of atmosphere.
The upper limit of troposphere is called tropopause. Here, temperature stops dropping with increasing height and begins climbing with increasing height.	This layer acts as a transitional ozone between the atmosphere and the inter planetary space.

13. (i) Name the greenhouse gases.
(ii) How they are harmful?

Ans. (i) The greenhouse gases are carbon dioxide, methane, chlorofluorocarbons, nitrogen oxide and water vapour.
(ii) The greenhouse gases are harmful as they react with ozone and deplete the ozone layer.

14. How industrial revolution contributed in the global warming?

Ans. Industrial revolution has increased the number of factories which emits greenhouse gases in the atmosphere which has harmful effect for the depletion of ozone layer of the atmosphere.

Long Questions

1. Give any two importances of the atmosphere.

Ans. The two importance of the atmosphere are
(i) The presence of oxygen for human beings and animals as well as carbon dioxide for plants supports the life on the Earth.
(ii) The atmosphere is colourless, odourless and tasteless and it protects the Earth from millions of meteors and meteorites.

2. Explain the composition of atmosphere.

Ans. Refer to chapter theory on page no 100.

3. How carbon dioxide is important for atmospheric process?

Ans. Carbon dioxide is important for the atmospheric process because of its ability to absorb heat radiation from the Earth. Carbon dioxide allows radiation of short wave length to pass through atmosphere of Earth and absorbs the outgoing longwave raditions. It keeps the lower layers of the Earth warm. It is also useful for the productions of plant through the process of photosynthesis.

4. Give a brief account of structure of Earth's atmosphere.

Ans. Refer to chapter theory on page no 101-103.

5. Explain troposphere.

Ans. Refer to chapter theory on page no 101.

6. Give reasons why
(i) Temperature decreases with increasing height in troposphere.
(ii) Temperature increases with increasing height in stratosphere.

Ans. (i) The temperature decreases with increasing height in troposphere because the troposphere gases absorb very little of the incoming solar radiation while the ground absorbs this radiation and then heats the tropospheric air by conduction and convection. Since, this heating is most effective near the ground, the temperature in the troposphere gradually decreases with increasing height.
(ii) The temperature increases with increasing height in stratosphere because the ozone layer absorbs ultraviolet radiations in the lower atmosphere and once it is absorbed, it is radiated at different wave lengths, thereby warming the stratosphere.

7. How depletion of ozone layer takes place?

Ans. Refer to chapter theory on page no. 102.

8. What are chlorofluorocarbons (CFCs)?

Ans. Chlorofluorocarbons into the atmosphere play a major role in the depletion of ozone layer. CFCs are man-made synthetic industrial chemical compounds containing chlorine, fluorine and carbon atoms. They are widely used as cooling fluid in the refrigerators, air-conditioning and as cleaning agents, fire extinguishing fluids, spray cans, car propellants and in insulating foams.

9. Define the following
(i) Global warming (ii) Effects of global warming

Ans. (i) Refer to chapter theory page no. 103.
(ii) Refer to chapter theory page no. 103.

Chapter Assessment

Section-I

Multiple Choice Questions

1. Which of the following are variable component of atmosphere?
   (a) Smoke (b) Argon
   (c) CO_2 (d) O_2
2. What is the upper limit of troposphere called?
   (a) Stratospause (b) Exobase
   (c) Tropopause (d) Turbulence
3. The tropospheric ozone is generated by the action of .... on molecules of nitrogen dioxide and become pollutant.
   (a) greenhouse gases (b) CFC
   (c) Ozone (d) UV rays
4. The coral reefs are destructed due to the formation of ....
   (a) hydrochloric acid (b) carbonic acid
   (c) CFC (d) ozone

Section-II

Short Questions

1. What is atmosphere?
3. Define the significance of ozone in the atmosphere.
4. Name the uppermost layer of the atmosphere and give its importance.
5. Which layer has the lowest temperature in the atmosphere?
6. Which layer protects the Earth from meteors and meteorites?

Long Questions

1. What is the role of water vapour in the atmosphere?
2. State the composition of oxygen in atmosphere and how is it important for us?
3. Explain any three layers of atmosphere.
4. What is the significance of global warming in the atmosphere?
5. What are the impacts of global warming on the Earth?
7. Give reasons, why?
   (i) Carbon dioxide is also useful for us
   (ii) CO_2 is responsible for global warming
8. Distinguish between
   (i) Troposphere and stratosphere
   (ii) Ionosphere and exosphere

CHAPTER

12

Insolation

SYLLABUS

Insolation Meaning of insolation and terrestrial radiation. • Factors affecting temperature: latitude, altitude, distance from the sea, slope of land, wind and ocean currents.

Solar Radiation

Solar radiation is the continuous heat and light energy radiated by the Sun in all directions. The only source of energy for the Earth's atmosphere comes from the Sun which has a surface temperature of more than 10,800°F (6000°C). This energy travel through space for a distance of 93 million miles and reaches us as solar energy or **radiant energy**[1].

Sun's energy takes approx 8 minutes to reach the Earth's surface. The flow of energy from the Sun to the Earth and then back into space is a complex process. The Sun emits radiation which is composed of three particles i.e. white light, infrared radiation and ultraviolet radiation. Apart from these three particles, Sun also emits atomic particles known as **solar wind.**

The Sun provides all the energy needed for movement and change on the Earth. The incoming solar radiation or Sun's energy is known as **insolation** and the outgoing infrared radiation from the Earth is known as **terrestrial radiation.**

Meaning of Insolation

It is the amount of solar energy received by the Earth. The energy emitted by the Sun is scattered before it reaches the Earth. The incoming solar energy is received on the Earth in the form of short waves.

Out of the total amount of solary energy, 51% reaches the Earth. A considerable amount i.e. 35% of the solar energy is reflected back into space by clouds, snowfields and ocean and only 14% is absorbed by the atmosphere during insolation.

Meaning of Terrestrial Radiation

It is the amount of heat radiated by the Earth in the form of long waves. After the Earth receives insolation from the Sun in the form of short waves, the Earth heated itself and becomes a radiating body. Thus, it radiates energy to the atmosphere in the form of long waves.

These long wave radiations are absorbed by the atmospheric gases particularly by carbon dioxide (CO_2) and the other greenhouse gases. So, the atmosphere is indirectly heated by the Earth's radiation. The atmosphere after being heated, radiates and transmits heat to the space.

1 **Radiant energy** It is the energy of electromagnetic waves. It can travel through space.

Thus, a constant temperature is maintained at the Earth's surface and in the atmosphere by radiating back the amount of heat into space received from the Sun.

> **Heat Budget**
> A heat budget is the perfect balance between incoming solar energy absorbed by the Earth and outgoing terrestrial radiation from the Earth. If the balance is disturbed, then Earth would get progressively warmer or cooler with each passing year.

Temperature

The interaction of insolation with the atmosphere and the Earth's surface creates heat, which is measured in terms of temperature. Heat represents the molecular movement of particles comprising a substance while the temperature is the measurement in degrees of how hot or cold a thing or a place is.

Factors affecting the Distribution of Temperature

The degree of warmth in the air refers to atmospheric temperature. The difference in the temperature varies from place to place, due to uneven distribution of heat. Major factors affecting the distribution of temperature are

Latitude

Temperature of a place depend on latitude of the place in the following ways

- Due to spherical shape of Earth and its revolution around the Sun, temperature decreases with increase in latitude on both sides of Equator.
- Latitude of a place determines the 'angle of incidence' of Sun rays.
- The Sun's rays are closest and vertical between the Tropic of Cancer and Capricorn. Therefore this zone gets maximum insolation.
- When Sun moves towards poles, the Sun's rays became increasingly slanting, which leads to decrease of temperature in polar areas.

Altitude

Height of the place above the sea level is called altitude. The atmosphere is mainly heated by terrestrial radiation from the Earth. Thus, it can be expected that places nearer to the Earth's surface are warmer than those higher up.

The temperature decreases with increasing height above sea level. Moreover this rate of decrease with altitude is never constant, varying from place to place and from season to season.

Density of atmosphere also decreases with increasing height. For every 1000 m, the temperature falls by 6.5°C. This is known as **normal lapse rate**. This is the reason why hill stations are cooler even in summer also. However, at times, the situation is reversed and the normal lapse rate is inverted. Due to this inversion, the temperature increases with increase in height/altitude.

Inversion is usually of short duration but quite common nonetheless. For example, a long winter night with clear skies and still air is ideal condition for inversion. Temperature inversion is normal over polar areas throughout the year.

Distance from the Sea

The temperature is influenced by the location of a place with respect to the sea. Land is heated more quickly than the sea because of higher specific heat of water. Therefore, during day time, land gets heated more than surrounding oceans. At night, the land radiates heat very rapidly and cools rapidly than the sea.

The places situated close to sea experience neither very high nor very low temperatures. The moderating influence of the sea and land breezes on temperature is called **maritime influence**.

On the other hand, the places situated in the interior of large continents experiences high temperature during day time and very low temperature at night. The annual range of temperature of these places are high.

Slope of Land

A steep slope shows difference in temperature from lower to the upper parts. Mountain ranges that have an East-West alignment like the Alps, shows a higher temperature on the South-facing sunny slope than the North-facing sheltered slope.

In hilly areas, a hot day is followed by a calm, cloudless night during which the air cools more rapidly over the higher areas. Due to this, cold and heavy air blows down the slope and gets accumulated in the bottom of valley by pushing the warmer air upwards. The temperature may then be lower in the valley and higher in the slopes. In this way, there is reversal in the vertical distribution of temperature. This is called a temperature inversion.

Winds

Winds also affect the distribution of temperature. During summer season, the winds blowing from land masses are warmer than those blowing from sea. In winter, the winds blowing over land are cooler than those blowing from sea.

Winds which blow from sea to land are known as the **on-shore winds**. These winds raise the temperature over the land in winters and lower the temperature on the land in summers.

The winds that blow from land to sea are known as the **off-shore winds**. These winds lower the temperature of land in winters and raise the temperature of land in summers.

Besides these winds, local hot and cold winds are also responsible for differential heating and cooling of land. For example, Chinook (South-Westerly wind), Foehn (Alps), Sirocco (Sahara to Mediterranean Sea), Loo (Northern India) are hot winds and Mistral (France) and Bora (East coast of Adriatic Sea and North Italy) are cold winds.

Ocean Current

A regular volume of water which flow like a river in a definite path is known as ocean current.

Ocean currents are of two types

(i) **Cold Currents** They move from polar regions to lower equatorial regions. They transport cool water to warmer regions.

(ii) **Warm Currents** They move from equatorial regions to polar regions. They transport warm water to cooler regions.

Thus, cold currents along the coast make the coastal areas cooler and warm currents make the coastal areas warmer.

Check Your LEARNING...

1. What do you mean by insolation?
2. Which gas absorbs long wave radiation in the environment?
3. What do you mean by off-shore winds?
4. Name any two factors that affect the temperature of a place.

QUiCK Revision

- The Sun continuously radiates heat and light energy in all directions which is called solar radiation.
- The Sun is the ultimate source of energy through which the Earth gets its amount of energy and light.
- Amount of solar energy received by the Earth is called insolation.
- Solar radiation strikes the surface of the Earth, which radiates this back into the atmosphere in the form of long waves. Thus, it is called terrestrial radiation.
- Factors affecting distribution of temperature are latitude, altitude, distance from the sea, slope of land, ocean currents and winds.
- Due to spherical shape of Earth and its revolution around the Sun, temperature decrease with increasing height.
- Atmosphere is heated by terrestrial radiation from Earth, this makes the surface more warm then the higher ups.
- Land heats up more rapidly and to higher temperatures than water and cools more rapidly and to lower temperatures than water.
- A steep slope shows difference in temperature from lower to the upper parts.
- During summer season, the wind blowing from land masses are warmer than those blowing from sea and this effects the distribution of temperature.
- A regular volume of water which flows in a definite path is known as ocean current.
- Cold currents and warm currents are the two types of ocean currents.

Chapter Practice

Section-I

Multiple Choice Questions

1. The Sun has a surface temperature more than ....

(a) 6000°C (b) 7500°C
(c) 5000°C (d) 3800°C

Ans. (a) 6000°C

2. Which of the following terms is identical to radiant energy ?

(a) Wind energy (b) Solar energy
(c) Light (d) Tidal energy

Ans. (b) Solar energy

3. Apart from white light, ultraviolet and infrared radiation, the Sun also emits atomic particles which is known as ....

(a) wind energy (b) tidal energy
(c) solar energy (d) yellow light

Ans. (c) solar energy

4. What is the percentage of incoming insolation which is absorbed by atmosphere?

(a) 13 per cent (b) 14.5 per cent
(c) 11 per cent (d) 14 per cent

Ans. (d) 14 per cent

5. The degree of warmth in the air refers to ....

(a) atmospheric temperature
(b) insolation
(c) radiation
(d) solar temperature

Ans. (a) atmospheric temperature

6. Which of the following terms defines the angle of incidence of Sun rays?

(a) Altitude (b) Longtitude
(c) Latitude (d) Insolation

Ans. (c) Latitude

7. The moderating influence of the sea and land breezes on temperature is called ....

(a) Maritime influence (b) Temperature inversion
(c) Continental influence (d) Land influence

Ans. (a) Maritime influence

8. In which of the following regions, a hot day is followed by calm, cloudless night during which the air cools more rapidly over the higher areas?

(a) Sea coast (b) Hilly areas
(c) Islands (d) Plains

Ans. (b) Hilly areas

9. .... blow from land to sea which lower the temperature of land in winter and raise the temperature in summers.

(a) On shore winds
(b) Tidal winds
(c) Chinook
(d) Offshore winds

Ans. (d) Offshore winds

10. Give reason for the following.
Only one part out of two billion parts of Sun energy reaches the sun.

(a) Earth rotation around the Sun.
(b) Scattered energy received by Sun.
(c) Heat waves of Earth.
(d) Charged particles of solar wind.

Ans. (b) Scattered energy received by Sun.

11. Give reason for the following.
Land surface is heated more quickly than water surface.

(a) Land receives energy in form of insolation.
(b) Land has reversal lapse rate.
(c) Higher specific heat of water.
(d) Land has steep slope.

Ans. (c) Higher specific heat of water.

12. Consider the following statement regarding altitudes and choose the correct ones

(i) Temperature increases with increasing altitudes above sea level.
(ii) The rate of decrease of temperature with altitude is never constant.
(iii) Due to high altitudes, hill stations are cooler even in summer.

Codes

(a) (i) and (iii) (b) (ii) and (iii)
(c) (i) and (ii) (d) None of these

Ans. (b) (ii) and (iii)

13. Consider the following statements regarding effect of wind on temperature and choose the correct ones

(i) In summer seasons, wind blowing form land masses are warmer than those blowing on sea.
(ii) Winds in winter decreases the temperature.
(iii) Winds in summer increases the temperature

Codes

(a) (i), (ii) and (iii) (b) (ii) and (iii)
(c) Only (ii) (d) Only (i)

Ans. (d) Only (i)

14. Match the following.

List I	List II
A. Radiant energy	1. Solar energy received by Earth
B. Insolation	2. Energy of electro-magnetic waves
C. Terrestrial radiation	3. Energy absorbed by atmosphere
D. Offshore wind	4. Movement of any weather feature moving toward the shore

Codes

	A	B	C	D		A	B	C	D
(a)	4	3	2	2	(b)	2	1	4	2
(c)	3	1	2	4	(d)	4	2	3	1

Ans. (c)

Section-II

Short Questions

1. (i) What is solar radiation?
   (ii) What is the source of solar radiation?

Ans. (i) The Sun continuously radiates heat and light energy in all directions which is called solar radiation.

(ii) The only source of energy for the Earth's atmosphere come from the Sun which has a surface temperature of 6000°C.

2. How many types of radiation particles are there? Name them.

Ans. The Sun's radiation comprises of three particles i.e.
(i) The white light
(ii) The ultraviolet rays
(iii) The infrared rays

3. (i) What do you mean by terrestrial radiation?
   (ii) Name the main elements of atmosphere absorbing the terrestrial radiation.

Ans. (i) The Earth receives insolation from the Sun in the form of short waves that heats up its surface. After receiving these short waves, the Earth is heated itself and becomes a radiating body. Thus, it radiates energy to the atmosphere in the form of long wave. This energy heats up the atmosphere too from below. This process is known as terrestrial radiation.

(ii) The main elements of atmosphere absorbing the terrestrial radiation are atmospheric gases particularly carbon dioxide (CO_2) and other greenhouse gases.

4. How much insolation is absorbed by the atmosphere?

Ans. The insolation absorbed by the atmosphere are about 51% radiation received by the Earth, i.e. 14% absorbed by insolation and 35% from terrestrial radiation.

5. Explain the role of altitude in influencing the temperature of a place.

Ans. Height of the place above the sea level is called altitude. The atmosphere is mainly heated by terrestrial radiation from the Earth, thus it can be expected that places near to the Earth's surface are warmer than those higher up. However, this rate of decrease with altitude is never constant, varying from place to place and from season to season.

6. How temperature is lower in the valley and higher in slopes? Explain.

Ans. In hilly areas, a hot day is followed by a calm, cloudless night during which the air cools more rapidly. The high ground may induce cold, heavy air to flow down the slope and accumulate at the valley bottom pushing the warmer air upwards and the temperature may then be lower in the valley and higher in the slopes.

7. How land and water surface have different properties in absorption and radiation of heat?

Ans. Land and water surface have quite different properties in absorption and radiation of heat as land heats up more rapidly and to higher temperature than water and cools more rapidly and to lower temperature than water. That's why temperature contrasts are great over the land masses, but only moderate over sea.

8. What do you mean by normal lapse rate?

Ans. The decrease in temperature with increase in height is called normal lapse rate. For every 1000 m, the temperature falls by 6.5°C.

9. State the two categories of ocean currents.

Ans. The two categories of ocean currents are
(i) Cold currents which move from polar regions to lower equatorial latitudes.
(ii) Warm currents which blows from equatorial to polar regions.

Long Questions

1. Give reasons for the following.
   (i) The vertical rays of the Sun provide more heat at the Equator.
   (ii) Temperature decreases from the Equator to the Poles.
   (iii) Hot deserts have high temperature range.

Ans. (i) The vertical Sun's rays cover small area with intense heating thus gives maximum insolation. So, the energy received per unit area is more in the Equator. It is compared to slanting rays which cover larger area where Sun rays dispersed more.

(ii) The Sun's rays become increasingly slanting from the Equator to the Poles. As slanting rays cover larger area where heat disperse, it leads to decrease in temperature.

(iii) The sky is clear in hot deserts. Insolation is received without obstruction in the day and lost it without obstruction in the night. This make the days warmer and night colder in deserts.

2. What is inversion of temperature? When it takes place?

Ans. Inversion of temperature is the reverse situation of the normal lapse rate (temperature decreases with increasing height) where temperature increases with increasing height.

It takes place under certain conditions which are

- A long winter night with clear sky and still air is ideal situation for inversion. The heat of the day is radiated off during the night and by early morning hours, the Earth is cooler than the air above. Over polar areas, temperature inversion is normal throughout the year.
- In hills and mountains, the inversion take place due to air drainage. This is because cold air at the hills and mountains produce during night flows under the influence of gravity. Being heavy and dense, the cold air moves down the slope like water and displaces the warmer air towards up. So, when we go in a valley, the temperature seems to getting increased.

3. How does distance from the sea affect the temperature distribution?

Ans. Refer to chapter theory page no. 110.

4. Explain in brief the factors affecting distribution of temperature.

Ans. Refer to chapter theory page no 110.

5. Define annual range of temperature on
(i) Equator (ii) Poles

Ans. (i) **Equator** The lowest annual temperature range is found in equatorial areas as the duration of the day or night is the same in equatorial region. The Sun's rays are vertical throughout the year. Hence, there is no worthwhile difference between the summer and winter seasons.

(ii) **Poles** Towards the poles, the annual temperature range goes on increasing, as the duration of the day and the inclination of the Sun's rays go on increasing. It causes a lot of difference between the temperature of the two seasons.

Chapter Assessment

Section-I

Multiple Choice Questions

1. The atmosphere gets the energy radiated by the Earth by the process of ....
(a) radiation
(b) terrestrial radiation
(c) insolation
(d) greenhouse effect

2. .... represents the molecular movement of particles comprising a substance, while the temperature is the measurement in degree of how hot or cold a place is.
(a) Rotation (b) Energy
(c) Heat (d) Wind

3. Which of the following factors are not responsible for variation's in Earth's temperature?
(a) Gravitational force (b) Temperature
(c) Ocean currents (d) Sea breeze and Land breeze

4. .... influences the actual amount of water vapour present in the air.
(a) Insolation (b) Sea breeze
(c) Temperature (d) Ocean currents

Section-II

Short Questions

1. Define insolation.
2. Give the meaning of
(i) Terrestrial radiation (ii) Heat budget
3. Which region receives maximum insolation?
4. How many units, the Earth surface receives from the Sun as insolation?
5. What do you mean by ultraviolet rays?

Long Questions

1. What is the role of energy transmission of the terrestrial radiation of the Earth?
2. What happen if the energy would not continuously received from the Sun?
3. What is the role of energy of the Sun in the atmosphere?
4. Explain the role of winds and ocean currents on the distribution of temperature.
5. Why radiation of the heat by the Earth continues during the night?

CHAPTER

13

Atmospheric Pressure and Winds

SYLLABUS

Atmospheric Pressure and Winds Meaning and factors that affect atmospheric pressure. •Major pressure belts of the world. •Factors affecting direction and velocity of wind-pressure gradient, Coriolis effect. •Permanent winds - Trades, Westerlies and Polar Easterlies. •Periodic winds - Land and Sea breezes, Monsoons. •Local winds - Loo, Chinook, Foehn and Mistral. •Variable winds - Cyclones and Anticyclones. •Jet Streams - Meaning and importance.

Air is an integral part of the atmosphere which expands on heating and get compressed on cooling. This process of heating and cooling of air results in variations in the atmospheric pressure. This causes the movement of air from high pressure to low pressure, setting the air in motion.

Meaning of Atmospheric Pressure

The weight of a column of air contained in a unit area from the mean sea level to the top of the atmosphere is called the atmospheric pressure. The pressure of the air is equal to the weight of a column of air above a unit area on the land surface.

The unit used by meteorologists for expressing atmospheric pressure is called **Millibar**[1] (mb) and Pascals or Kilopascal (kPa). Atmospheric pressure is measured by means of an instrument called barometer.

There are two types of barometers i.e. Aneroid barometer and Fortin's barometer. The average atmospheric pressure at sea level is 1013.25 mb or 760 mm. The atmospheric pressure reduces with height.

Factors affecting Atmospheric Pressure

Temperature

Atmospheric pressure decreases with increase in temperature. This is because when the temperature rises, air expands and the molecules of the air move fairly apart which results in less pressure.

On the contrary, with decrease in temperature, the air gets compressed and the space between the molecules decreases, thus exerts more pressure. This is the main reason behind the formation of low pressure belts of equatorial regions and high pressure belts of polar regions.

1 **Millibar** It is defined as exactly equal to 100000 Pa, which is slightly less than the current average atmospheric pressure on the Earth at sea level.

Altitude

Air pressure is generated due to the weight of the air, therefore, sea level has the highest air pressure. As we move upwards from the sea level, air pressure decreases because the upper air is light and low in density. The decrease in pressure is about 1 cm of mercury for every 110m of altitude.

Decrease in the pressure also results to the decrease in oxygen. At high altitudes, the atmospheric pressure and available oxygen gets low, which makes people feel breathless. For example, in mountain regions, the atmospheric pressure falls with increase in altitude and therefore, mountaineers carry oxygen cylinders on their expeditions.

Moisture in Air

The quantity of water vapour present in air affects atmospheric pressure as the molecular weight of air (about 29 g/mol) is greater than the molecular weight of water (18 g/mol). When water vapour enters the atmosphere as a gas, the molecules of water vapour takes the place of other gases molecules in the air. Conversion of water from the liquid state to gaseous state because of evaporation is known as **atmospheric humidity**. Water vapours are light in weight, therefore they rise up and pressure of humid air decreases as compared to dry air.

Rotation of the Earth

Rotation of the Earth produces **centrifugal force**[2] which has more effect in the equatorial region while lesser effect on polar regions. Centrifugal force pushes things away from its core. Same is the effect on air pressure which results into lesser pressure in equatorial regions as compared to that in polar regions.

As the equatorial region receives plenty of heat throughout the year, the air of this region becomes warm and light, creating a low atmospheric pressure. At the polar regions, there is scarcity of heat so the cold and heavy air sink down and creates high atmospheric pressure.

Major Pressure Belts of the World

The unequal heating of the Earth and its atmosphere by the Sun during the revolution of the Earth on its tilted axis causes difference in pressure. The distribution of atmospheric pressure across the latitudes is termed as global horizontal distribution of pressure. The differences in pressure leads to the formation of pressure belts around the Earth.

The major belts among them are

(i) **Equatorial Low Pressure Belt** This belt extends from 0° to 5° North and South of the Equator. Due to the excessive heating at equatorial region, the horizontal movement of air is absent and only conventional currents are there. As there is excessive heating in this belt, the air gets warm and rises to produce equatorial low pressure. This belt is also known as **doldrums** due to absence of surface winds.

(ii) **Sub-tropical High Pressure Belt** This belt is located around 30° North and South of the Equator, where the air is comparatively dry and the winds are calm and light. Thus, this belt is an area of high pressure. It is also called **Horse latitude**. This belt is characterised by anticyclonic conditions which cause atmospheric stability and aridity. Thus, most of the hot deserts of the world are present in this belt.

(iii) **Sub-Polar Low Pressure Belt** This belt is located between 60° and 70° in each hemisphere. It is more developed in the Southern hemisphere than the Northern hemisphere. In sub-tropical region, the descending air gets divided into two parts. One part blows towards the Equatorial Low Pressure Belt and the other part blows towards the Circum-Polar Low Pressure Belt.

This belt is marked by the ascent of warm sub-tropical air over cold polar air, blowing from the poles. The winds surrounding the polar region blow towards the Equator due to the Earth's rotation. The centrifugal forces operating in this region create the low-pressure belt appropriately called the Circum-Polar Low Pressure Belt. Violent storms occur in this belt in winter.

(iv) **Polar High Pressure Belt** This belt is located at both the North Pole and the South Pole between 70° and 90° North and South, where the temperature is extremely low. The cold air of the polar regions gave rise to high pressure over the poles. These areas of polar high

2 **Centrifugal Force** The apparent force that is felt by an object moving in a curved path that acts outwardly away from the centre of rotation.

pressure are known as the **polar highs**. These regions are characterised by permanent ice caps.

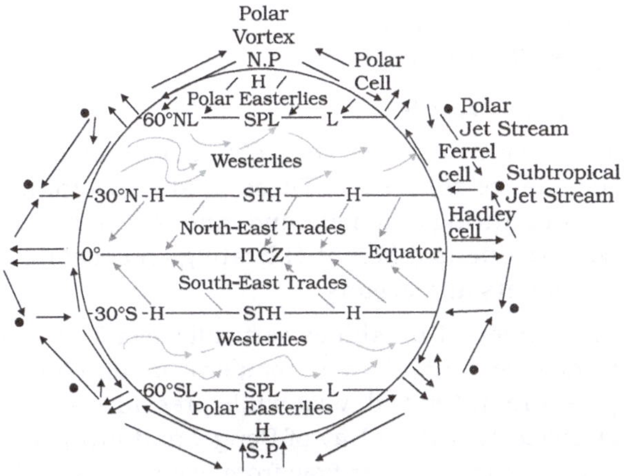

Pressure Belts

Check Your LEARNING...

1. Which instrument is used by meteorologists for the purpose of measuring atmospheric pressure?
2. Name two factors which affects the atmospheric pressure.
3. What is atmospheric humidity?
4. What is the latitude at which equatorial pressure belt situated?
5. Which zone is characterised by anticyclonic conditions?

Wind

Wind is referred to as horizontal movement of air. It blows from high pressure to low pressure. Its direction and speed are controlled by number of factors. The factors affecting the velocity and direction of wind are

Pressure Gradient Force

The changing rate of pressure with respect to distance is called pressure gradient and the force that actually causes air to move is called the pressure gradient force. As winds blow from the high pressure to low pressure, their direction is parallel to the direction of pressure gradient. It initiates the blow of the wind. Winds are named on the basis of the direction from which they blow, *viz*, Easterly, Westerly, etc.

Coriolis Force

Rotation of the Earth creates a force which causes the deflection of the free moving objects on the Earth. This force is called the coriolis force. It deflects the wind to the right direction in the Northern hemisphere and to the left direction in the Southern hemisphere.

The wind blowing from North becomes North-Easterly in Northern hemisphere and the wind blowing from South becomes South-Easterly in Southern hemisphere. The deflection is more when the wind velocity is high.

Types of Winds

Permanent Winds

These winds are the large air masses that are created mainly as a result of the Earth's rotation and the Sun's heating power. These are also known as **prevailing** or **planetary winds**. They blow from high pressure to low pressure over the Earth's surface throughout the year. These winds are categorised into three categories which are

(i) Trade Winds

These winds blow from Sub-tropical High Pressure Belt to Equatorial Low Pressure Belt. The trade winds cover the entire area between 30°N and 30°S latitudes on both side of the Equator.

These winds have the following characteristic features

- These are steady winds. They have fixed velocity and are regular.
- Since they travel from high latitude to low latitude area, they become gradually hot and dry and hence, have a great capacity to hold moisture.
- They cause considerable rainfall on Eastern margins of the continents as they get moisture after blowing over the oceans.
- These winds converge near the Equator and form **Inter-Tropical Convergence Zone (ITCZ)**[3]. Here, these winds rises and causes heavy rainfall.
- They are known as North-East trades in Northern hemisphere and South-East trades in Southern hemisphere.

(ii) Westerlies

The westerlies blow between 35° and 60° North and South latitudes from the Sub-Tropical High Pressure Belts, towards the Sub-Polar Low Pressure Belts.

3 **Inter-Tropical Convergence Zone (ITCZ)** It is the area encircling the Earth near the equator where the North-East and South-East trade winds converge.

The westerlies generally blow from South-West to North-East in Northern hemisphere and from North-West to the South-East in Southern hemisphere. It has the following important characteristic features

- It causes considerable rainfall particularly on Western margins of the continents.
- It is more consistent in direction or blow with stronger force in Southern hemisphere due to lesser obstructions from the continents.
- It is also known as **brave winds or roaring forties, furious fifties** and **shrieking sixties**, according to the varying degree of storminess in the latitudes in which they blow.

(iii) Polar Winds

These winds originate in the North and South polar regions and blow towards Circum-Polar Low Pressure Belt. These winds blow from polar high pressure zone and originate from ice-capped landmass in Arctic and Antarctic latitude.

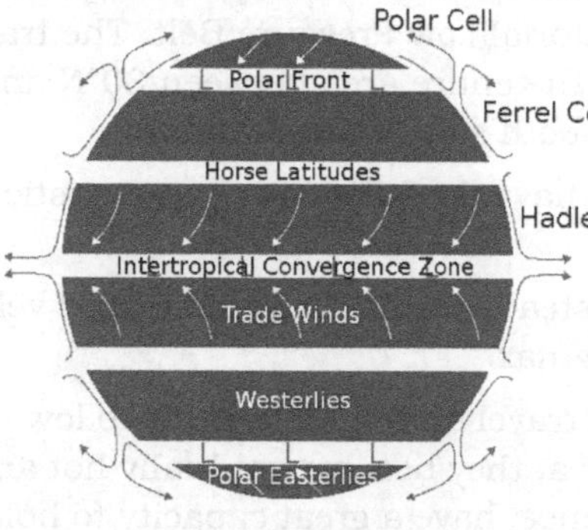

Polar Winds

The following are the important characteristic features of polar winds

- These winds are deflected to the West in both hemispheres and hence are known as **Polar Easterlies.**
- These are dry and cold winds because these winds originate in polar areas.
- These winds do not cause much rainfall.
- These winds causes temperature cyclones when they come in contact with westerlies.
- These winds blow from North-East in the Northern hemisphere and are called North-East Polar Winds and they blow from South-East in the Southern hemisphere and are called South-East Trade winds.

Periodic Winds

These winds change their direction periodically due to change in pressure and temperature. These winds are blown at regular intervals in regular cycles. These winds are

Monsoon Winds

These winds reverses their direction completely with the change of seasons. These winds blow from sea to land during summers and land to sea during winters due to differential heating and cooling of continents and oceans.

In summers, Sun shines vertically over Tropic of Cancer resulting in high temperature and low pressure in Central Asia, while pressure is sufficiently high at Bay of Bengal and Arabian sea. This induces air flow from sea to land and causes heavy rainfall in India and neighbouring countries. The summer monsoon winds blow South-West and are known as South-West Summer Monsoon.

In winters, high pressure develops over Central Asia up to the North-West Indian plain and low pressure develops in the Indian ocean. This induces winds to flow from land to sea. These winds are not capable of producing rainfall, but when they blow over sea and pass over adjoining land, they bring some rainfall. The winter monsoon winds blow North-East are known as North-East Winter Monsoon.

Land Breeze and Sea Breeze

These winds are caused by differential rate of heating of the land and sea. During the day, the land heats up faster and become warmer than the sea. Thus, the pressure gradient from sea to land is created and the wind blows from the sea to land as the sea breeze.

At night, the reversal of this condition takes place. The land loses heat faster and is cooler than the sea. Here, the pressure gradient is from land to sea and results in land breeze.

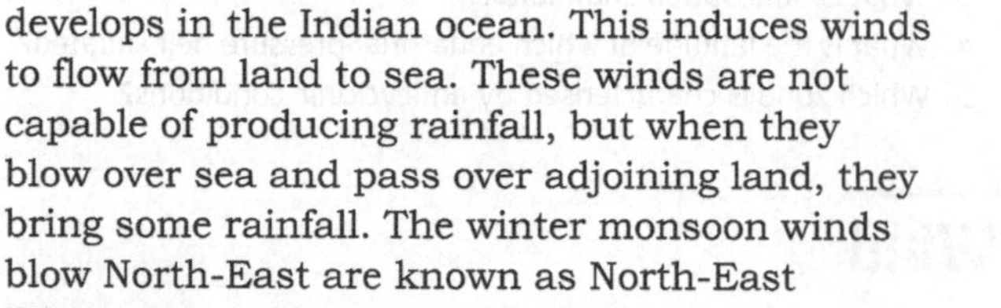

Land Breeze and Sea Breeze

Local Winds

These winds are restricted to a certain region and only blow for a short period of time. They may be warm or cold, depending upon the area from which they blow. Some of the local winds are

- **Loo** In the plains of North India, sometimes a very hot and dry wind blows which is known as loo. It blows from the West in summer in the afternoons. Its temperature invariably ranges between 45°C and 50°C. It may cause heatstroke and sunburn to people.
- **Chinook** (Snow Eater) This is the hot and dry wind blowing along the Eastern slope of the Rockies mountain in North America. It covers an area from the Southern part of Colorado in the South to British Columbia in Canada in the North. Due to its effect, the snow melts and green grass sprouts even in winter.
- **Foehn** This is similar to Chinook and blows along the Northern slope of the Alps. It is a warm and dry wind descending on the leeward side of the mountain. It melts the snow, makes the weather pleasant and helps in early ripening of the grapes.
- **Mistral** During winter, a local cold wind originates over the snow-capped mountains or highlands and blow down the valley. It is known as mistral wind. It blows from the Alps over France towards the Mediterranean Sea. It can cause variations in the temperature.

Variable Winds

These winds blow in small areas and are related to pressure systems. They are called variable because they do not blow in any definite direction and their directions varies with the movement of the pressure system. Two major types of variable winds are

(i) Cyclones

Cyclone is a part of the atmosphere in which the pressure is lowest in the centre and the wind blows inward in the opposite direction. The cyclone causes rising of moisture laden air which results in the heavy rain at the centre of the depression.

Cyclones originate in low latitude. They are known by different names like Tropical Cyclone in Indian Ocean, Hurricanes in Caribbean, Typhoons in China and Willy-Willies in Australia. They cause heavy damage to property and loss of human lives. Due to coriolis force, cyclone blow in anti-clockwise direction in the Northern hemisphere and clockwise direction in the Southern hemisphere.

The cyclones are classified into two types

(a) **Tropical Cyclone** These are violent storms that originate over oceans in tropical areas and move over to the coastal areas. They bring about large scale destruction caused by violent winds, very heavy rainfall and storms.

Tropical cyclones are one of the most devastating natural calamities in the world. These cyclone originate and intensify over warm tropical oceans, for example Pacific, Atlantic and Indian ocean. The conditions favourable for the formation and intensification of torpical storms are

- Large sea surface with temperature higher than 27°C.
- Presence of coriolis force.
- Small variations in vertical wind speed.
- A pre-existing weak low pressure area of low level cyclonic circulation.
- Upper divergence above sea level system.

(b) **Temperate Cyclone** These cyclones are also known as **extratropical** or **wave cyclones**. These cyclones are active above the mid-latitudinal region between 35° and 65° latitude in both the hemispheres. The direction of movement is from West to East and more pronounced in winter seasons. It is in these latitudes that the polar and sub-tropical air masses meet and form fronts.

Differences between Tropical and Temperate Cyclone

Tropical	Temperate
They originate between 8° and 20° North and South of the oceans in tropical regions.	These are active over mid-latitudinal regions between 35° and 65° latitudes in both the hemispheres.
These are produced and developed mainly over sea.	These are produced over both land and sea.
They are limited to small area and travel from East to West.	They cover a large area and move from West to the East.
Winds are calm at the centre of tropical cyclone with no rainfall.	Winds are strong and rainfall takes place at the centre of temperate cyclone.
They are largely intense in summer.	They are mosty intense in winter.
They are forecasted by high temperature and humidity.	They are forecasted by fall in temperature and pressure, wind shifts and a halo around the Sun and the Moon.

(ii) Anticyclones

Anticyclone is an atmospheric condition which is just opposite of cyclone. There is high pressure in the core or center and low pressure around it.

It blow in clockwise direction in the Northern hemisphere and anti-clockwise direction in the Southern hemisphere. Since anticyclones are the centres of high pressure, they are found in the region of descending air currents. They are very common in Sub-Tropical High Pressure Belts.

Jet Streams

These refer to the concentrated bands of high velocity winds located at 10-15 km above the surface of the Earth. They are strong and rapidly moving circum-polar Westerly air circulation in a narrow belt in the upper troposhere. There are two major types of jet streams which are

(i) **Sub-tropical Jet Streams** These jet streams occur at about 30° latitude and they are best developed in winters and early spring. During winters, these are more pronounced in Southern hemisphere. In summers, over Asia, the sub-tropical jet stream is replaced by the tropical Easterly jet stream because the Sun is directly vertical to Tropic of Cancer in summers.

(ii) **Tropical Easterly Jet Streams** These jet streams are closely connected to the Indian summer monsoons. These mainly occurs due to the differential heating and cooling of the land and sea as well as due to the superseding pressure gradient.

Importance of Jet Streams

- In terms of commercial usage, the jet stream is important for the airline industry.
- The position and strength of the jet stream helps meteorologists to forecast future weather events.
- The monsoon of South Asia is largely affected and controlled by jet streams.
- Jet streams are used to predict the climate change phenomena because they get influenced by El-Nino and La-Nina. During El Nino, for example, precipitation usually increases in California because the polar jet stream moves further South and brings more storm with it.

Check Your LEARNING...

1 What is the full form of ITCZ?
2 Which force influences the velocity of the wind?
3 Give the direction of flow of westerlies.
4 Name two cold winds and two warm winds.

QUiCK Revision

- The weight of a column of air per unit of area is called atmospheric pressure.
- The instrument used to measure atmospheric pressure is called barometer.
- Temperature is the main reason behind the formation of low pressure betls of equatorial regions and high pressure belts of polar regions.
- The height of an object or point in relation to sea level or ground level is called altitude.
- Conversion of water from the liquid state to gaseous form because of evaporation is known as atmospheric humidity.
- The unequal heating of the Earth, its atmosphere by the Sun and revolution of the Earth on its tilted axis creates pressure belts of varied nature around the Earth.
- Frictional force influences the velocity of the wind.
- The changing rate of pressure with respect to distance is called pressure gradient. The spacing of isobars on a map indicates the pressure gradient.
- Rotation of the Earth creates a force which causes deflection of wind in both the hemispheres. The force generated in this process is called coriolis force.
- Permanent wind blows from high pressure to low pressure over the Earth's surface throughout the year.
- Westerlies blow from South-West to North-East in Northern hemisphere and from North-West to South-East in Southern hemisphere.
- Polar winds are dry and cold winds because these winds originate in polar areas.
- Trade winds are the winds which blow from Sub-tropical high pressure belt to Equatorial low pressure belt.
- Periodic winds are the winds which change their direction periodically due to change in pressure and temperature.
- Local winds are restricted to a certain region and only blows for a short period of time.
- Variable winds don't blow in a definite direction and their direction varies with the movement of the pressure system.
- Tropical cyclones are the violent storms that originate over oceans in tropical areas.
- Temperate cyclones are active over mid-latitudinal region between 35° to 65° latitude in both hemisphere.
- Anticyclones blow in clockwise direction in the Northern hemisphere and anti-clockwise in the Southern hemisphere.
- Jet streams refers to the concentrated bands of high velocity winds located at 10-15 km above the surface of the Earth.
- Sub-tropical jet streams and tropical Easterly jet streams are the two major types of jet streams.
- El-Nino is associated with the warming of the Central and the Eastern tropical pacific.

Chapter Practice

Section-I

Multiple Choice Questions

1. The weight of a column of air contained in a unit area from the mean sea level to the top of atmosphere is called ....
   (a) atmospheric density
   (b) air pressure
   (c) atmospheric pressure
   (d) topospheric pressure

Ans. (c) atmospheric pressure

2. Which of the following devices are used to measure atmospheric pressure?
   (a) barometer (b) anemometer
   (c) thermometer (d) hydrometer

Ans. (a) barometer

3. What is the average atmospheric pressure at sea level?
   (a) 1023.25 mb (b) 1013.25 mb
   (c) 1093.25 mb (d) 765.20 mb

Ans. (b) 1013.25 mb

4. Give reason for the following.
   Atmospheric pressure decreases with increase in temperature.
   (a) Temperature decreases when air expands and molecule of air move fairly apart which results in less pressure.
   (b) Air get compressed with decrease in temperature.
   (c) Air pressure is generated due to weight of the air which may cause decrease in pressure.
   (d) Air expands when the temperature rises and molecules of the air move fairly apart which results in low pressure.

Ans. (d) Air expands when the temperature rises and molecules of the air move fairly apart which results in low pressure.

5. Which of the following statement is the correct definition of atmospheric humidity?
   (a) Conversion of water from gaseous state to liquid state by evaporation.
   (b) Conversion of water from the liquid state to gaseous state by evaporation.
   (c) Conversion of water vapour into solid form by evaporation.
   (d) Conversion of water vapour into gaseous form by condensation.

Ans. (b) Conversion of water from the liquid state to gaseous state by evaporation.

6. Which factor of atmospheric pressure is responsible for high atmospheric pressure at polar region and low atmospheric pressure at equatorial region due to centrifugal force?
   (a) Gravitational force (b) Rotation of Earth
   (c) Temperature (d) High altitude

Ans. (b) Rotation of Earth

7. Given reason for the following.
   The poles experience more air pressure than equator.
   (a) Distance of the equator from Earth's centre is more than that of pole.
   (b) Due to centrifugal force.
   (c) Less distance between Earth's centre and the equator.
   (d) Strong gravitational force at the South and North pole.

Ans. (a) Distance of the equator from Earth's centre is more than that of Pole.

8. Which of the following pressure belt of the world is located around 30° North and South of the Equator?
   (a) Polar Low Pressure Belt
   (b) Equatorial Low Pressure Belt
   (c) Sub-Tropical High Pressure Belt
   (d) Sub-Polar Low Pressure Belt

Ans. (c) Sub-tropical High Pressure Belt

9. .... are also known as Circum-Polar Low Pressure belt.
   (a) Polar Low Pressure Belt
   (b) Equatorial Low Pressure Belt
   (c) Sub-tropical High Pressure Belt
   (d) Sub-Polar Low Pressure Belt

Ans. (d) Sub-Polar Low Pressure Belt

10. What is the main reason behind changing in the direction of wind?
   (a) Change in atmospheric pressure
   (b) Change in gravitational force
   (c) Change in temperature
   (d) Both (a) and (c)

Ans. (d) Both (a) and (c)

11. Which of the following force causes the deflection of the free moving objects on the Earth?
   (a) Coriolis force
   (b) Rotational force
   (c) Gravitational force
   (d) Pressure gradient force

Ans. (a) Coriolis force

12. .... is the area encircling the Earth near the equator where North-East and South-East trade winds converge.
(a) Pressure gradient
(b) Sub-tropical high pressure
(c) Low pressure belt (d) ITCZ

Ans. (d) ITCZ

13. Give reason for the following.
Westerlies winds are more consistent in direction with stronger force in Southern hemisphere.
(a) Varying degree of stormines in the latitudes
(b) Lesser obstruction from continents
(c) Considerable rainfall in Southern hemisphere
(d) Lesser atmospheric pressure

Ans. (b) Lesser obstruction from continents

14. What is the main reason behind the formation and intensification of tropical cyclone?
(a) Upper divergence below sea level system.
(b) Presence of coriolis force.
(c) Small variations in horizontal wind speed.
(d) Large sea surface with maximum temperature of 27°C.

Ans. (b) Presence of coriolis force.

15. Which of the following local winds are referred to as mid-latitude depressions?
(a) Loo (b) Sub-tropical cyclone
(c) Tropical cyclone (d) Temperate cyclone

Ans. (d) Temperate cyclone

16. .... refers to the concentrated bands of high velocity winds located at 10-15 km above the surface of the Earth.
(a) Jet stream (b) Loo
(c) Mistral (d) Anti cyclone

Ans. (a) Jet stream

17. Consider the following statements about atmospheric pressure and altitude and choose the correct option.
(i) Air pressure is generated due to weight of air that's why sea level has higher air pressure.
(ii) In mountain region, the atmospheric pressure increases with increase in altitude.
(iii) Decrease in atmospheric pressure at high altitudes causes decrease in oxygen.

Codes
(a) (i) and (ii) (b) (ii) and (iii)
(c) (i) and (iii) (d) Only (ii)

Ans. (c) (i) and (iii)

18. Consider the statement about trade winds and choose the correct option.
(i) These are steady winds.
(ii) These wind covers the entire area between 40°N and 40°S latitudes on both side of equator.
(iii) These wind travels from high latitude to low latitude area and can become generally hot and dry.

Codes
(a) (i) and (ii) (b) Only (iii)
(c) (ii) and (iii) (d) (i) and (iii)

Ans. (d) (i) and (iii)

19. Match the following.

List I (Pressure Belts)	List II (Location)
A. Sub-Tropical High Pressure Belt	1. 0°-5°N and S
B. Sub-Polar Low Pressure Belt	2. 30°N and S
C. Polar High Pressure Belt	3. 60°N, 70°S
D. Equatorial Low Pressure Belt	4. 70°-90°N and S

Codes

	A	B	C	D		A	B	C	D
(a)	2	1	3	4	(b)	3	1	4	2
(c)	2	3	4	1	(d)	3	2	4	1

Ans. (c)

20. Match the following.

List I	List II
A. Monsoon winds	1. Blows in Northern part of India
B. Chinook	2. Blow from land to sea during winters
C. Loo	3. Leds the sprouting of green grass in winter
D. Foehn	4. Responsible for ripening of grapes

Codes

	A	B	C	D		A	B	C	D
(a)	4	3	2	1	(b)	1	4	2	3
(c)	2	3	1	4	(d)	3	4	2	1

Ans. (c)

Section-II

Short Questions

1. What do you mean by atmospheric pressure?

Ans. The weight of a column of air contained in a unit area from the mean sea level to the top of the atmosphere is called the atmospheric pressure.

2. Which instrument is used to measure atmospheric pressure?

Ans. The instrument used by meteorologists to measure the atmospheric pressure is called barometer.

3. Name the factors that affects the atmospheric pressure.

Ans. The factors that affects the atmospheric pressure are temperature, altitude, moisture in air, gravitational pull of the Earth and rotation of the Earth.

4. How the temperature impacts the atmospheric pressure?

Ans. The temperature and the atmospheric pressure have an inverse relationship. When the temperature increases, the atmospheric pressure decreases and *vice-versa*.

5. How the pressure belts on the Earth are formed?

Ans. The pressure belts on the Earth are created due to the combination of the following factors
- Unequal heating of the Earth and the atmosphere by the Sun.
- Revolution of the Earth on its tilted axis.

6. What is Polar-High Pressure Belt?

Ans. At the North and South poles (70° and 90°N and S), where the temperature is permanently low, there exists Polar-High Pressure Belt because of high pressure due to cold climate.

7. Name the factors that affects the direction and the velocity of the wind.

Ans. The factors that affects the direction and velocity of the wind are
- Coriolis force affects the direction.
- Frictional force affects the velocity.

8. (i) What do you mean by permanent winds?
(ii) Give two characteristics of polar winds.

Ans. (i) Permanent winds are the large air mass that are created mainly as a result of the Earth's rotation and Sun's heating power.
(ii) Two characteristics of polar winds are
- These winds do not cause much rainfall.
- These are dry and cold winds, because these winds originate in polar areas.

9. Differentiate between trade winds and Westerlies.

Ans. Differences between Trade winds and Westerlies are

Trade Winds	Westerlies
They blow from sub-tropical high pressure belt to the equatorial low pressure belt.	They blow from sub-tropical high pressure belt to sub-tropical low pressure belt.
They causes rainfall on the Eastern margin of the continent.	They causes rainfall on the Western margin of the continent.

10. (i) What do you mean by local wind?
(ii) Mention any two local winds.

Ans. (i) Local winds are defined as the winds blow due to local variation in the temperature and pressure and influence a very small area. These local winds blow in the lower layers of the troposphere.
(ii) The two local winds are loo and chinook.

11. What do you understand by mistral?

Ans. During winter, areas adjacent to highlands may experience a local cold wind, which originates over the snow capped mountains or highlands and blows down the valley. It is known as mistral wind.

12. Why the variable winds are considered as variable in nature?

Ans. The variable winds are called variable in nature because they do not blow in any definite direction and their direction varies with the movement of the pressure system. The two chief types of variable winds are cyclones and anticyclones.

13. (i) What is cyclone?
(ii) Name two types of cyclone.

Ans. (i) Cyclones are local winds that originate in low latitude. They can cause heavy damage to property and loss of human. These are caused by coriolis force which is blown in an anticlockwise direction in Northern hemisphere and clockwise in Southern hemisphere.
(ii) Two types of cyclone are tropical cyclone and temperate cyclone.

14. What do you understand by term 'Anticyclone'?

Ans. Anticyclone is an atmospheric condition which is just opposite to cyclone. There is a high pressure in the core or centre and low pressure around it. Anticyclone blow in clockwise direction in the Northern hemisphere and in anticlockwise direction in the Southern hemisphere.

15. (i) Explain the term 'jet streams'.
(ii) Mention any one importance of jet streams.

Ans. (i) The term jet stream refers to concentrated bands of high velocity winds located at 10-15 km above surface of the Earth. It is strong and rapidly moving circum-polar Westerly air circulation in a narrow belt in the upper troposphere.
(ii) Jet streams are used to predict the climate change phenomena.

Long Questions

1. Explain any three factors that impacts the atmospheric pressure.

Ans. Three factors that impacts the atmospheric pressure are
(i) **Temperature** Atmospheric pressure decreases with increase in temperature. This is because when the temperature rises, air expands and the molecules of the air move far apart and hence, exert less pressure. On the contrary, with decrease in temperature the air gets compressed and the space between the molecules decreases, thus exerts more pressure.
(ii) **Altitude** Increase in altitude, decreases the temperature, whereas the decrease in altitude, increases the temperature.
(iii) **Moisture in Air** Conversion of water from the liquid state to gaseous state because of evaporation is known as atmospheric humidity. Water vapours contain the latent heat, which make the air lighter. It makes the dry air into humid air thus, making it lighter and pressure of humid air decreases as compared to dry air.

2. How gravitational pull of the Earth and rotation of the Earth influence atmospheric pressure?

Ans. Earth holds its atmosphere with the help of its gravitational force. The Poles experience more air pressure than the Equator because the distance of the Equator from the center of the Earth is more than that of the poles.

Rotation of the Earth produces centrifugal force which has more effect in the equatorial region while lesser effect on polar regions. It pushes things away from its core. Same is the effect on air pressure which results into lesser pressure in equatorial regions as compared to that in polar regions.

3. How pressure belts are formed?

Ans. The process through which pressure belts shift is the unequal heating of the Earth and its atmosphere by the Sun because of the revolution of Earth on its tilted axis, causes difference in pressure. This leads to the formation of pressure belts around the Earth. The pressure belts shifts along the Northward or Southward movement of Sun during summer solstice and winter solstice, respectively as well as with the apparent movement of the Sun.

4. Differentiate between pressure gradient force with coriolis force with respect to velocity and direction of wind.

Ans. Differences between pressure gradient force and coriolis force are

Pressure Gradient Force	Coriolis Force
The changing rate of pressure with respect to distance is the pressure gradient and the force that actually causes air to move is called the pressure gradient force.	Rotation of the Earth creates a force which causes the deflection of the free moving objects on the Earth and the force applied is the coriolis force.
As winds blow from the high pressure to low pressure, their direction is parallel to the direction of pressure gradient. It initiates the blow of the wind.	It deflects the wind to the right direction in the Northern hemisphere and to the left in Southern hemisphere. The deflection is more when the wind velocity is high.

5. What is Westerlies? Give the characteristics of Westerlies.

Ans. Westerlies blows from sub-tropical high pressure belts towards sub-polar low pressure belts. It causes considerable rainfall particularly on the Western margins of the continents.

The important characteristics of westerlies are

- It causes considerable rainfall particularly on Western margins of the continents.
- It is more consistent in direction or blow with stronger force in Southern hemisphere due to lesser obstructions from the continents.
- It is also known as brave winds or roaring forties, furious fifties and shrieking sixties, according to the varying degree of storminess in the latitudes in which they blow.

6. Explain the following terms.

(i) Loo (ii) Variable winds
(iii) Land breeze

Ans. (i) **Loo** These are the hot and dry winds that blow from the West in summers particularly in the Northern India.

(ii) **Variable Winds** These winds are related to pressure systems and blow over small area. These are of two types i.e. cyclones and anticyclones.

(iii) **Land Breeze** At night, the land loses heat faster and is cooler than the sea. Thus, the pressure gradient is created from land to sea and results in land breeze.

7. Explain the following terms.

(i) Chinook and Foehn (ii) Monsoon winds
(iii) Trade winds

Ans. (i) **Chinook and Foehn** Both these winds are dry winds that are experienced on the leeward side of the mountains when the descending air becomes compressed under pressure.

(ii) **Monsoon Winds** These are the seasonal winds of the Indian Ocean and Southern Asia, blowing from the South-West in summer and from the North-East in winter.

(iii) **Trade Winds** These are the winds that blows from the Sub-Tropical High Pressure Belts towards the Equator. Due to the coriolis force, these winds blow pre-dominantly from the North-East direction in the Northern hemisphere and from the South-East direction in the Southern hemisphere.

8. Differentiate between the following

(i) Lands breeze and sea breeze
(ii) Cyclones and anticyclones
(iii) Planetary winds and variable winds.

Ans. (i) Differences between land breeze and sea breeze are

Land Breeze	Sea Breeze
The flow of air is from land to sea.	The flow of air is from sea to land.
At night, the land loses heat faster and is cooler than the sea, this situation give rise to land breeze.	During the day, the land heats up faster and becomes warmer than the sea, this situation gives rise to the sea breeze.

(ii) Differences between cyclones are anti-cyclones are

Cyclones	Anticyclones
It has low pressure at the centre.	It has high pressure at the centre.
It blows anticlockwise in Northern hemisphere and clockwise in Southern hemisphere.	It blows clockwise in Northern hemisphere and anticlockwise in Southern hemisphere.

(iii) Differences between planetary winds and variable winds are

Planetary Winds	Variable Winds
The general distribution of winds throughout the lower atmosphere is known as planetary winds.	Variable winds are those which don't blow in any definite direction and their direction varies with the movement of the pressure system.
Planetary winds is of three types i.e. trade winds, westerlies and polar easterlies.	Major types of variable winds are cyclones and anticyclones.

9. Differentiate between temperate cyclone and tropical cyclones.

Ans. Refer to chapter theory page no. 119.

10. What are jet streams? How jet streams are important?

Ans. Jet streams refers to the concentrated bands of high velocity winds, located at 10-15 km above the surface of the Earth.

The importance of jet streams are

- In terms of commercial usage, the jet stream is important for the airline industry.
- The position and the strength of jet stream helps the meteorologists to forecast future weather events.
- These are also used to predict the climate change phenomena because jet streams get influenced by El Nino and La Nina.

Chapter Assessment

Section-I

Multiple Choice Questions

1. Which of the following units are used to express the atmospheric pressure?
   (a) Millibar (b) Nanobar
   (c) Barometer (d) Isobar
2. Earth hold its atmosphere with the help of its .... force.
   (a) coriolis
   (b) pressure gradient
   (c) rotational
   (d) gravitational
3. Which of the following winds can cause considerable rainfall in Western margins of continent?
   (a) Trade winds
   (b) Westerlies
   (c) Loo
   (d) Jet streams
4. .... are active over mid latitudinal regions between 35° and 65° latitudes in both the hemisphere.
   (a) Tropical cyclone
   (b) Jet stream
   (c) Sub-tropical cyclone
   (d) Temperate cyclone

Section-II

Short Questions

1. How the atmospheric pressure is being forward in the atmosphere?
2. What is the normal pressure at sea level?
3. Explain the term atmospheric humidity.
4. How gravitational force is important for atmospheric pressure?
5. What do you mean by pressure belt?

Long Questions

1. Define the term
   (i) Equatorial low pressure belt
   (ii) Sub-tropical high pressure belt
   (iii) Polar high pressure belt
2. How winds can be classified? Explain in details.
3. Give accounts of the local winds found in the world.
4. Explain two types of jet streams.
5. Explain the term
   (i) La-Nina (ii) El-Nino.

CHAPTER

14

Humidity

SYLLABUS

Humidity Meaning and difference between relative and absolute humidity.

- Condensation-forms (clouds, dew, frost, fog and mist).
- Precipitation-forms (rain, snow and hail).
- Types of rainfall-relief/orographic, convectional, cyclonic/frontal with examples from the different parts of the world.

Meaning of Humidity

Water vapour present in the atmosphere is known as humidity. The term humidity, is used to express the wetness of the atmosphere, i.e. the pressure of the water vapour in the atmosphere. Humidity is inversely proportional to heat which means the hotter the air, the more the water vapour is present in it. When the atmospheric temperature is low, water vapour is less.

The instrument used for measuring the water vapour in the atmosphere is known as **Hygrometer**. It is also known as Dry and Wet Bulb Thermometer. Humidity measuring instruments usually rely on the measurement of some other quantities also such as temperature, pressure, etc. It is expressed quantitatively in different ways such as absolute humidity and relative humidity.

Absolute Humidity

The actual amount of water vapour present in the atmosphere is known as absolute humidity. It differs from place to place on the surface of the Earth and is measured in gram per cubic metre.

Absolute humidity is not taken into account while calculating weather calculations and forecasts.

Relative Humidity

The percentage of moisture presents in the atmosphere as compared to its full capacity at a given temperature is known as the relative humidity. Relative humidity is greater over oceans and least over the continents.

Relative humidity is the ratio between absolute humidity of a given mass of air and maximum amount of water vapour that it can hold at the same temperature.

$$\text{Relative humidity} = \frac{\text{Absolute humidity}}{\text{Humidity at saturation point}} \times 100$$

When the air containing moisture to its full capacity at a given temperature is said to be saturated, it is called saturation point. When there is more water vapour in the atmosphere, the relative humidity increases. It decreases, when there is a reduction in the level of water vapour in the atmosphere. When the air is fully saturated, relative humidity is 100%. The temperature at which air is fully saturated is called **dew point**.

Relative humidity is the most essential characteristic of climate. It generally helps to determine the amount of precipitation. When there is a high relative humidity, the human being feels warm and uncomfortable while the low relative humidity makes the weather pleasant in which human feel comfortable and happy.

Difference between Absolute Humidity and Relative Humidity

Absolute Humidity	Relative Humidity
Absolute humidity gives actual amount of water in the air.	Relative humidity is the amount of water vapour in the air at a given temperature compared with the maximum amount that can be held by the air at a given temperature.
Absolute humidity is expressed as grams per cubic meter.	Relative humidity is expressed as percentage.
Absolute humidity does not take temperature into consideration.	Relative humidity takes temperature into consideration.
Absolute humidity does not give any idea about the water vapour needed in the air to become saturated.	Relative humidity gives idea about the water vapours needs by the air to become saturated.

Condensation

The transformation of water vapour into water is called condensation. It is caused by the loss of heat. When the moist air is cooled, it may reach a level where its capacity to hold water vapour ceases, then the excess of water vapour condenses into liquid form. When it is directly condenses into solid form, it is known as **sublimation**.

The process of condensation is crucial to the water cycle because it is responsible for the formation of clouds. Condensation takes place when the following atmospheric conditions exist

- The temperature of air must be below dew point temperature so as to encourage condensation.
- High amount of water vapour should be present at the atmosphere.
- Tiny particles of dust, salt and smoke can act as a condensation nuclei (i.e. particles around which water vapour condenses).

Forms of Condensation

Condensation can take various forms like dew, frost, fog, mist and clouds.

Dew

When the moisture is deposited in the form of water droplets on the cooler surfaces of solid objects such as stones, grass blades and plant leaves, it is known as dew. For the formation of dew, it is necessary that the dew point is above the freezing point.

Frost

Frost forms on the cold surfaces when condensation takes place below the freezing point (0°C), i.e. the dew point is at or below the freezing point. In this condition, the excess moisture is deposited in the form of minute crystals instead of water droplets.

Fog and Mist

When the temperature of air mass contains large quantity of water vapour, the condensation takes place within the fine dust particles. This results in the formation of fog and mist. They are prevalent where warm air currents comes in contact with the cold air currents.

The difference between fog and mist is that the visibility in mist is less than 2000 metres and exceeds 1000 metres, but in case of fog, the visibility is less than 1000 metres. Thus, fog is denser than mist and visibility of mist is better.

Clouds

Cloud is a mass of minute water droplets or tiny crystals of ice. It is formed by the condensation of the water vapour in free air at considerable elevations above the earth's surface. Clouds are formed mainly by the **adiabatic cooling**[1] of the air below its dew point. When a cloud is fully saturated and relative humidity reaches 100%, precipitation occurs.

On the basis of the height, expanse, density and transparency or opaqueness, etc, the clouds are classified into various forms such as cumulus, cumulonimbus, stratus, stratocumulus etc.

1 **Adiabatic Cooling** It is the process of reducing heat through a change in air pressure caused by increase in the volume of air.

These are

- **Cirrus Clouds** They are formed at high altitudes (8,000 - 12,000 m). They are thin and detached clouds having a feathery appearance. They are always white in colour.
- **Cumulus Clouds** They are generally formed at a height of 4,000-7,000 m. They look like cotton wool. They exist in patches and can be seen scattered here and there. They have a flat base.
- **Stratus cloud** They are layered clouds covering large portions of the sky. They are generally formed either due to loss of heat or the mixing of air masses with different temperatures.

Precipitation

It has been defined as water in liquid or solid forms falling on the Earth under gravity. It is the process by which products of condensation i.e. water drops, ice crystals, sleet, etc fall to the ground. This process take place only when tiny particles of water join together to form large sized particles which become too heavy to be contained by the clouds.

Forms of Precipitation

- **Rain** It is a precipitation in liquid state. When the resistance of the air fails to hold the water vapours against the force of gravity, it falls on the Earth's surface in the form of rain.
- **Snow** When the temperature is lower than 0°C, precipitation takes place in the form of fine flakes of snow and is called snowfall. Moisture is released in the form of ice crystals and these crystals form flakes of snow.
- **Hail** It is a type of precipitation which falls in the form of small pellets or small balls of ice with a diameter between 5 to 50 mm and sometimes more. The pellets of ice start falling on the ground, passing through clouds having water droplets. These droplets of water coming in contact with ice freeze around the pellets of ice. Thus, the size of pellets becomes larger and they ultimately fall on the ground as hail which damages crops and houses in villages.

Types of Rainfall

Convectional Rainfall

The air when being heated up becomes light and rises up in convection currents. As the air rises, it expands and cools down slowly. Subsequently, condensation takes place and **cumulonimbus clouds**[2] are formed, which causes heavy rainfall. This rainfall is known as convectional rainfall. Such rain is common in summers. This type of rainfall occurs in after noon at about 4 o' clock, thus it is also known as **4 o' clock shower.**

Example Conventional rainfall is common in the equatorial regions and the interior parts of the continents, particularly in the Northern hemisphere.

Relief/Orographic Rainfall

When the rainfall occurs due to rising up of air by relief features like mountains, it is called relief rainfall. When the **saturated air**[3] mass comes across a mountain, it is forced to rise. The rising air expands, the temperature falls and the moisture is condensed. The windward slope of mountain receives the maximum rainfall, whereas the leeward side remains dry.

When the air reaches the leeward slope, its temperature increases and its ability to take in moisture increases which results in rainfall. The region situated on the leeward side is known as the rain shadow area.

Example This kind of rainfall is common on the Western slope of Western Ghats (India), on the windward slope of North-East part of West Malaysia, Western New Zealand, etc.

Cyclonic/Frontal Rainfall

Cyclonic rain is caused by cyclonic activity and it occurs along the fronts of the cyclone. It is formed when two air masses of different densities, temperatures and humidity meet. A layer which separate two air masses is called **front**. This front may be warm or cold.

2 **Cumulonimbus Clouds** They are clouds formed at lower altitude and they cause heavy rainfall.
3 **Saturated Air** It is the air that holds water vapour at its highest level.

At the warm front, the warm lighter wind rises slightly over the heavier cold air. As the warm air rises, it cools and the moisture present in it condenses to form clouds. The rain finally falls gradually for a few hours to a few day.

A cold front is formed when a cold air mass is moving faster and it starts replacing the warm air mass by occupying the area formerly occupied by warm air. In case of cold front, the rainfall is heavier and it occurs in a relatively narrow zone.

Example Winter rain in North-West India is a typical example of cyclonic rainfall.

Check Your LEARNING...

1. Which instrument is used to measure humidity?
2. Name different forms of condensation.
3. What are the common forms of precipitation?
4. Convectional rainfall is the phenomenon of which region?

QUICK Revision

- Water vapour present in the atmosphere is known as humidity.
- The actual amount of water vapour present in the atmosphere is called absolute humidity.
- Relative humidity is the percentage of moisture present in the atmosphere as compared to its full capacity at a given temperature.
- Hygrometer is the instrument used for measuring the water vapour in the atmosphere.
- Condensation is the transformation of water vapour into water.
- Dew point is the temperature at which air gets saturated.
- Conduction is the transfer of heat through matter by the collision of one atom with another.
- Clouds are visible mass of tiny droplets of water high above the ground.
- Water in liquid or solid form falling on the Earth under gravity is known as precipitation. Rain, snow and hail are forms of precipitation.
- There are three types of rainfall i.e. convectional, orographic and cyclonic.
- When subsequent condensation takes place and cumulonimbus clouds formed, it causes heavy rainfall which is known as convectional rainfall.
- When a relief feature like mountain obstruct the path air, the condensation takes place to release weight of air, this rainfall is known as orographic rainfall.
- When the rainfall happen due to cyclones in the oceans, it is known as cyclonic rainfall.

Chapter Practice

Section-I

Multiple Choice Questions

1. .... is present in the atmosphere which is known as humidity.
(a) Water vapour (b) Air pressure
(c) Rainfall (d) Fog

Ans. (a) Water vapour

2. Which of the following instruments are used to measure the actual amount of vapour present in the atmosphere?
(a) Anemometer (b) Hydrometer
(c) Seismometer (d) Hygrometer

Ans. (d) Hygrometer

3. Give reason for the following.
Relative humidity is the most essential characteristics of climate.
(a) It helps in the determination of climate.
(b) It makes pleasant weather.
(c) It determines the amount of precipitation.
(d) It helps in determining the drought and flood of the area.

Ans. (c) It determines the amount of precipititation.

4. The relative humidity is expressed in the form of ....
(a) cubic meter (b) gram per cubic meter
(c) percentage meter (d) decimals

Ans. (c) percentage meter

5. Which of the following is the process of reducing heat through a change in air pressure caused by volume expansion?
(a) Adiabatic cooling (b) Latent cooling
(c) Precipitation (d) Condensation

Ans. (d) Condensation

6. Consider the statement about condensation and choose the correct options.
(i) The temperature of air must be above dew point temperature to encourage condensation.
(ii) High amount of water vapour should be present at the temperature to encourage condensation.
(iii) The process of condensation is important in the formation of water cycle.

Codes
(a) (i) and (ii) (b) (ii) and (iii)
(c) (i) and (iii) (d) Only (ii)

Ans. (b) (ii) and (iii)

7. .... is the moisture which is deposited in the form of water droplets on the cooler surface of stone, grass and plant leaves.
(a) Mist (b) Fog
(c) Dew (d) Clouds

Ans. (c) Dew

8. The temperature of dew point is ....
(a) 100°C (b) 90°C
(c) −10° C (d) 0°C

Ans. (d) 0°C

9. Which of the following clouds has a flat base and are formed at height of 4000 to 7000 m?
(a) Cirrus (b) Cumulus
(c) Stratus (d) Nimbus

Ans. (b) Cumulus

10. Consider the following statements regarding rain and choose the correct option.
(i) It is precipitation in liquid state.
(ii) Rain releases moisture in the form of hexagonal crystals.
(iii) It is caused by the resistance of air when it fails to hold the water against the force of gravity.

Codes
(a) Only (i) (b) Only (ii)
(c) (ii) and (iii) (d) (i) and (iii)

Ans. (d)

11. It is the form of the precipitation which are formed by the rainwater passing through the colder layers and are generally round balls of ice. Which of the following forms of precipitation has been referred here?
(a) Snow (b) Rain (c) Ice (d) Hail

Ans. (d) Hail

12. Give reason for the following.
Reason behind occurrence of convectional rainfall
(a) Formation of stratus cloud
(b) Formation of cool air currents
(c) Formation of Cumulonimbus clouds
(d) Formation of Cumulus clouds

Ans. (c) Formation of Cumulonimbus clouds

13. Winter rain in North-West India is the typical example of
(a) orographic rainfall
(b) convectional rainfall
(c) relief rainfall
(d) frontal rainfall

Ans. (d) frontal rainfall

14. Match the following.

List-I (Rainfall)	List-II (Area)
A. Frontal rainfall	1. New Zealand
B. Orographic rainfall	2. Northern Hemisphere
C. Convectional rainfall	3. North-West India

Codes

	A	B	C		A	B	C
(a)	3	2	1	(b)	2	1	3
(c)	1	3	2	(d)	3	1	2

Ans. (d)

Section-II

Short Questions

1. (i) What do you mean by humidity?
(ii) How it can be measured?

Ans. (i) Water vapour present in the atmosphere is known as humidity. The amount of water changes with time and weather conditions.
(ii) It is measured in gram per cubic meter.

2. Define the following.
(i) Absolute humidity
(iii) Relative humidity

Ans. (i) The actual amount of water vapour present in the atmosphere is known as absolute humidity.
(ii) The percentage of moisture present in the atmosphere as compared to its full capacity at given temperature is known as relative humidity.

3. What is the difference between dew and frost?

Ans. When the moisture is deposited in the form of water droplets on the cooler surfaces of solid objects such as stones, plant leaves, it is known as dew. On the other hand, frost forms on the cold surfaces when condensation takes place below the freezing point (0°C).

4. (i) What is saturation point?
(ii) How the fog and mist are formed?

Ans. (i) The saturation point is a point at which the air contains moisture to its full capacity.
(ii) When the temperature of the air mass containing the large quantity of water vapour falls all of a sudden, condensation takes place within itself on the fine dust particles. This results in the formation of fog and mist.

5. What is cloud? Name any three types of clouds.

Ans. Cloud is a mass of minute water droplets of ice formed by the condensation of water vapour in free air at considerable elevation above earth's surface.
Cumulus, cumulonimbus, stratus, stratocumulus are some common clouds.

6. Define snow and hail.

Ans. When the temperature is lower than 0°C, precipitation takes place in the form of fine flakes which is called snow.
Hail is a type of precipitation which falls in the form of small pellets of ice.

7. (i) What do you mean by convectional rainfall?
(ii) What do you mean by orographic rainfall?

Ans. (i) As the air rises, it expands and cools down slowly. Subsequently condensation takes place and cumulus clouds are formed, this causes heavy rainfall. This rainfall is known as convectional rainfall.
(ii) When the rainfall occurs due to rising up of air by relief features like mountains, it is called orographic rainfall.

8. (i) What is cyclonic rainfall?
(ii) What are the major factors affecting the distribution of rainfall?

Ans. (i) Cyclonic rainfall is caused by cyclonic activity and it occurs along the fronts of the cyclone. It is also known as frontal rainfall. It is formed when two air-masses of different densities, temperatures and humidity meet.
(ii) Latitude, continents, oceans and mountain barriers are the major factors affecting the distribution of rainfall.

Long Questions

1. Differentiate between the following pairs.
(i) Relative humidity and absolute humidity
(ii) Condensation and evaporation
(iii) Convectional rainfall and orographic rainfall

Ans. (i) The differences between relative and absolute humidity are

Relative Humidity	Absolute Humidity
The percentage of moisture present in the atmosphere as compared to its full capacity at a given temperature is known as relative humidity.	The actual amount of water vapour present in the atmosphere is known as absolute humidity.
It is measured in terms of gram per cubic meter.	It is always expressed in terms of percentage.

(ii) The differences between condensation and evaporation are

Condensation	Evaporation
It is a process by which the water vapour present in the atmosphere gets converted into water droplets or ice.	It is a process by which water vapour enters the atmosphere.
It usually occurs due to the cooling of the saturated air.	It occurs due to heating of water bodies by solar radiation.

(iii) The differences between convectional and orographic rainfall are

Convectional Rainfall	Orographic Rainfall
It is caused due to the upliftment of air due to temperature.	It is caused due to the upliftment of moisture laden wind along the mountain barrier.
It is common in the equatorial regions and interior parts of the continents, particularly in the Northern hemisphere.	It is common on the Western slope of Western Ghats (India), on the windward slope of North-East part of West Malaysia, Western New Zealand, etc.

2. Explain the following terms
(i) Absolute humidity (ii) Precipitation
(iii) Measurement of humidity

Ans. (i) Refer to short questions 2 (i).

(ii) Precipitation has been defined as water in liquid or solid form falling on the Earth under gravity. Rain, snow and hail are the common forms of precipitation. It involves the process of evaporation, condensation and saturation.

(iii) The instrument used for measuring the water vapour in the atmosphere is known as Hygrometer. Humidity measurement instruments usually rely on the measurement of some other quantities also such as temperature, pressure, etc.

3. Answer the following questions.
(i) What is condensation?
(ii) What are the conditions required for condensation to take place?

Ans. (i) The process of transformation of water vapour into water is called condensation. It is caused by the loss of heat.

(ii) Conditions required for condensation to take place are

- When the temperature of air is reduced to dew point with it volume remaining constant.
- When the moisture is added to the air through evaporation.
- When both the temperature and volume are reduced.
- Most favourable condition is the decrease in temperature.

4. Differentiate between the following
(i) Dew and frost
(ii) Snowfall and hail
(iii) Fog and mist

Ans. (i) The differences between dew and frost are

Dew	Frost
Dew is formed when the water droplets are deposited on the cooler surfaces of solid objects such as stones, grass blades, leaves, etc.	Frost is formed when condensation takes place on the cold surface below the freezing point (0°C).
For its formation, it is necessary that the dew point is above the freezing point.	For its formation, the dew point must be at or below the freezing point.

(ii) The differences between snow and hail are

Snowfall	Hail
When the precipitation occurs in the form of ice crystals, it is called snowfall.	When the precipitation occurs in the form of pellets, it is called hail.
It is generally experienced in the high latitudes and in high mountain region.	It occurs in the regions which experience strong vertical air currents.
It is hexagonal in shape.	It is generally round in shape.

(iii) The differences between fog and mist are

Fog	Mist
It is more drier.	It is less drier.
It contains thin layer of moisture.	It contains thick layer of moisture.

5. Explain the concepts of fog and dew. What are the ideal conditions required for the formation of dew?

Ans. When the temperature of air mass containing the large quantity of water vapour falls all of a sudden, condensation takes place within itself on the fine dust particles. This results in the formation of fog.

When the moisture is deposited in the form of water droplets on the cooler surfaces of solid objects such as stones, grass blades and plant leaves, it is known as dew.

Ideal conditions required for the formation of dew are clear sky, calm air, high relative humidity and cold and long nights.

6. Explain any three types of cloud in brief.

Ans. Refer to chapter theory page no. 128.

7. Explain the following
(i) Rain
(ii) Cyclonic rain
(iii) Convectional rainfall

Ans. (i) **Rain** It is precipitation in liquid state. When the resistance of the air fails to hold the water vapours against the force of gravity, they fall on the Earth's surface in the form of rain.

(ii) Refer to short questions. Q. 8 (i)

(iii) Refer to chapter theory page no. 128.

8. Give examples of different forms of rainfall.

Ans. On the basis of the origin, rainfall may be classified into three main types i.e. convectional, orographic and cyclonic rainfall. Examples of all these three forms are

(i) **Convectional Rainfall** This kind of rainfall is common in the equatorial regions and the interior parts of the continents, particularly in the Northern hemisphere.

(ii) **Orographic Rainfall** Much of the rainfall of this kind is experienced on the Western slope of Western Ghats, windward slope of the North-East part of West Malaysia, Western New Zealand and Western Scotland and the Assam hills of the Indian sub-continent.

(iii) **Cyclonic Rainfall** Winter rainfall in North-West India is a typical example of cyclonic rainfall.

Chapter Assessment

Section-I

Multiple Choice Questions

1. .... is the ratio between absolute humid of a given mass of air and maximum amount of water vapour that it can hold at the same temperature
(a) Humidity (b) Relative humidity
(c) Absolute humidity (d) Atmospheric pressure

2. In which of the following form of condensation the excess moisture is deposited in the form of minute crystals instead of water droplets?
(a) Snow (b) Frost
(c) Dew (d) Clouds

3. Which of the following types of rainfall is caused by the cumulonimbus clouds?
(a) Convectional rainfal
(b) Orographic rainfall
(c) Frontal rainfall
(d) Relief rainfall

4. Which kind of rainfall is prominient in the windward slope of North-East part of Western Malaysia?
(a) Cyclonic rainfall (b) Relief rainfall
(c) Winter rainfall (d) Frontal rainfall

Section-II

Short Questions

1. How the dampness of the atmosphere is determined?
2. In which unit the absolute humidity is determined?
3. What do you mean by
(i) Sublimation (ii) Freezing point
4. What are the ideal conditions for the formation of dew and frost?
5. How cloud is formed in the atmosphere?

Long Questions

1. What is precipitation? Briefly explain the forms of precipitation.
2. Give an account of types of rainfall.
3. Winter rain in the North-West India is a typical cyclonic rainfall. How?
4. Answer the following questions.
(i) How organphic rainfall takes place
(ii) What are the conditions for cyclonic rainfall.

CHAPTER

15

Pollution and its Sources

SYLLABUS

Pollution Types-air, water (fresh and marine), soil, radiation and noise.
• Source-Noise traffic, factories, construction sites, loudspeakers, airports.
• Air : Vehicular, industrial, burning of garbage • Water : Domestic and industrial waste.
• Soil : Chemical fertilisers, biomedical waste and pesticides. • Radiation : X-rays, radioactive fallout from nuclear plants.

Meaning of Pollution

Pollution is defined as an addition or excessive addition of certain materials to the physical environment making it less fit or unfit for life. Poor management of resources and careless human activity leads to environmental damage. Hence, pollution is the contamination of the natural environment that badly affects human health and ecosystem.

The elements, molecules and particles involved in pollution are called pollutants. They are the materials or factors, which cause adverse affect on the natural quality of the environment.

On the basis of degradation, pollutants are divided into biodegradable and non-biodegradable pollutants. Biodegradable pollutants can be degraded by biological or microbial actions while non-biodegradable pollutants cannot be degraded by these actions.

On the basis of origin, pollutants are divided into primary and secondary pollutants. Primary pollutants are those that are directly introduced into the environment while secondary pollutants are those that are formed by the chemical reaction between primary pollutants in the environment.

Types of Pollution

Air Pollution

Air pollution is the addition of harmful and injurious matter in the air which cause acute problems to the environment, human health and the quality of life.

Air pollution is **aggravated**[1] because of increasing traffic, growing cities, rapid economic development and industrialisation. Air pollution can results in poor air quality, both in cities and countryside.

Air pollution is caused by the pollutants of solid, liquid and gas particles of both organic and inorganic chemicals. Some air pollutants make people ill, causing breathing problems and increasing the likelihood of cancer. Other air pollutants are harmful to plants, animals and the eco-systems in which they live.

Many air pollutants return to the surface of the Earth in the form of acid rain which are very harmful for the buildings, statues and monuments.

1 **Aggravate** To make a problem injury, etc. more serious or severe.

Sources of Air Pollution

Vehicular Pollution

Carbon monoxide and hydrocarbons, compounds of nitrogen and oxygen are the chief pollutants of the air emitted from vehicles, aeroplanes, ships and trains.

Nitrogen oxide produced due to fuel combustion in automobiles may cause deterioration of the ozone layer. Smog is also formed due to automobile emission.

Vehicles are the major consumer of oil in the world. They emit substantial amount of carbon dioxide and other gases, which contribute to global warming. Due to expanded chlorofluorocarbons (CFCs) use in vehicles, they are playing a significant role in the stratospheric ozone depletion.

In the major metropolitan cities like Delhi, Mumbai, Kolkata and Chennai, vehicular exhaust account for 75 per cent of all CO (Carbon Monoxide), 45 per cent of all hydrocarbons CnH $(2n+2)$, 40 per cent of all oxides, e.g. CO_2, SO_2, CO, H_2O, etc and 30 per cent of all suspended particulate matter.

Industrial Pollution

Burning of coal, fuel wood, petroleum and waste which are generated and collected from industries contains sulphur and nitrogen. This waste reacts with oxygen and then further with water vapour present in the atmosphere and causes acid rain. It is very harmful for the buildings and statues, especially the valuable monuments of historic importance.

The cement manufacturing industries generate various waste particles. Carbon dioxide is produced from the coal and limestone which are used for the cement manufacturing. It creates dusty air and it is also a potential health threat. The cement factories causes huge environmental impact in all stages of the production process.

Oil refineries and petrochemical industries generates hydrocarbons, oil sludge and oil slicks that are hazardous in nature. The construction and demolition of commercial buildings like shops, offices, hotels, etc creates huge pollution. The manufacturing industries, fertilisers, pesticides and other chemical producing industries generates many environmental threatening chemicals.

Burning of Garbage

Burning of garbage from home or local area causes huge amount of smoke and releases many harmful gases which severely pollutes the atmosphere. The smoke emitted from it contains many harmful gases such as carbon dioxide, carbon monoxide, sulphur dioxide, nitrogen oxide, etc.

The open burning of garbage releases sulphur dioxide which is a chief gas, contributing in acid rain phenomena. The rise in the quantity of harmful gases like carbon dioxide lead to global warming. It causes the temperature of the atmosphere to rise and leads to melting of ice which in turn causes rise in the sea level and submergence of many small islands.

Water Pollution

The addition of chemicals, garbage or any other waste material in the water bodies which reduces the quality of the water by changing its colour, odour and composition of any degree is termed as water pollution.

Water is typically referred to as polluted when it is impaired by anthropogenic contaminants. The polluted water usually contains **pathogens**[2] like virus, bacteria, parasitic protozoa and worms. Therefore, it is a source of waterborne diseases like dysentery, polio, trachoma, malaria, jaundice, cholera, typhoid, amoebiasis, etc.

Mercury compounds in waste water are converted by bacterial action into extremely toxic methyl mercury, which can cause deafness, blurring of vision and mental unstability. Water containing cadmium can cause itai-itai disease which causes pain in bones and joints. It also causes cancer of lungs and liver. It is also known as ouch-ouch disease.

Water pollution affects the entire biosphere i.e. plants and organisms living in effected water bodies. In almost all cases, the effect is damaging not only to individual species and population, but also to the natural biological communities.

Water pollution is of two types, fresh water pollution and marine pollution.

2 **Pathogens** A bacteria, virus or other micro-organism that can cause danger.

Freshwater Pollution

It is the contamination of streams, rivers, lakes and groundwater. About 70 per cent of untreated industrial waste is dumped into freshwater bodies in most of the developing countries.

Thereby, polluting the useable water supply which become unsafe for drinking, bathing, fishing and swimming and threatened the human and marine life.

Sources of Fresh Water Pollution

Industrial Waste

The industries discharges several inorganic and organic pollutants, which may prove highly toxic to the living beings. The industrial wastes contain pollutants such as lead, mercury, sulphur, asbestos, nitrates and many other harmful chemicals.

The toxic chemicals have the capability to change the colour of water, increase the amount of minerals also known as **eutrophication**[3]. Pollutants such as arsenic, lead, mercury, fluorides, etc are released from industries which posses harmful effects on environment and human life.

Lead can enter water from many sources like the mining and smelting of lead-bearing ores and metals, disposal of lead-zinc batteries in garbage, etc.

Methyl mercury is another toxic chemical which is very damaging for human life. It contaminated the water of Minamata (Japan) which caused serious health problems. This harmful chemical was consumed by smaller fishes and crabs which was later consumed by humans. This led to a crippling and often fatal disease called **Minamata disease.**

In addition, numerous manufacturing plants drain away undiluted corrosives, poisons and other **noxious**[4] byproducts. The construction industry discharges slurries of gypsum, cement, abrasives, metals and poisonous solvents. Another pervasive group of contaminants entering food chain is the Polychlorinated Biphenyl (PCB) compounds, components of lubricants, plastic wrappers and adhesives.

Domestic and Sewage Waste

The sewage and domestic waste water that is produced by each household is chemically treated and released into sea with freshwater. The sewage water carries harmful bacteria and chemicals that can cause serious health problems.

Micro-organisms in water spread deadly diseases and become the breeding grounds for other creatures that act like carriers. These carriers inflict these diseases via various forms of contact into an individual.

The domestic waste water which is mixed with other wastes such as human faecal material, plastic, animal dung and detergents, is called **municipal waste.** In general, the major concerned pollutants of domestic waste water include suspended solids, organic matter measured as BOD (Biochemical Oxygen Demand), COD (Chemical Oxygen Demand) or TOC (Total Organic Carbon), micro-organisms, pathogens, nutrients and refractory organic matter.

Marine Pollution

It is the contamination of sea and ocean by the combination of chemicals and trash, most of which comes from land sources and is washed or blown into the ocean. This pollution results in damage to the environment, health of all organisms and to the economic structures worldwide.

The International Oceanographic Commission (IOC) of the United Nations has defined marine pollution as the introduction (directly or indirectly) of substances or energy by man to the marine environment resulting in harmful effects. These effects are hazards to human health, hindrance to marine activities, impairment of the quality of seawater for various uses and reduction of amenities.

Sources of Marine Water Pollution

The increasing urbanisation, industrialisation and the rise in pollution has threatened the life of organisms in oceans and seas.

The ships and boats often dispose plastic material which is very harmful for marine life. Around 3.25 million metric tonnes of oil is discharged annually into the sea.

3 **Eutrophication** It is the process of depletion or reduction of oxygen content from water bodies due to direct or indirect activities of human being.

4 **Noxious** Something which is very harmful to living things.

Many dangerous metals such as mercury, lead, copper as well as heavy metal are a great concern as they enter the food chain. Copper is dangerous to marine organisms and has been used in marine anti-fouling paints.

The main sources of marine pollution are

- Commerce and trade practiced in the ocean/sea.
- Effluents coming from industries and factories.
- Discarding radioactive substances into sea water.
- Riverine flows into the sea carrying pollutants from the entire catchment area.
- Global atmospheric inputs to the sea from air discharges.
- Many recreational activities including sea sports.
- Various agricultural pollutants brought to the sea by rain and rivers.

Check Your LEARNING...

1. What is pollution?
2. Mention some effects of air pollution.
3. How water is being polluted by industrial waste?
4. Mention some sources of marine pollution.

Soil Pollution

The process of degradation and deterioration of soil quality due to addition of certain solid and semi-solid wastes by agriculture practices, industrial works, household works, etc is termed as soil pollution. It is also defined as the contamination of soil with harmful substance that can adversely effect the quality of the soil.

Soil or land pollution occurs due to deposition of solid waste, accumulation of biodegradable material, toxification of chemicals into poisonous chemical compositions, etc. The pollutants remain in the soil for longer periods as compared to air and water.

Sources of Soil Pollution

Chemical Fertilisers and Pesticides

Chemical utilisation has gone up tremendously as technology has provided modern pesticides and fertilisers. They are full of chemicals that are not produced in nature and cannot be broken down by it. As a result, they seep into the ground after they mix with water and slowly reduce the fertility of the soil.

Some chemicals in fertilisers and pesticides damage the composition of the soil and make it easier to erode by water and air.

Plants absorb many of these pesticides and when they decompose, they cause soil pollution since they become a part of the land.

Biomedical Wastes

It refers to the solid or liquid waste or their byproducts including their containers generated from hospitals, clinics, pathology labs, medical colleges and industries.

Plastics, bottles, polythene bags, tubes, gloves, syringes, needles, soiled dressings, expired medicines (pills, capsules), wastes from surgery and postmortem are the hospital and biomedical wastes which when disposed off carelessly cause soil pollution.

Radioactive Pollution

The harmful level of radiations emitted by naturally occurring or artificially produced radioactive materials is called radioactive pollution. These radiations are emitted by radioactive decay of unstable heavy atoms nuclei. Exposure of these radiations can cause damage to living cells and environment.

The concern for radioactive pollution increased after the discovery of artificial radioactivity, development of nuclear weapons and installation of nuclear reactors for generating electricity.

Living organisms are continuously exposed to a variety of radiations called background radiation. If the level of the radioactive radiations increases above a certain limit, it causes harmful effects on living beings.

Sources of Radioactive Pollution

Natural Sources

The natural sources of radioactive pollution include cosmic radiations reaching on the Earth's surface from the outer space and the terrestrial radiations originating from the radioactive substances in the Earth's atmosphere.

Man-made Sources

- **Diagnostic Medical Applications** Radiations employed for diagnostic and therapeutic (therapy related) applications and X-rays used in general radiology and CT scan are some sources of radioactive pollution.
- **Nuclear Tests** Nuclear explosion tests, especially when carried out in the atmosphere are a major cause of radiation pollution. It is responsible for increasing the background level of radiation throughout the world. During atmospheric nuclear explosion tests, a number of long-lived radio nuclides are released into the atmosphere and cause severe radioactive pollution.
- **Nuclear Reactors** Radiations may leak from nuclear reactors and other nuclear facilities even when they are operating normally. Even with best design, proper handling and techniques, some radioactives are routinely released into the air and water.
- **Nuclear Wastes** The wastes of nuclear reactor emit harmful radiations. The wastes emitted by testing of nuclear weapons which involves using radioactive substance such as Plutonium-239 and Uranium-235 for **fission**[5], makes the surrounding materials radioactive.
- **Nuclear Material Processing** The processing of nuclear material is carried out to extract radioactive metals. Several compounds of radioactive elements are also produced and processed for various uses. All those who handle these materials are at a greater risk of man-made radioactive pollution.

Noise Pollution

It may be defined as regular exposure to elevated sound levels that may lead to adverse effects on humans or other living organisms. It is an unpleasant noise created by people or machines that can be annoying, distracting, intrusive and physically painful.

Sound becomes unwanted when it either interferes with normal activities such as sleeping, conversation or disrupts or diminishes one's quality of life. High noise level can result in cardiovascular effects.

Scientists also believe that besides humans animals are also affected by noise, e.g. water animals are subjected to noise by submarines and big ships on the ocean and chain-saw operations by timber companies also create extreme noise to animals in the forests.

Sound is measured in decibels (dB). An increase of about 10 dB approximately double the increase in loudness. A person's hearing can be damaged if exposed to noise level over 75 dB over a prolonged period of time. The World Health Organisation has suggested that the sound level indoors should be less than 30 dB.

Sources of Noise Pollution

Traffic and Airports

The main source of noise pollution is the rapidly increasing vehicles which led to traffic on the roads. Noise pollution is produced by movement of big trucks, vehicles and motorbikes on the road, and jet planes and helicopters **hovering**[6] over cities, if airport is nearer to the city.

Factories and Loudspeakers

The various machines and equipments installed in factories and industries and their whistling sounds, crushing noise and thundering sounds are also a source of noise pollution. Noise pollution is also caused by loudspeakers and bands used in the cities for various purposes like religious functions, marriage, elections, commercial advertising, etc.

Construction Sites

The construction and demolition of commercial buildings like shops, offices, hotels, etc create a big noise pollution which has to be minimised below prescribed limit.

Other Sources

Various gadgets like food mixers, grinder, vacuum cleaner, washing machines and dryer and cooler can create noise.

Other sources of noise pollution are agricultural equipments like tractors, harvesters, tube wells, etc and defence practices like explosions, launching of rockets, shooting practices, etc.

Check Your LEARNING...

1. How soil pollution occurs?
2. Give names of various biomedical wastes.
3. What do you know about nuclear waste?
4. What are the sources of noise pollution?

5 **Fission** The process in which the nucleus of a heavy atom is split apart.

6 **Hovering** It refers to remain in one place in the air.

QUiCK Revision

- Pollution is defined as an addition or excessive addition of certain materials to the physical environment (air, water, land, etc) making it less fit or unfit for life.
- Air pollution is the addition of harmful and injurious matter in the air which causes acute problems to the environment, human health and the quality of life.
- Some of the major air pollutants are carbon monoxide, carbon dioxide, sulphur dioxide, lead, ozone, etc.
- Chlorofluorocarbons (CFC) are gases that are released mainly from air-conditioning systems and refrigeration. The CFC molecules reacts with ozone which causes depletion of ozone layer.
- Methyl mercury is a toxic chemical which contaminated the water of Minamata (Japan) and caused a crippling disease called Minamata disease.
- Water pollution is the addition of chemicals and other waste material which makes water contaminated and unfit for use.
- The International Oceanographic Commission (IOC) of the United Nations has defined marine pollution as the introduction (directly or indirectly) of substances or energy by man to the marine environment resulting in deleterious effects such as hazards to human health, hindrance to marine activities, impairment of the quality of seawater for various uses and reduction of amenities.
- Soil pollution is the process of degradation and deterioration of soil quality due to addition of certain solid and semi-solid wastes.
- Sources of soil pollution are chemical fertilizers and pesticides, biomedical waste, garbage dumps, etc.
- The radiations emitted by naturally occurring or artificially produced radioactive materials is called radioactive pollution.
- Some sources of radioactive waste are nuclear tests, medical applications like X-rays and CT scan and waste from nuclear reactors.
- Noise pollution may be defined as the regular exposure to elevated sound levels that may lead to adverse effects in humans or other living organisms.
- Sources of noise pollution are traffic, construction sites, factories and loudspeakers.

Chapter Practice

Section-I

Multiple Choice Questions

1. .... is defined as an addition or excessive addition of certain materials to the physical environment making it less fit or unfit for life.
(a) Pollutant (b) Contamination
(c) Pollution (d) Waste

Ans. (c) Pollution

2. What is the reason behind badly affected human health and eco-system?
(a) Depression (b) Pollutants
(c) Bad health (d) Pollution

Ans. (d) Pollution

3. Which of the following types of pollution adds harmful matter into air?
(a) Air pollution (b) Water pollution
(c) Soil pollution (d) Noise pollution

Ans. (a) Air pollution

4. What is the reason behind acid rain?
(a) Water pollution (b) Noise pollution
(c) Soil pollution (d) Air pollution

Ans. (d) Air pollution

5. Consider the following statement with regard to vehicular pollution and choose the correct option.
(i) Carbon monoxide and hydrocarbons, compounds of nitrogen and oxygen are its chief sources.
(ii) It helps in the formation of smog.
(iii) Usage of CFC's in vehicle also causes vehicular pollution.
Codes
(a) (i) and (ii) (b) (ii) and (iii)
(c) (i) and (iii) (d) (i), (ii) and (iii)

Ans. (d) (i), (ii) and (iii)

6. What is the main reason behind smoke?
(a) Burning of garbage (b) Chlorofluorocarbon
(c) Limestone (d) Acid rain

Ans. (a) Burning of garbage

7. The advance incinerators releases .... which causes acid rain.
(a) sulphur dioxide (b) carbon monoxide
(c) nitrogen dioxide (d) sulphur dioxide

Ans. (d) sulphur dioxide

8. What is the reason behind causes of itai-itai or ouch-ouch disease?
(a) Water containing worms
(b) Water containing cadmium
(c) Water containing lead
(d) Water containing pathogens

Ans. (b) Water containing cadmium

9. Which of the following pollution changes the colour, odour and composition of groundwater?
(a) Marine pollution
(b) Groundwater pollution
(c) Freshwater pollution
(d) Air pollution

Ans. (c) Freshwater pollution

10. Which of the following chemical contaminated the water of minamata which caused serious health problems?
(a) Methyl mercury (b) Ethyl mercury
(c) Cadmium (d) Lead

Ans. (a) Methyl mercury

11. What is the full form of PCB compound?
(a) Polyhydrated Biphenyl
(b) Polychloride Bioenzymes
(c) Polychlorinated Biphenyl
(d) Polyhydroxide Biphenyl

Ans. (c) Polychlorinated Biphenyl

12. Consider the following statements regarding marine pollution and choose the correct option.
(i) Copper, which is used as anti-fouling paint is beneficial for the marine water bodies.
(ii) Marine pollution can be caused by discarded radioactive substances which are dumped into the oceans.
(iii) Agricultural pollutants can cause marine contamination of oceans.
Codes
(a) Only (ii) (b) (ii) and (iii)
(c) (i), (ii) and (iii) (d) Only (i)

Ans. (b) (ii) and (iii)

13. Medical wastes like blood samples and tissues, unused drugs and samples from pathological labs can cause .... pollution if they are not disposed off properly.
(a) soil (b) marine
(c) air (d) radioactive

Ans. (a) soil

14. Which of the following types of pollution are caused by nuclear tests?
(a) Noise pollution (b) Soil pollution
(c) Radioactive pollution (d) Air pollution

Ans. (c) Radioactive pollution

15. What is the example of nuclear waste?
(a) CFC (b) Sulphur dioxide
(c) Nuclides (d) Plutonium-239

Ans. (d) Plutonium-239

16. High noise level can affect .... system of human body.
(a) digestive (b) respiratory
(c) cardiovascular (d) hormonal

Ans. (c) cardiovascular

17. The World Health Organisation has suggested that the sound level in indoors should be less than .... dB.
(a) 30 (b) 85 (c) 75 (d) 60

Ans. (a) 30

18. What is the main reason behind noise pollution?
(a) Traffic and airports
(b) Factories and loudspeakers
(c) Chirping of birds and roaring of animals
(d) Both (a) and (b)

Ans. (d) Both (a) and (b)

19. Match the following.

List-I (Pollution)	**List-II** (Causes)
A. Air pollution	1. Fertilizers
B. Water pollution	2. Plutonium-235
C. Soil pollution	3. CFC
D. Radioactive pollution	4. Oils

Codes

	A	B	C	D		A	B	C	D
(a)	2	4	1	3	(b)	4	3	1	2
(c)	3	1	2	4	(d)	3	4	1	2

Ans. (d)

20. Match the following.

Pollution	**Side effect**
A. Soil pollution	1. Respiratory disease
B. Water pollution	2. Cardiovascular disease
C. Air pollution	3. Cholera, typhoid
D. Noise pollution	4. Cancer

Codes

	A	B	C	D		A	B	C	D
(a)	4	3	1	2	(b)	3	4	2	1
(c)	1	2	3	4	(d)	3	2	4	1

Ans. (a)

Section-II

Short Questions

1. (i) Define the word pollution.
(ii) How pollution is caused?

Ans. (i) Pollution is defined as an addition of certain material to the physical environment making it less fit or unfit for life.
(ii) Pollution is caused by various garbages, waste and byproducts of domestic, industries, offices, hospital, automobiles, etc.

2. (i) How carbon monoxide is produced in the atmosphere?
(ii) What are the effects of air pollution in the atmosphere?

Ans. (i) Carbon monoxide is produced by the incomplete burning of carbon-based fuels including petrol, diesel and wood.
(ii) Air pollution can result in poor air quality, both in cities and country side. Some air pollutants make people ill, causing breathing problems and increasing the likelihood of cancer.

3. What is oil spill? How it is harmful?

Ans. Oil spill is one of the most dangerous of all water pollutants. It is the leakage of oil from tankers at sea or leaks from underground storage tanks on land.

Oil spill is harmful as it is very difficult to control it because oil tends to spread very fast, affecting a large area in a very short time.

4. What are the harmful chemical contents in smoke? Which pollutant causes cancer?

Ans. The burning of waste generates smoke which contains harmful gases such as carbon dioxide, carbon monoxide, sulphur dioxide, nitrogen oxide, etc.

The pollutants which causes cancer are asbestos dust raised during the mining and manufacturing of asbestos.

5. What is water pollution? Name any two sources of water pollution.

Ans. The addition of chemicals, garbage or any other waste material in the water bodies which reduces the quality of the water by changing its colour, odour and composition of any degree is termed as water pollution.

The two sources of water pollution are industrial waste and domestic and sewage waste.

6. Answer the following questions.
(i) How lead affects human life?
(ii) Define eutrophication.

Ans. (i) Lead affects human life as it is present in petrol, diesel, lead batteries, paints, hair dye products, etc and can cause nervous system damage and digestive problems.
(ii) Eutrophication is the process of depletion or reduction of oxygen content from water bodies due to direct or indirect activities of human work.

7. Mention any three sources of marine pollution.

Ans. Three sources of marine pollution are
(i) Commerce and trade practiced in the ocean/sea.
(ii) Effluents coming from industries and factories.
(iii) Discarding radioactive substances into sea water.

8. Evaluate the negative impacts of chemical fertilizers and pesticides on soil.

Ans. The negative impacts of chemical fertilisers and pesticides on soil are

- Pesticides and fertilisers are full of chemicals that are not produced in nature and cannot be broken down by it. As a result, they seep into the ground after they mix with water and slowly reduce the fertility of the soil.
- The chemicals in pesticides and fertilisers damage the composition of the soil and make it easier to erode by water and air.

9. Mention any two sources of radiation pollution.

Ans. Sources of radiation pollution are

(i) **Diagnostic Medical Applications** Radiations are employed for diagnostic and therapeutic (therapy related) applications. X-rays are used in general radiology and CT scan.

(ii) **Nuclear Tests** Nuclear explosion tests, especially when carried out in the atmosphere are a major cause of radiation pollution. It is responsible for increasing the background level of radiation throughout the world. During atmospheric nuclear explosion tests, a number of long-lived radio nuclides are released into the atmosphere.

10. Differentiate between the natural and man-made sources of pollution.

Ans. The differences between the natural and man-made sources of pollution are

Natural Sources	Man Made Sources
These include pollutants generated naturally like forest fires, volcanic eruptions, dust storms, etc.	These are the pollutants generated by human activities like automobiles, aeroplanes, chimney houses, bricks, kilns, etc.
These are difficult to manage or control by humans.	These sources can be controlled and minimised by careful supervision of human activities.

11. Answer the following questions.

(a) What is the unit of measuring sound?

(b) How is the noise pollution caused by construction sites?

Ans. (a) Sound is measured in decibels (dB).

(b) The construction and demolition of commercial buildings like shops, offices, hotels, etc create a big noise pollution which has to be minimised below prescribed limit.

Long Questions

1. What are the major air pollutants? Explain.

Ans. Some of the major air pollutants are

- **Carbon monoxide** (CO) It is produced by the incomplete burning of carbon-based fuels including petrol, diesel and wood.
- **Carbon dioxide** (CO_2) It is the principle greenhouse gas emitted as a result of human activities such as the burning of coal, oil and natural gases.
- **Sulphur dioxide** (SO_2) It is a gas produced from burning coal, mainly in thermal power plant.
- **Lead** It is present in petrol, diesel, lead batteries, paints, hair dye products, etc.

2. Explain in brief about industrial air pollution.

Ans. Refer to chapter theory page no.135

3. How does burning of garbage affects environment?

Ans. Burning of garbage from home or local area cause huge amount of smoke and releases many harmful gases which severely pollutes the atmosphere. The smoke emitted from it contains many harmful gases such as carbon dioxide, nitrogen oxides, etc. The rise in the quantity of harmful gases like carbon dioxide lead to global warming which causes the temperature of the atmosphere to rise and leads to melting of ice which in turn causes rise in the sea-level and sub-mergence of many small islands.

4. Throw some light on the following human sources of water pollution.

(i) Industrial waste

(ii) Domestic and sewage waste

Ans. Refer to chapter theory page no. 136.

5. Explain briefly about ouch-ouch disease and Minamata disease.

Ans. Water containing cadmium can cause itai-itai disease which is also known as ouch-ouch disease. It causes pain in bones and joints and also causes cancer of lungs and liver.

Minamata disease is caused by methyl mercury a toxic chemical which contaminated the water of Minamata (Japan) that caused serious health problems. This harmful chemical was consumed by small fishes and crabs which was later consumed by humans.

This led to a crippling (a lame or partly disabled person) and often fatal disease.

6. What are the sources of marine pollution?

Ans. Refer to chapter theory page no. 136-137.

7. Briefly explain about biomedical waste.

Ans. Refer to chapter theory page no. 137.

8. (i) What are the concerns regarding radioactive pollution?

(i) What are the anthropogenic or man-made sources of radioactive pollution?

Ans. (i) The concern for radioactive pollution increased after the discovery of artificial radioactivity, development of nuclear weapons and installation of nuclear reactors for generating electricity.

Living organisms are continuously exposed to a variety of radiations called background radiation. It causes various deformity and ill effects on living beings.

(ii) Refer to chapter theory page no. 137-138.

9. (i) How does noise pollution affect us?

(ii) What are the common sources of noise pollution?

Ans. (i) Noise pollution is an unpleasant noise created by people or machines that can be annoying, distracting, intrusive and physically painful. Sound becomes unwanted when it either interferes with normal activities such as sleeping, conversation or disrupts or diminishes one's quality of life. Even water animals are subjected to noise by submarines and big ships in the ocean.

(ii) Sources of noise pollution are

- Noise pollution is produced by big trucks, vehicles and motorbikes on the road and jet planes and helicopters hovering over cities.
- The various machines and equipments installed in factories and industries and their whistling sounds, crushing noise and thundering sounds are also a source of noise pollution.
- Burning of firecracker for celebration creates sound pollution and also environmental pollution.

Chapter Assessment

Section-I

Multiple Choice Questions

1. Carbon monoxide, CFCs and hydrocarbon are the bioproducts of which of the following pollutions?
   (a) Air pollution
   (b) Soil pollution
   (c) Water pollution
   (d) Radioactive pollution
2. Which of the following statements are not related to soil pollution?
   (a) Soil pollution affects the quality of soil.
   (b) Soil pollution causes soil erosion.
   (c) Biomedical wastes such as syringes and surgical equipments deteriorates the quality of soil.
   (d) Soil pollution also effects the growth of vegetation.
3. X-rays and CT scans are responsible for which of the following pollutions?
   (a) Air pollution
   (b) Soil pollution
   (c) Radioactive pollution
   (d) Water pollution
4. .... defined as the regular exposure to elevated sound levels that may lead to adverse effect in humans or living body.
   (a) Air pollution
   (b) Noise pollution
   (c) Soil pollution
   (d) Water pollution

Section-II

Short Questions

1. Name the different sources of air pollution.
2. What is the meaning of water pollution?
3. How nuclear tests add to the source of radioactive pollution?
4. List the source of sulphur oxide, nitrogen oxide, carbon monoxide and their health effects.
5. How has industrialisation affected our environment?
6. Explain about
   (i) Minamata disease
   (ii) Sources of marine pollution

Long Questions

1. How does water get polluted from agricultural waste?
2. Why are nuclear research and experiments need to be supervised carefully?
3. How has domestic waste led to the degradation of soil?
4. Many agricultural activities has led to the pollution of soil. Explain.
5. Explain various sources of noise pollution.
6. Explain
   (i) Soil pollution and its sources
   (ii) Importance of reducing pollution

CHAPTER
16

Effects of Pollution and Preventive Measures

SYLLABUS

Pollution Effects-on the environment and human health.
• Preventive Measures- Carpools, promotion of public transport, no smoking zone, restricted use of fossil fuels, saving energy and encouragement of organic farming.

Effects of Pollution

Environment pollution is one of the severe problems being faced by both the developed as well as developing countries of the world. Pollution in our environment is affecting the normal life of human. Pollution also affects animals and marine life and also degrades the normal quality of air, water and soil.

Pollution occurs in different forms like air, water, soil, radioactive and noise. Every form of pollution has two sources of occurence i.e. the **point** and the **non-point** sources. The point sources are easy to identify, monitor and control, whereas the non-point sources are hard to control.

Effects of Air Pollution

Air pollution is harmful to the health and also impacts the environment. The pollutants which are released by air pollution is responsible for many deaths around the globe.

Effects of Air Pollution on Environment

- **Change in Composition of Air** The rapid industrialisation, human activities and also the natural calamities changes the composition of the air. The addition of undesirable and unwanted matters in the air causes harm, discomfort and **affliction**[1] to living organisms directly or indirectly.
- **Acid Rain** It is the precipitation containing harmful amounts of nitric and sulphuric acids. These acids are formed primarily by nitrogen oxides and sulphur oxides released into the atmosphere when fossil fuels are burned. In the environment, acid rain damages trees and causes soils and water bodies to acidify, making the water unsuitable for some fish and other wildlife.
- **Eutrophication** It is a condition in a water body where high concentrations of nutrients (such as nitrogen) stimulate blooms of algae, which in turn can cause fish kills and loss of plant and animal diversity. Air emissions of nitrogen oxides from power plants, cars, trucks, and other sources contribute to the amount of nitrogen entering aquatic ecosystems.
- **Crop and Forest Damage** Air pollution can damage crops and trees in a variety of ways. Ground-level ozone can lead to reductions in agricultural crop and commercial forest yields, reduced growth and survivability of tree seedlings, and increased plant susceptibility to disease, pests and other environmental stresses (such as harsh weather).

1 **Affliction** It is something (such as a disease) that causes pain or suffering.

- **Global Climate Change** The Earth's atmosphere contains a delicate balance of naturally occurring gases that trap some of the Sun's heat near the Earth's surface. This greenhouse effect keeps the Earth's temperature stable. However, humans have disturbed this natural balance by producing large amounts of some of these greenhouse gases, including carbon dioxide and methane in the atmosphere. This led to increase in temperature and global warming.

Effects of Air Pollution on Human Health

Air pollution affects everyone's health, but certain groups may be harmed more. The effects of air pollution are

- **Respiratory Disease** Air pollution can affect lung development and is implicated in the development of emphysema, asthma and other respiratory diseases such as chronic obstructive pulmonary disease. Nitrogen oxide causes chronic bronchitis. Children who play several outdoor sports and live in high ozone communities are more likely to develop asthma.
- **Cancer** Occupational exposure to benzene, an industrial chemical and component of gasoline, can cause leukemia and is associated with **non-Hodgkin's Lymphoma**[2].
- **Neurological Disease** Air pollution was linked to a greater chance of developing several neurological disorders, including Parkinson's disease, Alzheimer's disease and other mental illnesses.
- **Cardiovascular Diseases** Air pollution can also have an inflammatory effect on the heart as it can elevate blood pressure and aggravate pre-existing conditions of the heart. The risk of death significantly increases with long term exposure to polluted air. For instance, people susceptible to heart disease are at higher risk.

The pollutants of air pollution also have some negative impacts on human health such as

- **Carbon Monoxide** It lowers the amount of oxygen that enters in the blood of a person.
- **Lead** It affects children in particular. It can cause nervous system damage and digestive problems.
- **Sulphur Dioxide** It causes smog and acid rain. It can lead to lung diseases.
- **Ozone** It is a pollutant at the ground level, with highly toxic effects. Vehicles and industries are the major sources of ground-level ozone emission. It lowers human's resistance to cold and pneumonia.

Effects of Water Pollution

Water pollution has been a great contributor to a wide range of health problems and disorders in humans. It also have negative impacts on the environment. The effects of water pollution are varied and depend on what chemicals are dumped.

Effects of Water Pollution on Environment

- **Contamination of the Food Chain** Fishing in polluted waters and the use of waste water for livestock farming and agriculture can introduce toxins into food which are harmful to a person's health when eaten.
- **Lack of Potable Water** Many people around the world have no access to clean water to drink or sanitation, particularly in rural areas.
- **Eutrophication** Chemicals in a water body encourage the growth of algae. These algae form a layer on top of the pond or lake. Bacteria feed on this algae and this decreases the amount of oxygen in the water body, severely affecting the aquatic life there.
- **Death of Aquatic Animals** Industrial wastes result in the addition of poisonous chemicals such as arsenic, mercury, cadmium, lead, etc which effects the aquatic organisms. These chemicals may reach the human body through using seafood for consumption.
- **High Temperature** Hot waste water released from power stations increases the temperature of water resources, reduces its oxygen level and makes it incapable of supporting life.
- **Biomagnification** It is the rise in concentration of various toxic substances like mercury, arsenic, DDT, etc in the food chain. These sustances are consumed by the organisms through the food. When the organisms in the higher food chain feed on these organisms, the toxic substances accumulated in the higher organisms. This concentration of toxic substances at higher trophic level is called bioaccumulation.

2 **Non-Hodgkin's Lymphoma** It is a cancer of the immune system.

- **Oil Spill** It takes place due to accidents of ships, sinking of oil tanker; leaking of pipelines, etc. Offshore drilling i.e. extracting resources, like oil and gas involves environmental risks. Oil spills spread immediately, block sunlight and reduce the amount of oxygen in water resulting into the death of marine organism. Spills even pollute the beaches and coastal marine life.

Effects of Water Pollution on Human Health

Drinking or using polluted water can result in health problems such as digestive issues, toxicity and death, or chronic toxicity and neurological issues from more serious chemical pollution.

There are various waterborne diseases which are

- **Jaundice** It is caused due to polluted water.
- **Cholera** It is caused by consuming dirty and contaminated water.
- **Diarrhoea** It is a severe intestinal disorder due to polluted water.
- **Typhoid** It is caused due to polluted water.
- **Hepatitis** It is caused by virus in the water.

The various chemical components of water which affects human health are

- **Mercury** Its compounds in waste water are converted into extremely toxic methyl mercury by bacterial action, which can cause numbness of limbs, lips and tongue, deafness, blurring of vision and mental derangement. Methyl mercury may also cause a disease called Minamata disease, which is a form of mercury poisoning.
- **Pathogens** It is a type of bacteria (or a virus) that causes disease. Waterborne pathogens are the most common cause of illness in humans from polluted water. Diseases from the consumption of contaminated water include giardia, typhoid, and cholera.
- **Cadmium** It causes cancer of lungs and liver.
- **Nitrate** Its presence in excess in drinking water may cause a disease called methamoglobinemia or blue baby syndrome.
- **Fluoride** It causes fluorosis neuro muscular disorders, gastro-intestinal problems, hunchback, stiffness of bone joints and dental fluorosis.
- **Lead** It is harmful to both central and peripheral nervous system. It causes anaemia, headache and loss of muscle power.
- **Arsenic** It causes diarrhoea, peripheral, neuritis, hyperkeratosis and lung and skin cancer.
- **Pesticides** It leads to turn chromosomal alternations, brain damage, impotency and cancer.

Effects of Soil Pollution

Soil is the upper layer of the Earth's crust, which is formed by weathering of rocks. During the time of cultivation, the soil is treated with various fertilisers, pesticides, insecticides, fungicides, etc which disturb the natural process taking place in soil.

Most of the insecticides and pesticides remain active for years and tend to accumulate in soil. This was absorbed by the plants growing there. When human beings consume these plants these pollutant reach to them. Soil pollution by various chemicals and organic materials produce various environmental problems as well as health hazards for humans.

Effects of Soil Pollution on Environment

- **Reduces Growth of Plants** The ecological balance of any system gets affected due to the widespread contamination of the soil. Most plants are unable to adapt when the chemical composition of the soil changes so radically in a short period of time. Fungi and bacteria found in the soil that bind it together begin to decline, which creates an additional problem of soil erosion.
- **Decreases Fertility of Soil** The fertility of the soil slowly diminishes, making land unsuitable for agriculture and any local vegetation to survive. The soil pollution causes large tracts of land to become hazardous to health. Such land cannot support most forms of life.
- **Changes in Soil Structure** The death of many soil organisms (e.g. earthworms) in the soil can lead to alteration in soil structure. Apart from that, it could also force other predators to move to other places in search of food.
- **Poisoning of the Underground Water Table** Soil pollution also leads to the poisoning of the underground water table. Since this water is stored beneath the layers of the soil, the toxins in the soil could easily percolate slowly and steadily into the water table.

Effects of Soil Pollution on Human Health

- The contaminants found in polluted soil can enter human body through nose, mouth or skin and can cause a variety of short-term health problems like headache, chestpain, cough, nausea and sking or eye irritation.

- Long term exposure to polluted soil can affect the genetic make-up of the body, causing congenital illnesses and chronic health problems that cannot be cured easily.
- Use of human and animal excreta manure pollutes the soil. Excreta contains pathogens that contaminates the soil and crops and affect the health of humans.

Effects of Noise Pollution

Noise pollution interferes with normal activities such as sleeping, conversation or disrupts or diminishes one's quality of life. The effects of noise pollution are

Effect of Noise Pollution on Environment

- Thousands of oil drills, **sonars**[3], seismic survey devices, coastal recreational watercraft and shipping vessels are now occupying the oceans which is a serious cause of noise pollution for marine life.
- The buildings and material may get damaged by exposure to infrasonic/ultrasonic waves and even get collapsed.
- The loud noise can cause cracks in national and archaeological monuments. Very high levels of noise are the cause of cracks in hills.

Effects of Noise Pollution on Human Health

- **Annoyance** Noise pollution creates annoyance to the receptors due to sound level fluctuations.
- **Physiological Effects** The physiological blood pressure, heart-beat rate, pulse rate, blood cholesterol are affected by noise pollution.
- **Loss of Hearing** Long exposure to high sound levels causes hearing loss. This is mostly unnoticed, but has an adverse impact on hearing functions.
- **Human Performance** The working performance of workers/humans will be affected as noise distracts the concentration.
- **Nervous System** Noise pollution causes pain ringing in the ears and feeling of tiredness, thereby affecting the functioning of human system.
- **Sleeplessness** Noise pollution affects the sleeping thereby inducing people to become restless and loose concentration and presence of mind during their activities.
- **Interference with Communications** Noise pollution causes disturbance while we communicate with other people.

Effects of Radiation

The effects of radiation on environment and human health are

Effects of Radiation on Environment

- Radiations emitting from radioactive materials and the disposal of radioactive wastes cause pollution and damage to the environment.
- Radioactive material in soil can prevent nutrient from being taken in by plants, causing it to be infertile.
- The effects of nuclear radiation can sometimes change the biodiversity of an area completely.

Effects of Radiation on Human Health

- Exposure to high amounts of radiation almost generate serious and chronic disease such as cancer which is the most common radiation induced disease or immediate death.
- Serious life-threatening disease may develop even from exposure to small amounts of radiation.
- Thyroid tumors/cancer may also develop due to effect of radioactive iodine that accumulates in the thyroid.
- Radiation causes genetic disorders, which may carry on from one generations to another.

Check Your LEARNING...

1. What happen to living organism by the effect of air pollution?
2. Mention any two problems caused by water pollution.
3. Mention any two effects of soil pollution.
4. What are the effects of noise pollution?
5. What are the effects of radioactive iodine?

Preventive Measures

Following are the measures that can be adopted to reduce the pollution

Car Pools

Car pooling is also known as car sharing. It means a number of people using a single car for their journey or travel instead of using individual cars if going on the same destination.

3 **Sonars** A system for the detection of objects under water by emitting sound pulses.

The main advantages of car pooling are

- **Reduced Carbon Emission** When people start car-pooling, fewer cars run on the road every day which means fewer carbon emissions into the air. A reduced amount of carbon emissions will help reduce air pollution as well.
- **Reduced Traffic** Reduced number of vehicles means less traffic on the road and people will reach their destinations on time. Sitting in traffic for long hours make individuals irritated and bored. Most importantly, it delays the arrival at the destination.
- **Allows Saving** Car pooling is an excellent way to save money and time. One can save money from the costs of travelling, including the fuels of cars. Time will also be saved, as there will be less traffic.
- **Fuel Costs will Reduce** If the number of cars goes less on roads, the demand for fuels will also decrease, and the reduced demand will not raise the fuel prices much.
- **An Opportunity to Socialise** Many people who work together do not get a chance to socialise much because they do not get the time or may not get the chance to do so. Car pooling together will allow them to spend time and socialise with each other.

Promotion of Public Transport

It offers alternative modes of transport. It is one of the best measures to reduce pollution arising out of vehicles on road, thus reducing traffic congestion in the cities and metropolitans. People should also be encouraged to use the public transport as means of primary mode to travel.

The main advantages of using public transportation are

- **Improves Fuel Efficiency** One of the most technical benefits of public transportation is the ability to outfit buses and other public transit vehicles with alternative fuel sources. Some systems are completely electric or utilise renewable resources for fuel.
- **Reduces Air Pollution** Public transportation reduces air pollution as if people use public transport, there will be less number of vehicles on roads and less fuel is burned which means better air quality for cities.
- **Improves Road Congestion** More people travelling from buses, trains and other public systems means there are fewer vehicles on the road to cause traffic.
- **Improves Community Mobility** Inter-city transit systems help travellers move throughout the area regardless of the area they live in. Many people do not have the capability to drive, so public transportation is sometimes the only option to help them get to their destination.
- **Improves Commuters Productivity** The travellers of public transportation have the ability to be more productive with their time during their commute. People can sleep, read and relax on their way to work while travelling from public transportation.

No Smoking Zones

Smoking is another means of increasing pollution affecting public health. This not only affects the smokers, but also the people around them who are not smoking and are called **passive smokers**. It causes heart disease, lung cancer, chronic bronchitis, asthma, etc.

The ill-effects of smoking can be eliminated or minimised if no smoking zones are created or marked. The closed spaces like offices, hospitals, restaurants, public malls, public transport, busy crossing, etc must be included in these zones and adequate signage must be put there. The law on prohibiting smoking in public places must be strictly followed.

The main advantages of no smoking zones are

- It reduces the possibility of second-hand tobacco smoke being inhaled by non-smokers.
- It reduces air pollution as areas which have prohibited smoking have been found to have better indoor air quality as compared to areas where smoking is allowed.
- It reduces healthcare costs by reducing the chances of diseases caused by smoking.
- It reduces the chances of influencing others, especially the youth, to take on the habit of smoking.

Restricted Use of Fossil Fuel

Fossil fuel comprises of coal, natural gas and mineral oil which are the world's primary and most important source of energy. When it is burnt to derive energy, it emits carbon dioxide (CO_2) in large quantities which causes global warming and led to acid rain. It can lead to kidney damage, reduces development of RBC and causes pulmonary malfunction.

Fossil fuels are also non-renewable source of energy and their continuous or unrestricted use will completely exhaust them. Thus, it is important to restrict their use for causing minimum impact and protect them for future generation. Their should be continuous research and promotion of renewable sources of energy as an alternative to fossil fuels. This will protect environment and reduce pollution.

Saving Energy

Saving energy will help to reduce consumption of fossil fuels. The following measures can help to save energy

- **Use of Renewable Sources of Energy** The use of renewable energy will help to save energy thereby to save natural resources. It can be obtained from the following
  - **Solar Energy** This is a great source of energy which can be generated and converted into electricity without causing any pollution. Countries like India, Pakistan, Bangladesh and many African countries can generate such energy in abundance due to the presence of solar energy in abundance. It can be used for lighting, water heating, cooking as well as can be put through in the power grid.
  - **Wind Energy** This is another source of energy to generate electricity which can be used for various purposes. Wind is used to move a wind mill and run electrical generators.
  - **Biogas** It is the most important energy in rural areas. Biogas plants produce enriched fertilisers as a by-product. The use of biogas improves sanitation and provide smokeless and efficient cooking fuel. It can also be used for power generation and lighting.
- **Turning off the Lights** A basic habit to develop and foster is to make sure to always turn off the lights when leaving a room. It can save a good percentage of a person's monthly electricity costs by doing this regularly.
- **Use LED Lights** Many homes are moving towards smart LED lights as they save more energy and are affordable. They are also way more efficient than halogen bulbs.
- **Using Efficient Appliances** Dryers and refrigeratiors are of the most energy-intensive appliances in a home and replacing these with better efficient models can cut the electricity usage by half, thereby reducing electricity bills. Installing heat pumps is another idea to reduce electricity consumption. In general, maintaining and replacing appliances every few years, will make less burden on electricity usage.
- **Unplug Devices** Unrequired devices should not be leaved on standby mode, but rather should be unplugged to save electricity.
- **Lessen Water Usage** Some easy steps to reduce water consumption could be, taking quick showers, using the required amount of water while cooking and turning off running taps when unused even for seconds.
- **Keep the Thermostat at a Lower Temperature** Keeping the thermostat at a lower temperature around 17 degrees, can make a big difference and save energy costs. Using a programmable smart thermostat is even better.
- **Use Smart Automated Devices** Smart automated devices can lower the energy bills as they will detect that a person is no longer using a device and turn off the power supply.
- **Use Double Glazing Door** Double glazing doors and windows are a perfect solution for a modern home as they can significantly reduce the emissions of greenhouse gases from heating and cooling, thereby reducing a person's carbon footprint and also lowering energy bills.
- **Cook with the Lid on Utensil** It will lessen the cooking time and water usage significantly.
- **Using Smart Meter** A smart meter is a great way to see how much power a person is consuming, which will help him keep a track of his consumption in real-time and where he can reduce it.
- **Washing at Low Temperature** Washing clothes at a cooler temperature and with a full load, can save a lot of water and electricity.
- **Solar-Powered Devices** These days solar-powered version of almost all electronics are available. Making small shifts and using more solar-powered electronics can go a long way and can also lower the maintenance and replacement costs of such electronics.

Encouragement of Organic Farming

Organic farming is a technique which involves production of food and fiber in natural ways without the use of synthetic substances. It is a system of cultivation with the help of integrated pest management, integrated nutrient supply and integrated natural resources management systems.

The features of organic farming are

- It aims at increasing productivity while reducing the production cost and minimising the environmental impact of farming.
- It aims at keeping mutual relationships between agricultural productivity and conservation of nature.
- It aims to bring together agricultural development and conservation of bio-diversity in the same landscapes.
- It relies on ecologically balanced agricultural principles like usage of organic waste, biological waste control, green manure, crop rotation, etc.
- The fertilisers and pesticides used in organic farming are bio-pesticides obtained from plant and animal waste and mineral sources.
- Organic manure used in organic farming improves structure aeration, water holding capacity of soils and reduces phosphorus fixation in acidic soil. For this, crop residue are to be left in the field for decomposition and this process is known as **bio-fertilisation.**

The advantages of organic farming are

- **Reduces Pesticides** Organic farming minimises the use of pesticides and chemicals, thereby reducing the major environmental issues. It ensures the health of soil, water, air and flora and fauna. It also reduces the major environmental issues like soil erosion, air pollution, water pollution, etc
- **Reduces Global Warming** The continuous use of organic farming practices reduces the carbon dioxide content in air and helps in slow climate change.
- **Control Water Pollution** Organic farming ensures water conservation and controls water pollution. It helps in keeping water supplies unpolluted and clean by stopping polluted chemical and pesticides runoff.
- **Preserves Animal Health** Pesticides and chemical sprays disturb and destroy the natural habitat of majority of insects, birds, fishes, etc. Thus, organic farming helps in preserving the natural habitat along with encouraging birds and other natural predators to live happily in the farmland which acts like natural pest control.
- **Encourages Bio-diversity** By encouraging organic farming, natural plants, insects, birds and animals will survive and be abundant in the natural environment, thereby maintaining the ecological balance.

Check Your LEARNING...

1. What do you mean by car pooling?
2. Mention any one preventive measure for minimising pollution?
3. What is the importance of biogas?
4. What is the aim of organic farming?

QUiCK Revision

- Environmental pollution is one of the severe problems being faced by the world community.
- The rapid industrialisation, human activities and also the natural calamities has changed the composition of the air which results in environmental hazards to the living being on the Earth.
- Air pollution increases global warming. It impacts human health and causes respiratory diseases.
- Ozone is an important gas which shields the Earth from the harmful UV rays of the Sun. However at the ground level, it is a pollutant with highly toxic effects.
- Vehicles and industries are the major sources of ground-level ozone emissions.
- Water pollution reduces drinkable water and reduces oxygen level in water bodies which impact marine life.
- Jaundice, cholera, diarrhoea, typhoid, hepatitis are some common diseases which occur due to contaminated water.
- Drinking contaminated water can cause digestive issues and other health problems.
- Methyl mercury might cause a disease called Minamata disease which is a form of mercury poisoning.
- Pesticides leads to tumours, chromosomal alteration, brain damage, impotency and cancer.
- Soil pollution reduces the soil fertility and increases erosion.
- Soil pollution reduce the growth of plant, decrease soil fertility, make underground water poisonous and changes soil structure.
- Some of the common effects of noise pollution are annoyance, loss of hearing, physiological effects, human performance, sleeplessness and interference with communications.
- Some of the preventive measures to reduce pollution are car pooling, promotion of public transport, no smoking zones, restricted use of fossil fuel, saving energy and encouragement of organic farming.
- Long term exposure to soil pollution can affect the genetic make-up of the body.
- Noise pollution highly effects marine life and other environment, as it causes irritation and mental health problems in them.
- Noise pollution affects the hearing, heart rate, blood pressure and mental health of humans.

Chapter Practice

Section-I

Multiple Choice Questions

1. The ....sources of pollution are hard to control.
   (a) point
   (b) non-pollutant
   (c) pollutant
   (d) non-point

Ans. (d) non-point

2. What is the reason behind changing composition of air ?
   (a) Industrialisation
   (b) Inhale and exhale of gases by plants and animals.
   (c) Natural calamities
   (d) Both (a) and (c)

Ans. (d) Both (a) and (c)

3. Which of the following gases can not be categorised under greenhouse gases ?
   (a) Oxygen
   (b) Methane
   (c) Nitrogen oxide
   (d) CFC

Ans. (a) Oxygen

4. Which of the following chemicals are responsible for causing non-Hodkins Lymphoma ?
   (a) Lead (b) Arsenic
   (c) Benzene (d) Methane

Ans. (c) Benzene

5. .... is an important gas which shields the Earth from harmful UV rays radiated from the Sun.
   (a) Oxygen (b) Carbon dioxide
   (c) Ozone (d) CFC

Ans. (c) Ozone

6. What is the reason behind oil spillage ?
   (a) Accidents of ships
   (b) Leaking of pipeline
   (c) Secretion of oils by marine organism
   (d) Both (a) and (b)

Ans. (d) Both (a) and (b)

7. Which of the following diseases are not caused by water pollution ?
   (a) Typhoid
   (b) Chickenpox
   (c) Hepatitis
   (d) Giardia

Ans. (b) Chickenpox

8. Consider the following statement regarding impact of water pollution on human health and choose the correct option.
   (i) Polluted water can cause jaundice, cholera typhoid and hepatitis.
   (ii) Polluted water contains arsenic which can cause neuritis, hyperkeratosis and lung cancer.
   (iii) Polluted water can cause Eutrophication.
   Codes
   (a) (i) and (iii)
   (b) (i) and (ii)
   (c) (i), (ii) and (iii)
   (d) (ii) and (iii)

Ans. (b) (i) and (ii)

9. Which of the following statements are not associated with consequences of soil pollution on environment.
   (a) Soil pollution decreases fertility of soil.
   (b) Soil pollution changes the structure of the soil.
   (c) Soil pollution can affect the genetic makeup of the body.
   (d) Soil pollution reduces the growth of plants.

Ans. (c) Soil pollution can affect the genetic makeup of the body.

10. What is the reason behind migration of animals to other places in the search of food ?
    (a) Change in soil structure.
    (b) Decreased fertility of soil.
    (c) Toisoning of the underground water table.
    (d) Chronic health problems of animal.

Ans. (a) Change in soil structure.

11. .... pollution reduces the concentration power and performances of the human body.
    (a) Soil (b) Noise (c) Water (d) Air

Ans. (b) Noise

12. What is the reason behind noise pollution in seas and oceans.
    (a) Coastal recreational watercraft
    (b) Shipping vessels
    (c) Huge noise created by aquatic animals
    (d) Both (a) and (b)

Ans. (d) Both (a) and (b)

13. .... pollution causes genetic disorders which may carry on year after year for generations.
    (a) Noise (b) Soil
    (c) Radioactive (d) Water

Ans. (c) Radioactive

14. Consider the following statements regarding preventive measures for controlling pollution and choose the correct option.
(i) Car pooling is an effective measure to control pollution as it helps in reduction of carbon dioxide and carbon monoxide.
(ii) Public transportation are to be used as it reduces air pollution.
(iii) Fossil fuels are to be used in large numbers as it helps in diminishing the ultra violet rays.

Codes
(a) Only (i)
(b) (ii) and (iii)
(c) (i) and (iii)
(d) (i) and (ii)

Ans. (d) (i) and (ii)

15. Which of the following is not the merit of biogas ?
(a) Improved sanitation
(b) Efficient cooking fuel
(c) Power generation
(d) Running wind mills

Ans. (d) Running wind mills

16. ....is a technique which involves production of food and fiber in natural ways without use of synthetic substances.
(a) Inorganic farming
(b) Organic farming
(c) Rotational farming
(d) Mixed farming

Ans. (b) Organic farming

17. What is the reason behind more and more implementation of organic farming practice ?
(a) It reduces use of pesticides.
(b) It increases global warming.
(c) It deteriorates human health.
(d) It discourages bio-diversity.

Ans. (a) It reduces use of pesticides.

18. Match the following.

Chemicals	Diseases
A. Cadmium	1. Neutritis
B. Nitrate	2. Hunchback
C. Fluoride	3. Lung Cancer
D. Arsenic	4. Blue Bay Syndrome

Codes

	A	B	C	D
(a)	1	2	3	4
(b)	2	3	1	4
(c)	3	4	2	1
(d)	4	1	2	3

Ans. (c)

19. Match the following.

Chemicals	Diseases
A. Air	1. Genetic disorder
B. Water	2. Respiratory diseases
C. Soil	3. Sleeplessness
D. Noise	4. Biomagnification
E. Radioactive	5. Eutrophication

Codes

	A	B	C	D	E
(a)	2	4	5	3	1
(b)	2	5	4	3	1
(c)	3	4	5	1	2
(d)	1	3	4	2	5

Ans. (b)

Section-II

Short Questions

1. (i) What do you mean by environment pollution?
(ii) What are the common forms of pollutants which affect our life?

Ans. (i) Environment pollution is one of the severe problems being faced by both the developed as well as developing countries. The environment, when appeared to be get polluted by various pollutants and caused various diseases, is called environment pollution.
(ii) Gases and smoke in the air, chemical and other substances in water and solid wastes on land are common forms of pollutants which affects our daily life.

2. How is pollution affecting our normal life?

Ans. Pollution of our environment is affecting the normal life of human, animals and marine life as it is degrading the quality of air we breathe, water we drink and soil we live upon.

3. State any one negative consequence of air pollution on the environment.

Ans. Burning of coal in power stations, vehicles on road and factory chimneys produces sulphur dioxide and nitrogen oxide. These oxides react with water vapour present in the air and form acids such as sulphuric acid and nitric acid. These often fall in the form of acid rain which is very harmful for both human life, agriculture and buildings.

4. How has air pollution affected our life?

Ans. Air pollution has affected the human health and environment by contaminating the air. Air pollution causes respiration diseases and effects the lungs of humans. Some pollutants like sulphur dioxide, Nitrogen oxide can cause nural diseases. Pollution in air also affects the plant growth, life of animals and birds.

5. What are the common problems caused by pollution in water?

Ans. The pollution in water can cause the following problems

- It kills life that depends on water bodies.
- It causes diseases by various micro-organisms.
- It disrupts the normal foodchain.

6. Write the negative impact of fluoride and lead which are components of water pollutants.

Ans. Fluoride causes fluorosis, neuromuscular disorders, gastro-intestinal problems, hunchback, stiffness of bone joints and dental fluorosis.

Lead is harmful to both the central and peripheral nervous system. It causes anaemia, headache and loss of muscle power.

7. What are the effects of soil pollution on agriculture?

Ans. The effects of soil pollution on agriculture are

- It reduces soil fertility.
- It reduces nitrogen fixation.
- It increases soil erosion.
- It reduces crop yield.

8. How does environment get affected by soil pollution?

Ans. The soil pollution has following effects on the environment

- It reduces vegetation.
- It creates ecological imbalances.
- It causes imbalance in soil fauna and flora.

9. How has soil pollution brought changes in health of humans?

Ans. The soil pollution has brought the following changes in health of human being

- It causes bio-magnification.
- It releases pollutant gases which caused various diseases.
- It releases radioactive rays causing health problems.

10. Briefly explain the impacts of noise pollution.

Ans. The impacts of noise pollution are

- It creates annoyance to the public.
- It creates loss of hearing.
- It causes many physiological effects.
- It causes sleeplessness.

11. Mention the side effects of radiation on human health.

Ans. The side effects of radiation on human health are

- Radiation causes genetic disorders which may carry on year after year for generations.
- Exposure to high amounts of radiation almost generates serious and chronic disease such as cancer which is the most common radiation induced disease or immediate death.

12. State anyone advantage of car pooling

Ans. An advantage of car pooling is reduced carbon emission. When people start car pooling, fewer cars run on the road every day, which means fewer carbons being released into the air. A reduced amount of carbon emissions will help reduce air pollution as well.

13. (i) What comprises fossil fuels?

(ii) State any one side effect of fossil fuel.

Ans. (i) Fossil fuels comprises coal, natural gas and mineral oil.

(ii) Fossil fuels cause global warming as it emits carbon dioxide in large quantities.

14. Write any two measures for saving energy at homes.

Ans. Two measures for saving energy at homes are

(i) Switching off lights, fans and other electrical appliances when not in use.

(ii) By seeing that electrical devices are operating efficiently. For example, defrosting refrigerator regularly and not keeping the refrigerator door open for longer than necessary.

15. (i) What do you understand by organic farming?

(ii) State one positive impact of organic farming on the environment.

Ans. (i) Organic farming is a technique which involves production of food and fiber in natural ways without the use of synthetic substances.

(ii) One positive impact of organic farming is that it involves use of organic manure which improves structure aeration, water holding capacity of soils and reduces phosphorus fixation in acidic soil.

16. (i) How can alternative fuel vehicles reduce air pollution?

(ii) In what way government can abate pollution?

Ans. (i) Alternative fuel vehicles reduce air pollution as these fuels like hydrogen, methane, methanol and CNG are low polluting and burns efficiently.

(ii) Government must have a very comprehensive approach to execute the required rules and regulation for common people in order to combat the problems of pollution. Government must focus on preventive aspects of pollution control and also promote technological inputs to minimise industrial pollutants which are emitted in the air.

17. How can public awareness and participation help in abating pollution?

Ans. Public must be made aware about judicious use of pesticides, fertilisers and detergents. Installation of proper sewage disposal methods must be ensured to abate pollution. Public must buy recycled products like paper bags, etc. Environment friendly goods must be used and harmful products like plastics must be discarded by the people.

Long Questions

1. What are the impacts of various air pollutants on human health?

Ans. The air pollutants has very serious impacts on human health which are

- **Carbon Monoxide** It lowers the amount of oxygen that enters the blood of a person.
- **Lead** It causes damage in nervous system.
- **Sulphur Dioxide** It causes lung diseases.
- **Ozone** It causes cold and pneumonia.
- **Suspended Particulate Matter** It can lodge in our lungs and cause lung damage and respiratory problems.

2. What are the various waterborne diseases?

Ans. The various waterborne diseases are

- **Jaundice** It is caused due to polluted water.
- **Cholera** It is caused by contaminated water.
- **Diarrhoea** It is a severe intestinal disorder due to polluted water.
- **Typhoid** It is caused by dirty water.
- **Hepatitis** It is caused by virus in the water.

3. What are the effects of various chemical components found in water?

Ans. The effects of various chemical components present in water are

- **Mercury** It causes numbness of limbs, lips and tongue, deafness and blurring of vision.
- **Cadmium** It causes cancer of lungs and liver.
- **Nitrate** It causes a disease called blue baby syndrome.
- **Lead** It causes anaemia, headache, loss of muscle power.
- **Arsenic** It causes diarrhoea and skin cancer.

4. How can we control the gaseous pollutants? Explain.

Ans. The gaseous pollutants from the air can be removed or regulated if we take some adequate measures. They are

- Carbon monoxide installation of catalytic converts in vehicle engines can help to convert CO to CO_2 and water.
- Sulphur dioxide restriction and control on the burning of coal and oil can reduce the emission of SO_2.
- Oxides of nitrogen can be diffused and scattered by constructing taller chimneys and factories.
- Incomplete burning of fuels must be avoided. Complete oxidation of hydrocarbons to carbon dioxide and water must be ensured.

5. What are the effects of radiation on human health?

Ans. The effects of radiation on human health are

- The exposure to high amount of radiation almost always generate serious and chronic diseases such as cancer, which is the most common radiation induced disease.
- Thyroid tumors may also develop due to the effect of radioactive iodine that accumulates in the thyroid.
- It causes genetic disorders which may carry on year after year for generations.

6. What are the main preventive measures to combat pollution? What is its aim?

Ans. The following are the preventive measures that can be adopted to combat the pollution

- Car pooling
- Promotion of public transport
- No smoking zone
- Restricted use of fossil fuel
- Saving energy
- Encouragement of organic farming

The aim of preventive measures is to reduce the pollution before its widespread.

7. Differentiate between physical effects and biological effects of pollution.

Ans. The physical effects of pollution are those that we can see, but they also include effects other than the actual physical damage. Burning oil and coal produce sulphur oxides, which cause steel to erode two to four times faster than normal. It also speeds the erosion of statues and buildings which in some instances, destroys work of art.

On the other hand, the most serious result of pollution is its harmful biological effects on human health and the foodchain of animals, birds and marine organism. It can destroy vegetation that provides food and shelter. It can seriously disrupt the balance of nature and in extreme cases, can cause the death of living beings. The widespread use of pollutants, such as soil chemicals and fertilisers pollutes our waterways. The biological effect of water pollution cause danger to our water supply and is also dangerous to all forms of marine life.

8. What is car pooling? How is it beneficial to reduce pollution?

Ans. Refer to chapter theory page no. 147 and 148.

9. Write short notes on the following.
(i) Public transport (ii) No smoking zone
(iii) Solar energy

Ans. (i) **Public Transport** It includes bus, metro-rail, railways, etc which is provided by the government on reasonable rate. It offers alternative mode of transport. It is one of the best measures to reduce pollution arising out of vehicles on road, thus reducing traffic congestion and the authority must improve the same in all cities and metros. People should also be encouraged to use the same as a means of primary mode of travel.

(ii) Refer to chapter theory page no. 148.

(iii) **Solar Energy** This is a great source of energy which can be generated and converted into electricity without causing any pollution. Tropical countries like India, Pakistan, Bangladesh and many African countries, etc can generate such energy in abundance. It can be used for lighting, water heating, cooking as well as can be put through in the power grid.

10. Write down the measures for protection of energy in our homes.

Ans. Refer to chapter theory page no. 149.

Chapter Assessment

Section-I

Multiple Choice Questions

1. .... lowers the amount of oxygen that enters in the blood of a person.
(a) CFC (b) CO_2
(c) Ozone (d) Carbonmonoxide

2. Which of the following term signifies the formation of algae on the top of a lake or a pond?
(a) Biomagnification (b) Derangement
(c) Eutrophication (d) Pollution

3. Which of the following pollution causes poisoning of the underground water table ?
(a) Noise pollution (b) Air pollution
(c) Soil pollution (d) Radioactive pollution

4. Which of the following statements are not associated with the preventive measures for controlling pollution?
(a) Car pooling
(b) Increased use of fossil fuels
(c) No smoking zones
(d) Promotion of public transport

Section-II

Short Questions

1. Explain how environmental pollution is the reflection of careless waste management.
2. What does healthy environment depend upon?
3. Mention any two effects of air pollution.
4. What is the effect of lead and sulphur dioxide on human health?
5. Give any two effects of water pollution.
6. What are the effects of radiation?
7. Explain the following terms
(i) Oil Spill
(ii) Eutrophication

Long Questions

1. How has careless littering by the public disturbed the compositions of the atmosphere?
2. How can preservation of forest help in combating pollution?
3. Explain the role of solar and wind energy in reducing the consumption of fossil fuels.
4. What is the effect of long-term exposure to contaminated soil?
5. Explain the following
(i) Effects of air pollution on human health.
(ii) Effects of water pollution on human health.
6. Describe the following
(i) Car pooling will reduce carbon emission.
(ii) Encouragement of organic farming will reduce soil pollution.

CHAPTER

17

Natural Regions of the World

SYLLABUS

Natural Regions of the World Location, area, climate, natural vegetation and human adaptation. • Equatorial region, Tropical Grasslands, Tropical Deserts, Tropical Monsoon, Mediterranean, Temperate Grasslands, Taiga and Tundra.

The structure, surface form and climate within the Earth's surface which has comparatively high degree of uniformity is called a natural region. A natural region is a homogeneous unit which has uniformity in its climatic conditions, soil, natural vegetation and human activities.

Classification of Natural Regions of the World

Every natural region of the world has a combination of different climatic element as compared to other. Thus, on the basis of climate, the world is divided into different natural regions which are

(i) Equatorial region (ii) Tropical Grasslands
(iii) Tropical Deserts (iv) Tropical Monsoon region
(v) Mediterranean region (vi) Temperate Grasslands
(vii) Taiga region (viii) Tundra region

(i) Equatorial Region

Location

The Equatorial region is found between 0-10° North and South of the Equator.

Area

The areas of Equatorial regions are

- **Asia** Indonesia, Papua New Guinea, Malaysia and the Southern part of the Philippines.
- **South America** The coastal lowlands between Guiana and Brazilian Highlands, Amazon basin and Coastal Columbia.
- **Africa** Zaire basin and the Guinea Coast in West Africa.

Climate

- **Temperature** The mean monthly temperature in Equatorial region is always around 80° F i.e. 20°C-30°C with very little variation. The high temperature in this region has high angle of incidence which lies between 66½° to 90°. The temperature rises in the afternoon while the nights are cool.
- **Rainfall** The Equatorial region receives heavy rainfall and has constant high temperature throughout the year. It lies in Torrid belt. Rainfall is heavy between 60 inches to 100 inches i.e. between 175 cm to 250 cm and well distributed throughout the year in Equatorial region. The mountainous regions receive relief rainfall while

the plains receive torrential rainfall. The amount of rainfall and temperature is modified according to relief and rainfall decreases with increase in distance from the Equator.

- **Season** There is equal duration of days and nights throughout the year. In Equatorial region within the tropics, the equatorial highlands have a distinctively cooler climate. There is no winter or dry season. Due to small differences in temperature, the region has a hot and wet season throughout the year.

Natural Vegetation

High temperature and abundant rainfall in the Equatorial regions support a heavy and thick growth of vegetation i.e. the Tropical Rainforest.

It is also called the **lungs of the world** because these rainforests absorbs large amount of carbon dioxide and produce oxygen.

In Amazon Basin, these rainforests are called **selvas.** The vegetation in these forests can be categorised into four layers i.e. emergent layer, canopy, forest floor and understorey.

The Equatorial vegetation comprises a multitude of evergreen trees that yield tropical hardwood, e.g. mahogany, ebony, green heart, cabinet woods and dyewoods, rosewood and rubber.

Wildlife

The Equatorial forest has a wide variety of animal species. Many animals can be found in this area such as snake, lizard, frog, elephant, rhinoceros, bills, parrots and macaws.

Human Adaptation

People of equatorial regions have adapted themselves for the survival by practicing shifting cultivation. In the Equatorial region, the primitive people practice hunting and gathering, whereas the advanced ones practice shifting cultivation and crops like yam, bananas, groundnuts and maize are grown. When the fertility of land is exhausted, people move on to a new place. Such farming practices are becoming more and more widespread even among the backward tribes.

With the coming of the Europeans, many large plantations have been established, especially in Java, Sumatra, Malaysia, West Africa and Central America. The most outstanding plantation is plantation of natural rubber called **Hevea brasiliensis**. The climate has proved to be very favourable for the cultivation of certain crops that are highly valued in the industrial West.

Cocoa is most extensively cultivated in West Africa, Ghana and Nigeria being important producers. Other crops that have been suitable for cultivation in Equatorial regions are coconuts, sugar, coffee, tea, tobacco, spices, cinchona, banana, pineapple and sago.

(ii) Tropical Grasslands or Savanna

Location

These are grassland biomes located within the tropics. They lie roughly between 7° to 20° North and South of the Equator. They consist more of long and short grass and less number of trees.

Area

Tropical grasslands includes half the surface of Africa (Generally Central Africa) and large areas of Australia, South America and Central America.

The areas of Tropical Grasslands are

- **South America** Llanos of the Orinoco Basin and the Campos of the Brazilian Highlands are the two distinct regions of Savanna, North and South of the Equator.
- **Africa** The regions where Savannas are found are Chad, Mali, Niger, Togo, Kenya, Sudan, Senegal, Cameroon, Tanzania, Angola, Uganda, Zaire, Zambia, Zimbabwe, Malawi, Ghana and Guinea.
- **Australia** The Australian Savanna is located South of the monsoon strip running from West to East in North of the Tropic of Capricorn and Queensland.

Climate

- **Temperature** The monthly temperature in Tropical Grasslands **hovers**[1] between 70° F to 90° F (22°C to 37°C) for lowland stations. An annual temperature range is of 20° F. There is a distinct drop in temperature in the rainy period, due to the overcast sky and the cooler atmosphere. Temperatures drop to well below 10°C and night frosts are not uncommon at this time of the year.
- **Rainfall** The Savanna climate is characterised by an alternate hot, rainy season and cool, dry season. Its annual precipitation of 32 inches also varies much from year to year.

1 **Hovers** To float in the air without moving in any direction or to stay very close to a person or place.

- **Season** In the Northern hemisphere, the hot rainy season normally begins in May and last until September as in Kano, Nigeria. The rest of the year is cool dry season. In the Southern hemisphere, there is rainy season from October to March.

Natural Vegetation

The Savanna landscape is characterised by tall grasses and short trees. The grass is rough and grows to the height of 3 to 6 feet at maturity.

The trees are deciduous and shed their leaves in the cool dry season to prevent excessive loss of water through transpiration, e.g. acacias. When there is no or less rainfall in this region, the Savanna merges into thorny scrub.

Trees grow best towards the equatorial humid latitude or along river banks, but decreases in height and density away from the Equator. Many trees are umbrella shaped, exposing only a narrow edge to the strong wind.

Human Adaptation

A large number of people in this region involve in pastoral and herding activities. These people keep large number of cattles which are fed on the tall grass or bush of Savanna region. Thus, Savannas are called **natural cattle country.**

The Masai is a nomadic tribe who once wandered with their cattle in the Central Highlands of East Africa in Kenya, Tanzania and Uganda. Cattle are kept by every Masai family and are considered as a symbol of wealth. Milking of cattle is done by women before day break and the dusk.

The people of Savanna region are involved in the farming and agricultural activities. Cotton, sugarcane, coffee, palm oil, groundnuts and tropical fruits are grown by the people of this region.

Wildlife

The Savanna particularly in Africa is the home of wild animals. The leaf and grass eating animal in this region includes the zebra, antelope, giraffe, deer, gazelle, elephant and okapi.

Check Your LEARNING...

1. Mention some areas of Equatorial regions throughout the year.
2. Name the crops suitable for cultivation in Equatorial regions.
3. Which tribe wandered in the central highland of East Africa in Kenya, Tanzania and Uganda?
4. Name the activities, on which people of grasslands are dependent.

(iii) Tropical Deserts

Location

The major Tropical Deserts of the world are located on the Western side of continents between 15° to 30° North and South latitudes. Amongst the mid latitude deserts, many are found on plateau and are at a considerable distance from the sea.

Area

The areas of Tropical Deserts are

- **Africa** Sahara Desert in North Africa is the largest single stretch of desert (3,200 miles from East to West and at least 1,000 miles wide). Other deserts found in Africa are Kalahari Desert and Namib Desert.
- **Asia** The Iranian Desert, Thar Desert and Arabian Desert.
- **North America** Mexican Desert, Sonoran, Mohave, Californian Desert are the deserts found in North America which is known to the world.
- **South America** The Atacama or Peruvian desert area.
- **Australia** The great Australian Desert covers almost half of the continent.

Climate

- **Temperature** The Tropical Deserts are rainless because of their interior location in the tropical latitude, away from the rain bearing winds. Tropical Deserts have hot summers and cool winters. The average summer temperature is around 30° to 45° C. The reasons for the high temperatures are clear, cloudless sky, intense **isolation**[2], dry air and a rapid rate of evaporation. The average winter temperature may be less than 20°C and sometimes, there may be frost at night.
- **Rainfall** Generally, Tropical Deserts receive less than 25cm of annual rainfall. However, some deserts have few areas with no rainfall at all. These areas are located in Western side in which trade winds become dry after bringing rainfall in areas of Eastern side. Precipitation is scarce and most unreliable in coastal stations like Massawa on the Red sea. The relative humidity is extremely low, decreasing from 60% in coastal areas to less than 30% in the desert interiors.

2 **Isolation** It is the rate of delivery of direct solar radiation per unit of horizontal surface.

- **Season** In this region, there are two seasons i.e. winter and summer. In the coastal areas of Tropical Deserts, there may be a short rainy season between summer and winter. Hot and dry winds like the Mistral, Bora and Sirocco may affect the seasons and bring pleasant weather conditions

Natural Vegetation

Plants that exist in Tropical Deserts are known as **xerophytic plants**. These plants are leafless and store water in their stems and roots. Some plants have leaves and many other plants have thorns. Leathery leaves is also a feature of vegetation in these areas.

Plants that exist in deserts have highly specialised means of adapting themselves to the arid environment. Intense evaporation increases the salinity of the soil so that dissolved salts tends to accumulate on the surface forming hard cracks.

The desert soils are very deficient in humus. Most desert shrubs have long roots and are well spaced out to gather moisture, in search of ground water. The most important plant of this region is thorny cacti.

Wildlife

Lifeforms like lizards, squirrels, snakes, rats, foxes and mice, hyenas and antelopes can be easily found in Tropical Deserts. Camels are used by people to travel in this region.

Human Adaptation

The primitive tribes, the **Bushmen** and **Bindibu** are best known in this region. Both the tribes are nomadic hunters and food gatherers. They does not grow crops and domesticate animals.

The Bushmen roam around the Kalahari Desert with their bows and poisoned arrows, spears, traps and snakes. The women and children collect insects, rodents and lizards and gather honey, roots, grass and shrubs. The **Aborigines**[3] or Bindibu of Australia live in the same way as the Bushmen.

In Tropical Deserts, crops cannot be grown without irrigation. The water for irrigation is obtained from rivers, dams, oasis or through canals, e.g. Nile in Egypt. The tribes in this region cultivate rice and cotton in summers and wheat, barley, beans and other minor crops in winters.

(iv) Tropical Monsoon Region

Location

The Tropical Monsoon region is located roughly between 10° to 30° North and South of the Equator. It is usually found in the Eastern part of the continents.

The Tropical Monsoon climate is found in Southern Asia with off-shore dry monsoon in winter and on-shore wet monsoon in summer. The Eastern coasts of tropical lands which experience on-shore trade winds all the year round and more evenly distributed rainfall, have Tropical Marine climate.

Area

The areas of Tropial Monsoon climate are

- **Asia** Indian-subcontinent including (India, Pakistan, Sri Lanka, Bangladesh, Southern China, Cambodia, Laos, Thailand Vietnam, Myanmar, the islands of Hainan, Taiwan and Philippines.
- **Australia** Northern Australia

The areas of Tropical Marine climate are

- **Africa** The parts of South-East Africa and Madagascar.
- **Central America** Nicaragua, Honduras, Jamaica and Belize.
- **South America** Eastern Brazil
- **Australia** The parts of North-Eastern Australia

Climate

The basic cause of Tropical Monsoon climate is the difference in the rate of heating and cooling of land and sea. The temperature, rainfall and seasons in Tropical Monsoon region are

- **Temperature** The temperature of summer varies between 27°C to 30°C in the coastal areas and 35° C to 38°C in the interior. The temperature of winter varies between 5°C to 18°C in the interior and 22°C to 25°C in the coastal areas.
- **Rainfall** The annual amount of rainfall varies from 75 to 200 cm. Cherrapunji in Meghalaya receives over 1200 cm rainfall. **Mawsynram** near Cherrapunji has recorded heaviest rain in the world. The rainfall is influenced by cyclonic disturbances in winter. The areas having Tropical Marine climate receive rainfall by trade winds and intense heat during the day in summer.

3 **Aborigines** A member of the original people to live in an area.

- **Season** There are basically three distinct seasons in regions with Tropical Monsoon climate.
  (i) The hot dry season from March to May,
  (ii) The rainy season from June to September
  (iii) The cool dry season from October to February
  In the areas with Tropical Marine type of climate, there are two main seasons, i.e. the wet season and dry season. There is no month without rainfall in the wet seasons.

Natural Vegetation

The Tropical Monsoon region has a wide variety of vegetation types. Tropical Evergreen forests are found in coastal areas and islands. Islands in the Indian Ocean, the slopes of the Western Ghats, Western parts of Maharashtra, Kerala and Tamil Nadu in India.

These forests consists of tall trees (above 60 m height) having broad leaves to give out excess moisture and receives more sunlight. For example, sisam, ebony, rosewood, etc. During the summer rains, there is heavy growth of climbers, bamboos, epiphytes, ferns, etc.

Areas where rainfall is not experienced throughout the year have a marked dry season and here, Tropical Monsoon Deciduous Forests are found e.g. Deccan Plateau and some areas in Southern China. These forests are found in areas with 150-200 cm of rainfall. For example, teak, sal, sandalwood and mahua.

Human Adaptation

Tropical rainforest provides the basis for many livelihoods. Farming or agriculture is the dominant occupation for the large number of people in these rainforests. Tropical agriculture is dependent on natural rainfall and a large labour force.

Food crops like rice, maize, millet, sorghum, wheat, gram and beans and cash crops like sugarcane, cotton, tea and coffee are grown in tropical monsoon regions.

Check Your LEARNING...

1. Name two deserts found in the African continent.
2. How much is the annual precipitation of tropical desert type of climate?
3. Which wind influences the climate of Tropical Monsoon?
4. At which place, Tropical Marine type of climate is found in the Central America?
5. What are the cash crops grown in Tropical Monsoon type of climate?

(v) Mediterranean Region

Location

The Mediterranean climate is found relatively in few areas in the world. They are entirely confined to the Western portion of continental masses between 30° to 45° North and South of the Equator. The large stretch of Mediterranean region lies along the Mediterranean Sea, thus it is known as Mediterranean region.

Area

The areas of Mediterranean region are

- **Europe** On the margins of South Portugal, Greece, Italy, France, Serbia, Spain, Romania and Montenegro.
- **Asia** Lebanon, Israel, Syria and parts of coastal Turkey.
- **North America** The coastal California around San Francisco.
- **South America** Central Chile
- **Africa** The coastal area of Algeria, Morocco, Libya, Tunisia and the region around Cape Town in South Africa.
- **Australia** Southern Australia around Adelaide and South-West area around Perth.

Climate

The Mediterranean type of climate is characterised by very distinctive climatic features. They are

- Hot dry summer with off-shore winds.
- Wet mild winter with on-shore westerlies.
- The Mediterranean region is also known as **Sub-tropical Winter Rain Zone** or the **Warm Temperate West Margin Climate** as it lies between the tropical deserts on the Equatorward side and cool temperate West margin region on the Poleward side.
- **Temperature** The Mediterranean climate have a relatively high temperature (76° F in July in Rome and 70° F in January in Cape Town) which ranges between 20°C to 28°C. The area close to the oceans experiences a lower temperature. In winter, the mean January temperature may be from 6° C to 10°C and in hottest month, the temperature may touch a maximum of 30° C. In winter, the temperature at night may fall below 0°C which led to destruction of forests in Mediterranean region.

- **Rainfall** The annual average rainfall in Mediterranean region varies from 35 cm to 75 cm. In the Northern hemisphere, the prevailing on-shore westerlies bring much cyclonic rain from the Atlantic to the countries bordering the Mediterranean sea. The Mediterranean lands receive most of their precipitation in winter when the westerlies shift towards the Equator.
- **Season** There are four climatic seasons in Mediterranean region i.e. winter, spring, summer and autumn. The good winter rain allows plants to adjust their growth with seasons. The plants flower in spring and fall their leaves in autumn in a rhythmic order.

Natural Vegetation

The Mediterranean region has a deciduous type of vegetation. The trees of these region have long roots and thick barks to retain moisture in the months of dry summer.

Higher and brighter intensity of light, moderate rainfall and dominant growing season makes this region suitable for growing trees, plants, crops, fruits and vegetables. Olive, eucalyptus oak, laurel, cork, beach ash, orange and lemon can be commonly found here.

Bushes are also grown in this region. Common species of bushes are lavender and rosemary, which can be seen in the region of the Mediterranean landscape.

The absence of shade is a distinct feature of Mediterranean lands. The growth of vegetation is slow in the cooler and wetter season, even though more rain comes in winter. The growth almost restricted to autumn and spring, when the temperature is higher and moisture is just sufficient.

Human Adaptation

Mediterranean region is particularly famous for orchard farming where a wide variety of citrus fruits like oranges, limes, lemons and grape fruits are grown. A wide variety of crops are cultivated in the Mediterranean region due to warm bright summers and cool moist winters.

The Mediterranean region accounts for 70% of the world's export of citrus fruits. Besides citrus fruits, the other important fruits cultivated in the Mediterranean region are olives, grapes, walnuts, hazelnuts and almonds. Other crops grown in the Mediterranean regions include wheat, barley, rice, cotton and tobacco.

(vi) Temperate Grasslands

The Temperate Grassland is also known as the **Continental** or **Steppe-Prairie** type of climatic region which lies in the westerly wind belt.

Location

The Temperate Grasslands lie between the foothills of the Rockies and the Great Lakes astride the American- Canadian border. They occupy the interior of the continents in mid-latitude zone of 40° to 55° North and South of the Equator. They are extended to vast areas in Northern hemisphere as compared to Southern hemisphere where they are small in extent.

Area

The areas of Temperate Grasslands are

- **Europe** In Europe, the Temperate Grasslands stretch Eastwards from the shore of Black Sea across the great Russian Plain to the foothills of the Altai mountain. They are also found in the area around Caspian sea and a small area in Hungarian plain known as the **Pustaz**.
- **Asia** The area around North-West China, Manchurian Plains and Western Siberia.
- **North America** In North America, the Grasslands are quite extensive and are called **Prairies**. They include a part of USA and Canada situated between the Great Lakes and the Rockies.
- **South America** In South America, the Temperate Grasslands are known as **Pampas** and found in the area around the pacts of Argentina and Uruguay.
- **South Africa** In South Africa, the grasslands are known as **Velds** and are situated between Drakensberg and Kalahari Desert.
- **Australia** In Australia, the grasslands are better known as **Downs** and are found in the Murray-Darling Basin of Southern Australia.

Climate

- **Temperature** The annual range of temperature in Temperate Grasslands varies between 18°C to 26°C. The temperature in summer varies between 15°C to 25°C and the maximum temperature during the day in the hottest month may exceed 30°C.
- **Rainfall** The average rainfall in Temperate Grasslands varies between 20 cm to 60 cm. The rainfall is conventional type accompanied by lighting and thunder. The heaviest rain comes in

the middle of the year with 3.1 inches each in June and July. Most of the winter months have precipitation brought by the occasional depressions of the westerlies in the form of snow. The local winds like chinook brings about an increase in temperature for few days.

Natural Vegetation

The Temperate Grasslands are practically treeless and the grasses are much shorter where the rainfall is moderate, above 20 inches. The grasses are tall, fresh and nutritious and are better described as long Prairie grass. The grasses are wiry and sparse, often found in discontinuous clumps, with bare soil between them.

In the high plains of USA, the Steppe grass can lie **dormant**[4] throughout the prolonged drought. They sprout and come to life as soon as temperature is warm enough for plant growth (43°F) and grow steadily with very little moisture.

In the cultivated regions (such as the wheat farms of Prairies), double rows of trees are planted around the house to shield the occupants from the strong winds.

Wildlife

The herbivorous animals are found in large numbers in Temperate Grasslands who feed on grass. Other animals include antelopes, horses, wild asses, kangaroo, etc.

Human Adaptation

The Temperate Grasslands were once the home of grazing animals, wild horses in the Asiatic Steppes, swift-footed bison in the Prairies and untamed buffaloes in the Pampas.

These grasslands were dominated by nomadic and semi-nomadic peoples like the Kirghiz of the Asiatic Steppes. They roamed far and wide with their herds and earned a certain living from whatever they could find.

Many of their home-made products were exchanged at trading posts or with the caravans for guns, canned food, grains, tea, coffee, sugar, medicines and other essential goods.

The Temperate Grasslands are known as the **granaries of the world**. They have ideal conditions for extensive wheat cultivation. Cotton and maize are also grown in this region.

4 **Dormant** Not doing anything or being active, but able to become active.

Check Your LEARNING...

1. Where do we find the Mediterranean climate in the world?
2. Which citrus fruits are grown in mediterranean region?
3. What are the regions of Temperate Grasslands in South America?
4. What do you understand by the term Pustaz?

(vii) The Taiga Region

It refers to the cool temperate continental or Siberian climate which is present in the Northern hemisphere.

Location

This region lies between 55° and 70° in the Northern hemisphere. On the poleward side of Northern hemisphere, the cool temperate continental climate merges into the Arctic Tundra of Canada and Eurasia at around the Arctic circle.

It stretches in a great, contiguous belt across North America, Europe and Asia.

Area

The areas of Taiga region are

- **Europe** Northern part of Russia, Finland and Sweden.
- **Asia** Sakhalin Island and Northern Siberia.
- **North America** In North America, this sub-Arctic belt stretches from Alaska across Canada to Labrador.

Climate

The Siberian type of climate is absent in the Southern hemisphere due to its narrowness in the high altitude. It only prevails in Northern hemisphere. The climate of the Siberian type is characterised by a bitterly cold winter of long duration and a cool brief summer.

The temperature, rainfall and season in Taiga region are

- **Temperature** The Taiga region is characterised by severe winters for long period and short summer for only 3 to 4 months. Occasionally, cold, Northerly polar winds such as **Blizzards** of Canada and **Buran** of Eurasia blow violently at 50 mph or more and at a temperature of 50°F below freezing point.

- **Rainfall** The total yearly precipitation in Taiga region varies from 25 cm to 100 cm. Most precipitation come in the summer months.
- **Season** In Taiga region, summers are rainy, warm and humid. In winter, the precipitation is in the form of snow, as mean temperature is below freezing point all the time.

Natural Vegetation

In Taiga region, vegetation include evergreen coniferous forests. The coniferous forest belts of Eurasia and North America are the richest sources of softwood used in building construction, furniture, matches, paper and pulp and other branches of the chemical industry.

There are four major species in the coniferous forests which are **pine**, (white pine, red pine, scots pine, jack pine, lodgepole pine), **Fir** (douglas fir and balsam fir), **spruce** and **larch**.

Only in the more accessible areas, the forests are cleared for **lumbering**[5]. The various species of pine, fir, larch and spruce are felled and transported to the saw mills for the extraction of softwoods.

Human Adaptation

The Taiga region is sparsely populated as farming is not an important activity here because the land remains covered with snow during the long winter seasons.

Crops like barley, oats, potoatoes and beetroots are grown only in the sheltered valley and the lands bordering the Steppes.

(viii) The Tundra Region

The word 'Tundra' has been derived from a Russian word which means a flat treeless plain. The Tundra type of climate is also known as the Arctic or Polar type.

Location

This region lies roughly beyond 65° North on the Northern side of the Taiga region.

Area

The areas of Tundra region are

- **Europe** Greenland, Iceland and Northern Scandinavia.
- **North America** Northern Canada and Alaska.
- **Asia** Siberia

Climate

- **Temperature** The Polar climate is characterised by a very low mean annual temperature and the hottest month is June where temperature rises to more than 10°C. Mid-winter temperatures are as low as –37°C and much colder in the interior.
- **Rainfall** Precipitation is mainly in the form of snow falling in winter and being drifted about during blizzards. Snowfall varies with locality. Conventional rainfall is generally absent because of the low rate of evaporation and the lack of moisture in the cold polar air. Most precipitation comes in the summer in the form of sleet. In coastal areas, where cyclones are more strongly felt, most of the rain fall in winter.

Natural Vegetation

Only few plants survive in such harsh climatic conditions in Tundra. The greatest inhibiting factor is the region's deficiency in heat. Such climatic conditions support only the lower form of vegetation which include mosses, lichens and sedges.

Drainage in the Tundra is usually poor as the subs-soil is permanently frozen. Ponds and waterlogged areas are found in hollows. Here, some hardy grasses are mostly found which provide the only pasturage for the herbivorous animals like reindeer. Mammals like the wolves, foxes, musk-ox, Arctic hare and **lemmings**[6] also live in Tundra regions.

Human Adaptation

Human activities of the Tundra region are largely confined to the coast. Areas where plateaus and mountains increase the altitude are uninhabitable as these are permanently snow covered. Few people who live in the Tundra region live a semi-nomadic life and have to adapt themselves to the harsh environment.

Invits, Sapmi, Samoyeds, Yakuts are major races that live in Tundra region. Invit people are known as Eskimos. They live in Greenland, Northern Canada and Alaska. They used to live as hunters, fishermen and food gatherers.

5 **Lumbering** It refers to felling of economically valuable trees in forest.

6 **Lemmings** A lemming is a small rodent usually found in or near the Arctic in Tundra biomes.

In winter, Invits or Eskimos live in round houses made from blocks of snow called **igloos**. In the summer, when the snow melts, they live in tent-like huts made of animal skins stretched over a frame. In recent years more and more of them are settling in permanent huts.

Yakus live in the North-Eastern part of Siberia, Sapmi live in Tundra region of Norway, Sweden, Finland and Western Russia.

Semoyeds live in European Russia and part of North-Western Siberia.

Check Your LEARNING...

1. What type of climate is experienced in the Taiga region?
2. What are the natural vegetation found in Taiga region?
3. What are the crops grown in Taiga region?
4. Where can we find Tundra climate in North America?
5. What is the type of precipitation in Tundra climate?

QUiCK Revision

- The structure, surface form and climate within the Earth's surface having comparatively high degree of uniformity is called natural region.
- The equatorial region is found between 0-10° North and South of the Equator. The equatorial region receives heavy rainfall and has constant high temperature throughout the year.
- High temperature and abundant rainfall in the equatorial region support a luxuriant type of vegetation.
- Tropical grassland is confined within the tropics and is best developed in the Sudan where the dry and wet seasons are most distinct. Hence, it is also called Sudan or savannas.
- The Sudan type of climate is characterised by an alternate hot, rainy season and cold, dry season.
- In the Northern hemisphere, the hot, rainy season begins in May and last until September and in the Southern hemisphere, the rainy season is from October to March.
- The Masai are nomadic tribe who once wandered with their cattle in the central highlands of East of Africa in Kenya, Tanzania and Uganda.
- The major hot deserts or tropical deserts of the world are located on the Western coasts of continents between 15° to 30° North and South.
- The predominant vegetation of Tropical desert is xerophytic or drought-resistant scrub. This includes the bulbous, cacti, thorny bushes, long rooted wiry grasses and scattered dwarf acacias.
- The temperature of summer varies between 27°C to 30°C in the coastal areas and 35°C to 38°C in the interior in the tropical monsoon type climate. A wide range of lowland tropical cash crops are cultivated for the export market. A number of cash crops like sugarcane, cotton, tea and coffee are also grown.
- The Mediterranean type of climate is characterised by very distinctive climatic features which are
  - A day, warm summer with off-shore trades.
  - A concentration of rainfall in winter with on-shore westerlies.
  - Bright, sunny weather with hot day summers and wet, mild winters.
- The temperate grassland is also known as the continental or Steppe-Prairie type of climatic region which lies in the Westerly wind belt.
- Steppe grassland of the mid-latitudes, is also known as Tropical Grassland, Prairies, Pampas, Veld and Downs.
- The Taiga region experience the cool temperate continental or Siberian climate which is present in the Northern hemisphere.
- The Tundra type of climate is also known as the Arctic or polar type. The word 'tundra' has been derived from Russian word which means a flat treeless plain.
- The polar type of climate and vegetation is found mainly North of the Arctic Circle in the Northern hemisphere. This region lies roughly beyond 65° North on the Northern side of the Taiga region.

Chapter Practice

Section-I

Multiple Choice Questions

1. The structure, surface form and climate within the Earth's surface having comparatively high degree of uniformity is called ....
(a) tundra region (b) island
(c) coastal areas (d) natural region

Ans. (d) natural region

2. Which of the following cannot be considered as natural region?
(a) Man-made island (b) Taiga region
(c) Deserts (d) Tundra region

Ans. (a) Man-made island

3. Consider the following statement regarding equatorial region and choose the correct option.
(i) The equatorial region is found between 0-30° North and South of the equator.
(ii) The equatorial region receives heavy rainfall.
(iii) There is equal distribution of day and night in equatorial region.

Codes
(a) (i) and (ii) (b) Only (iii)
(c) (ii) and (iii) (d) (i), (ii) and (iii)

Ans. (c) (ii) and (iii)

4. What is the reason behind adopting of shifting cultivation in equatorial region?
(a) High degree of fertility
(b) Exhausted fertility
(c) Favourable condition for crops
(d) Large number of backward tribes

Ans. (b) Exhausted fertility

5. Cocoa is most extensively cultivated in ....
(a) South America (b) India
(c) West Africa (d) Malaysia

Ans. (c) West Africa

6. Which of the following term is identical to Tropical Grasslands?
(a) Manioc (b) Savanna
(c) Vegetation (d) Deciduous

Ans. (b) Savanna

7. What is the reason behind distinct drop in temperature in the rainy period of Savanna region?
(a) Overcast sky, cooler atmosphere
(b) Dry atmosphere
(c) High degree of precipitation
(d) Polar winds

Ans. (a) Overcast sky, cooler atmosphere

8. .... are located on the Western side of continents between 15° and 30° North and South latitudes.
(a) Equatorial region (b) Savanna
(c) Tropical monsoon (d) Tropical Desert

Ans. (d) Tropical Desert

9. Give reason for the following.
Tropical Deserts are rainless.
(a) Intense isolation
(b) No cold season
(c) Interior location on temperate latitude
(d) Direct solar radiation

Ans. (c) Interior location on temperate latitude

10. Thorny Cacti is important plant of which region?
(a) Tropical Desert
(b) Tropical Monsoon
(c) Tundra
(d) Taiga

Ans. (a) Tropical Desert

11. Consider the following statement regarding tropical monsoon, and choose the correct options.
(i) This region is located roughly between 10° to 30° North and South of equator.
(ii) The climate of this region is modified by the influence of the on-shore trade winds all the year around.
(iii) This climate of this region is similar to marine type of climate.

Codes
(a) (i) and (iii) (b) Only (i)
(c) (i) and (ii) (d) (i), (ii) and (iii)

Ans. (d) (i), (ii) and (iii)

12. .... has recorded heaviest rain in the world.
(a) Himalayas
(b) Cherrapunji
(c) Chennai
(d) Shillong

Ans. (b) Cherrapunji

13. Give reason for the following.
Reason behind distinctive climate of Mediterranean region.
(a) Shifting of wind belts
(b) Western margin of the region
(c) Bright sunny weather
(d) None of the above

Ans. (a) Shifting of wind belts

14. The Mediterranean region is also known as ....

(a) Tropical Desert
(b) Sub-Tropical zone
(c) Deciduous region
(d) Sub-Tropical winter rain zone

Ans. (d) Sub-Tropical winter rain zone

15. Which of the following region is particularly famous for orchard farming?

(a) Temperate Grassland (b) Equatorial region
(c) Tropical Desert
(d) Mediterranean region

Ans. (d) Mediterranean region

16. Prairies, Pampas and Pustaz belongs to which of the following region?

(a) Taiga (b) Equatorial
(c) Temperate Grassland (d) Tropical Desert

Ans. (c) Temperate Grassland

17. Give reason for the following.
Reason behind small amounts of natural coniferous forests in Germany, Australia and Poland of Taiga region.

(a) Low altitude
(b) High altitude
(c) Scanty rainfall
(d) Cool temperature

Ans. (b) High altitude

18. In which region of Asia, the Tundra type of climate is found?

(a) India
(b) East Asian countries
(c) Siberia
(d) UAE

Ans. (c) Siberia

19. .... live in round house made from ice called igloo.

(a) Eskimos (b) Nomads
(c) Hunters and gatherers (d) Yaknts

Ans. (a) Eskimos

20. Match the following.

Region	Location
A. Equatorial	1. 10°to 30° N and S
B. Savanna	2. 55° to 70° N and S
C. Tropical Monsoon	3. 0-10° N and S
D. Taiga	4. 7°–20° N and S

Codes

	A	B	C	D
(a)	1	4	3	2
(b)	2	4	1	3
(c)	3	4	1	2
(d)	4	3	1	2

Ans. (c)

21. Match the following.

Area	Natural Region
A. New Guinea	1. Tropical Desert
B. Kalahari Desert	2. Tropical Monsoon
C. India	3. Taiga
D. Eurasia	4. Equatorial region

Codes

	A	B	C	D		A	B	C	D
(a)	4	1	2	3	(b)	1	3	4	2
(c)	3	2	1	4	(d)	2	1	4	3

Ans. (a)

Section-II

Short Questions

1. What do you mean by the term natural region? List three natural regions of the world.

Ans. The structure, surface form and climate within the Earth's surface having high degree of uniformity comparatively is called natural region.

Three natural regions of the world are

(i) Equatorial region (ii) Savanna region
(iii) Tropical region

2. What is the importance and significance of climate?

Ans. The climate is very important and plays a significant role as it influences the soil, flora and fauna and vegetation of the region. There are different climatic conditions, so we find slight variations in each climatic region.

3. (i) What are the locations of Equatorial region in Asia?

(ii) What is the rainfall distribution of Equatorial region?

Ans. (i) The locations of equatorial region in Asia are Indonesia, Papua New Guinea, Malaysia and the Southern part of the Philippines.

(ii) Rainfall in the Equatorial region is heavy between 60 inches and 100 inches i.e. between 175 cm to 250 cm and well distributed throughout the year.

4. What are the climatic conditions of Equatorial region?

Ans. The Equatorial region receives heavy rainfall and has constant high temperature throughout the year and lies in torrid belt. The high temperature in this region has high angle of incidence of sun's rays in this region which is between 66½° to 90°.

5. What are the dominant types of vegetation of the Equatorial region?

Ans. The vegetation in Equatorial region forest can be categorised as emergent layer, canopy and forest floor. The Equatorial vegetation comprises a multitude of evergreen trees that yield tropical hardwood, e.g. mahogany, ebony, greenheart, ivorywood, dyewoods, rosewood, rubber, cinchona, etc.

6. (i) Specify the areas where Tropical Grasslands exists.
(ii) How is the wildlife of Tropical Deserts?

Ans. (i) The areas where Tropical Grasslands exist includes half the surface of Africa (generally Central Africa) and large areas of Australia, South America and Central America.
(ii) The animals which find their life form in Tropical Desert's hot weather condition are squirrels, snakes, foxes, lizards and mice. These animals burrow their holes to escape heat.

7. What are the temperature and rainfall conditions of Tropical Grasslands?

Ans. The monthly temperature of Tropical Grasslands, hovers between 22°C to 37°C for lowland station. The range increases as one moves further away from the equator. In Tropical Grasslands, the rainfall of 32 inches varies much from year to year.

8. What is the natural vegetation of Tropical Grasslands?

Ans. The natural vegetation of Tropical Grasslands is characterised by tall grass and short trees. The trees in Tropical Grasslands are deciduous, shedding their leaves in the cool, dry season to prevent excessive loss of water through transpiration.

9. What is the temperature condition of Tropical Desert?

Ans. The deserts are some of the hottest spots on the Earth and have high temperature throughout the year. There is no cold season in the hot deserts and the average summer temperature is around 30°C to 45°C.

10. Describe the areas experiencing Tropical Deserts.

Ans. The areas where Tropical Deserts are found are Africa, Asia, North America, South America and Australia. In Asia, Tropical Deserts are found in Iran, India and Arabia. In North America, they found in Mexico, Arizona, Nevada states and California. In South America the Atacama or Peruvian deserts are Tropical Deserts.

11. (i) What are the locations of Tropical Monsoon region?
(ii) Describe the areas covered under Tropical Monsoon region.

Ans. (i) The Tropical Monsoon region is located roughly between 10° to 30° North and South of the Equator. It is usually found in the Eastern part of the continents.
(ii) The areas covered by the Tropical Monsoon region include

- **Asia** This comprises the areas of India, Pakistan, Bangladesh, Thailand, Vietnam, Sri Lanka and South-China.
- **Africa** It covers the areas of South-East Africa and Madagascar.
- **Australia** North Australia

12. What are the typical climatic features of the Tropical Monsoon region?

Ans. The features of Tropical Monsoon region are

- The temprature of summer in this region varies between 27°C to 30°C in the coastal areas and 35°C to 38°C in the interior.
- Temperature in this region in winter varies between 5°C to 18°C.
- Annual rainfall in Tropical Monsoon regions is 75 to 200 cm.

13. What is the temperature condition of Tropical Monsoon type of climate?

Ans. Being located near the Equator, the Tropical Monsoon climate experiences warm temperature throughout the year. In this region, the average temperature varies from 27°C to 32°C and annual range of temperature varies from 12°C to 17°C depending on the location of the place. The temperature of summer varies between 27°C to 30°C in the coastal areas and 35° to 38°C in the interior. The temperature of winter varies between 15°C and 18°C in the interior and 22°C to 25°C in the coastal areas.

14. Describe the characteristics of the vegetation of the Tropical Monsoon region.

Ans. The characteristics of the vegetation of Tropical Monsoon region are

- This region is characterised by a wide variety of vegetation types. Many of the islands and coastal areas have forests.
- The natural vegetation of Tropical Monsoon climate consists of trees having broad leaves to give out excess moisture and receives more Sunlight. For example, sal, teak, bamboo, mahua, jamun, neem, shisham, etc.

15. (i) What is the main occupation of people in the Tropical Monsoon region?
(ii) What are the crops grown in Tropical Monsoon region?

Ans. (i) Agriculture is the main occupation of the majority of the population in the Tropical Monsoon region.
(ii) The major crops grown in Tropical Monsoon region include rice, wheat, maize, millets, sorghum, gram and beans.

16. What is the location of Temperate Grasslands?

Ans. The Temperate Grasslands lies between the foothills of the rockies and the great lakes astride the American-Canadian border which occupy the interior of the continents in mid-latitude zone of 40° to 55° North and South of the Equator. In the Southern hemisphere, due to the narrowness of the temperate portions of the Southern continents, the grasslands are rather restricted and less continental.

17. How is rainfall distributed in the Temperate Grasslands?

Ans. The annual precipitation of the Tempratre grasslands in its continental position can be expressed to be light. The average rainfall may be taken as about 20 cm to 60 cm. The heaviest rain comes in the middle of the year with 3.1 inches each in June and July.

18. Name six Temperate Grasslands of the world.

Ans. Temperate Grasslands are known by different names in different continents. These are

Name of Grasslands	Country/Continents
(i) Steppes	Euro-Asia
(ii) Pustaz	Hungary
(iii) Velds	Africa
(iv) Prairies	North America
(v) Pampas	South America
(vi) Downs	Australia

19. Explain Taiga and its location.

Ans. The Taiga region experience the cool temperate continental or Siberian climate which is present in the Northern hemisphere where the continents within the high latitude have broad East-West spread.

Taiga region lies between 55° and 70° in the Northern hemisphere. It stretches in a great, contiguous belt across North America, Europe and Asia.

Long Questions

1. Give an account for the climatic condition and temperature exists in equatorial region.

Ans. Refer to chapter theory page no. 156-157.

2. Differentiate between Mediterranean type of climate and Temperate Grasslands climate.

Ans. The differences between Mediterranean type of climate and Temperates Grasslands climate are

Mediterranean Type of Climate	Temperate Grasslands Climate
The Mediterranean type of climate is found in Western portion of continental masses between 30° and 45° North and South of the Equator.	The Temperate Grassland lies between the foothills of the Rockies and the Great Lakes astride the American Canadian border which occupy the interior of the continents in mid-latitude zone of 40° to 55° North and South of the Equator.
The basic cause of Mediterranean type of climate is shifting of the wind belts. The area around the Mediterranean Sea has the greatest extent of this type of winter rain climate.	Their location in the heart of continents means that they have little maritime influence. It is also known as the continental or Steppe-Prairie type of climatic region which lies in the westerly wind belts.
The Mediterranean type of climate is found in Africa on the coastal area of Algeria, Morocco and the region around Cape Town in South-Africa.	In Europe, the Temperate Grasslands stretch Eastwards from the shore of Black Sea across the great Russian plain to the foothills of the Altai mountains. It is also found in the area around Caspian sea and a small area in Hungarian Plain known as Pustaz.

3. Why Mediterranean region is known as sub-tropical winter rain zone or warm temperate West margin climate?

Ans. As the Mediterranean region lies between the tropical desert on the equatorward side and cool temperate West margin region on the poleward side, that is why this climate region is also known as sub-tropical winter rain zone or the warm temperate West margin climate. Hot dry summers and wet mild winter is one prime character of Mediterranean region.

4. Describe the natural vegetation of the Temperate Grasslands.

Ans. Refer to chapter theory page no. 162.

5. Explain the human adaptation of the Temperate Grasslands.

Ans. Refer to chapter theory page no. 162.

6. Describe the human adaptation in Taiga region.

Ans. Refer to chapter theory page no. 163.

7. Describe the natural vegetation on the Tundra region.

Ans. Refer to chapter theory page no. 163.

8. How has human adapted their life and activities in the Tundra region?

Ans. Refer to chapter theory page no. 163-164.

9. Explain the following.

(i) Natural vegetation in Tropical Deserts

(ii) Human adaptation in Equatorial region.

Ans. (i) Refer chapter theory page no. 159.

(ii) Refer chapter theory page no. 157.

Map Based Question

1. On the map of world, shade the following.
   (i) Equatorial region
   (ii) Tropical monsoon region
   (iii) Mediterranean region
   (iv) Tropical grasslands
   (v) Temperate grasslands
   (vi) Tropical Desert region
   (vii) Taiga region
   (viii) Tundra region

Ans.

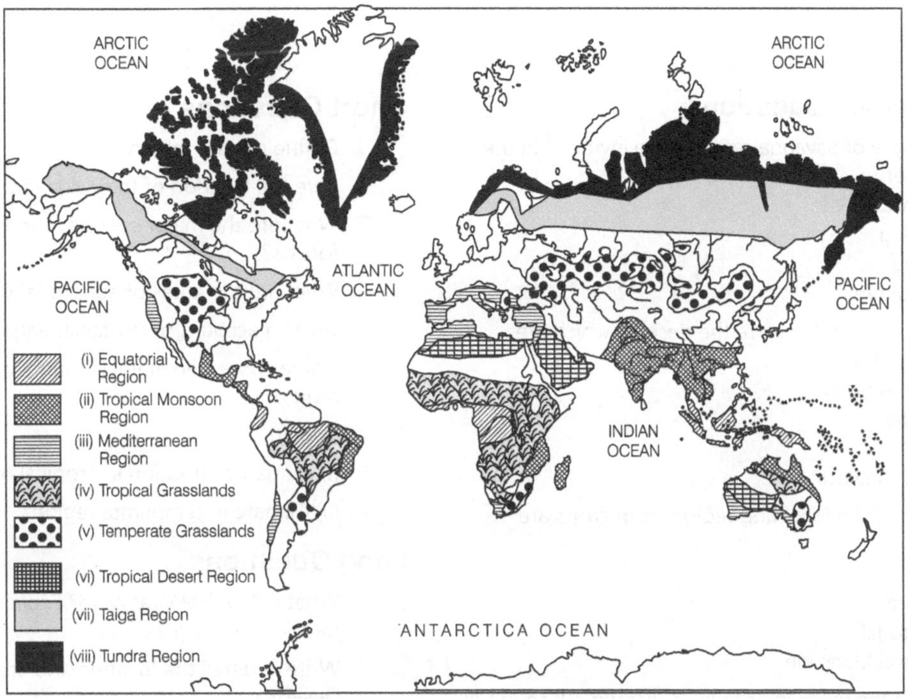

Chapter Assessment

Section-I

Multiple Choice Questions

1. The people of Savanna region were involved in the activity of ....
   (a) business
   (b) farming
   (c) fishing
   (d) sericulture
2. Sonoran and Mahave are the deserts, which are located in the ....
   (a) South America
   (b) Europe
   (c) Asia
   (d) North America
3. In which of the following region, cash crops are grown?
   (a) Taiga
   (b) Tundra
   (c) Equatorial
   (d) Tropical Monsoon
4. Which of the following region is located 30° to 45° N and S?
   (a) Tropical Desert
   (b) Mediterranean
   (c) Tundra
   (d) Tropical Monsoon
5. Spruce and larch are grown in ....
   (a) Tundra (b) Taiga
   (c) Deserts (d) Coastal areas

Section-II

Short Questions

1. Define natural region.
2. Give the location of the Taiga region.
3. What are the major species found in the coniferous forests?
4. What are the areas of equatorial region?
5. Give an account of rainfall in equatorial region.
6. Name some wild animals found in equatorial region.
7. Explain
   (i) Human adaptation in Tropical region
   (ii) Climate in temperate regions.

Long Questions

1. What is Tropical Grassland? Explain the area and location of this grassland.
2. Write in detail the location and area of Tropical Deserts.
3. Describe the human adaptions of Tropical Desert.
4. Explain the area, location and climate of Mediterranean region.
5. Explain the following.
   (i) Evergreen vegetation in tropical climate.
   (ii) Different human adaptations in different climate zones.

Allinone®

ICSE Sample Papers

SAMPLE QUESTION PAPER 1

A HIGHLY SIMULATED Sample Question Paper for ICSE Class IX

Geography (Unsolved)

General Instructions

1. Answers to this Paper must be written on the answer sheet provided separately.
2. Attempt seven questions in all. Part I is compulsory. All questions from Part I are to be attempted. A total of five questions are to be attempted from Part II.
3. The intended marks for questions or parts of questions are given in brackets ( ).

Time : 2 Hrs **Max. Marks : 80**

Part - I

(30 Marks)

Attempt all questions from this part

Question 1

(a) Give a reason for each of the following. (2)

(i) Why noon is the hottest time of the day? **(Analyse)**

(ii) Why does the Sun rise in the East? **(Analyse)**

(b) Divide the crust based on its composition. **(Understand) (2)**

(c) Name any two structural plains with their cause of formation. **(Remember) (2)**

(d) How the humans are involved in the weathering of rocks? **(Understand) (2)**

(e) Name the major relief features of the oceans. **(Recall) (2)**

Question 2

On the outline map of the world provided **(Recall)**

(a) Shade and label the Equatorial region in the continent of Africa. (1)

(b) Shade and label the Caribbean Sea. (1)

(c) Mark and label the Rockies. (1)

(d) Locate and label the River Yangtse Kiang. (1)

(e) Mark and label the Zagros. (1)

(f) Shade and label the Persian Gulf. (1)

(g) Shade and label the Bering Strait. (1)

(h) Shade, mark and label the Canadian Shield. (1)

(i) Mark and label the Pyrenees. (1)

(j) Locate and label the River Nile. (1)

Question 3

Choose the correct answers to the questions from the given options. **(10)**

(i) 21st June is the longest day in the Northern hemisphere because **(Apply)**

(a) The Sun is located overhead the Tropic of Cancer.

(b) The Sun is located overhead the Tropic of Capricorn.

(c) The Sun is located overhead the Antarctic Circle.

(d) The Sun is located overhead the Arctic Circle.

(ii) Which category of rocks is characterised by a distinct layered formation? **(Remember)**

(a) Igneous rocks (b) Metamorphic rocks

(c) Sedimentary rocks (d) Extrusive igneous rocks

(iii) The wearing away of the Earth's surface is called .... **(Remember)**

(a) mountains (b) plateau

(c) erosion (d) deposition

(iv) Hygrometer: Humidity **(Remember)**

(a) Barometer: Air Pressure (b) Anemometer: Temperature

(c) Thermometer: Wind Speed (d) Rain gauge: Direction of winds

(v) **Assertion (A)** Hill stations are cooler than the plains. **(Analyse)**

Reason (R) Temperature decreases with increasing altitude.

(a) Both A and R are true and R is the correct explanation of A.

(b) Both A and R are true, but R is not the correct explanation of A.

(c) A is true, but R is false.

(d) A is false, but R is true.

(vi) If a scientist detects an abrupt change in seismic wave velocity at a depth of 2,900 km, which geological boundary is being examined? **(Apply)**

(a) Mohorovicic discontinuity (b) Asthenosphere boundary

(c) Gutenberg discontinuity (d) Crustal Plate boundary

(vii) Which of the following tides take place twice in a month at the time of the full Moon and the new Moon ? **(Remember)**

(a) Low tide (b) Diurnal tide

(c) Mixed tide (d) High tide

(viii) Depletion of oxygen in water bodies is known as .... **(Recall)**

(a) Eutrophication (b) Biomagnification

(c) Bioaccumulation (d) Eburnification

(ix) The given below picture shows chalk. It is an example of which type of rock? **(Apply)**

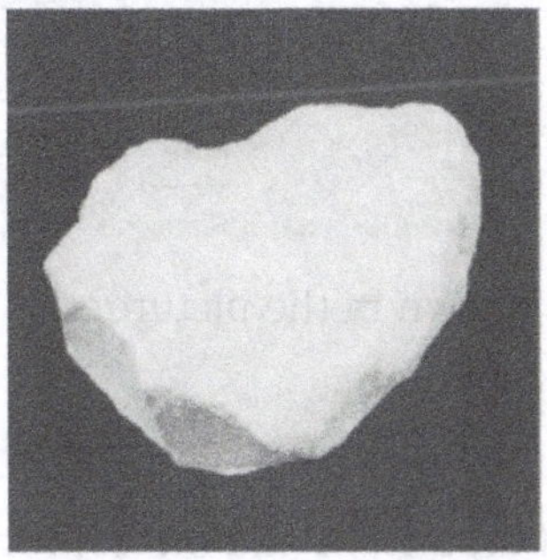

(a) Metamorphic rock (b) Riverine rock

(c) Mechanically formed rock (d) Sedimentary rock

(x) Which pressure belt is commonly referred to as the Doldrums? **(Remember)**

(a) Equatorial low pressure belts (b) Sub-tropical high pressure belts

(c) Circum-polar low pressure belts (d) Polar high pressure areas

Part - II

(50 Marks)

Attempt any five questions from this part

Question 4

(a) 'Geysers are a reliable source of renewable energy.' Explain this statement. **(Understand) (2)**

(b) Distinguish between active volcanoes and dormant volcanoes. **(Analyse) (2)**

(c) State any three destructive effects of volcanoes. **(Understand) (3)**

(d) Give reasons for each of the following. **(Evaluate) (3)**

(i) Volcanic eruption is associated with water.

(ii) Volcanic activity leads to earthquakes.

(iii) Tectonic plates responsible for volcanic activity.

Question 5

(a) With reference to landforms of the Earth, answer the following **(2)**

(i) Explain the formation of fold mountains. **(Understand)**

(ii) Give two examples of residual mountain. **(Remember)**

(b) Define the landform and mention its three main types. **(Remember) (2)**

(c) Based on the given below picture, answer the following questions **(Understand, analysis and analysis) (3)**

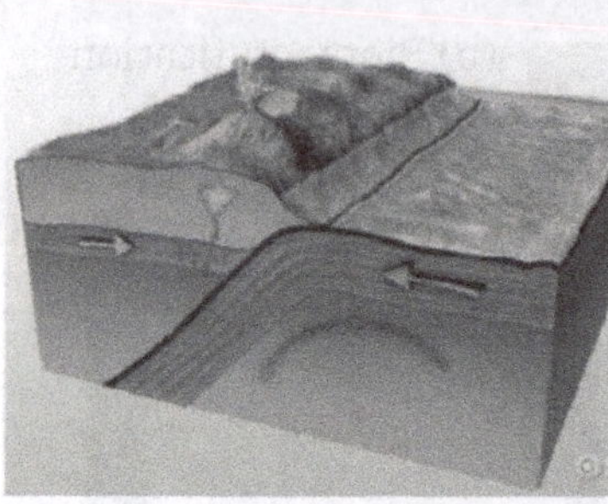

(i) Identify the type of mountain shown in the picture?

(ii) Explain the formation of this mountain.

(iii) This mountain has two types. Mention the difference between them.

(d) Distinguish between young fold mountain and old fold mountain. **(Analyse) (3)**

Question 6

(a) State any two types of local winds. **(Recall) (2)**

(b) Why the variable winds are considered as variable in nature? **(Evaluate) (2)**

(c) Distinguish between tropical cyclone and temperate cyclone. **(Analyse) (3)**

(d) Give a reason for each of the following **(3)**

(i) Polar regions have high atmospheric pressure. **(Analyse)**

(ii) Land breezes occur at night. **(Analyse)**

(iii) There is low atmospheric pressure in the equatorial region. **(Analyse)**

Question 7

(a) Explain relative humidity. **(Understand) (2)**

(b) Distinguish between dew and frost? **(Analyse) (2)**

(c) Give one reason to explain each of the following **(3)**

(i) Absolute humidity not used in weather forecasts. **(Analyse)**

(ii) Condensation occurs when air cools below its dew point. **(Analyse)**

(iii) Orographic rainfall occurs on the windward side of mountains. **(Analyse)**

(d) With reference to humidity, answer the following **(3)**

(i) Mention the names of the four chief forms of condensation. **(Recall)**

(ii) Explain how humidity measures. **(Analyse)**

(iii) State three types of rainfall. **(Understand)**

Question 8

(a) Despite being moderate earthquake with strength of 4 on Richter scale, the quake on Monday rattled parts of the Delhi-NCR, reigniting worries of the impact of the 'great Himalayan earthquake.' Since 2015, the earthquake in Nepal has seismologists, scientists who study quakes, have expressed their worries about a big earthquake in the coming Himalayan region. **(3)**

(Source: The Economic Times, Date 18th Feb, 2025)

(i) Describe the fault lines? **(Understand)**

(ii) How do seismologists study earthquake patterns? **(Analyse)**

(iii) 'Prevention is better than cure.' How does this statement apply to earthquakes? **(Evaluate)**

(b) Mention any two natural causes of an earthquake. **(Remember) (2)**

(c) Sayonika was reading about the 2011 Pacific ocean earthquake, which triggered a series of devastating tsunamis that affected countries such as Japan, Philippines and North American countries causing widespread damage. **(3)**

(i) Sayonika read about the effects of earthquakes on the coastal region. How did the earthquake affect coastal regions? **(Analyse)**

(ii) How does an earthquake cause a tsunami, and where are they most likely to occur? **(Evaluate)**

(d) 'Aftershocks occur after major earthquakes.' Explain. **(Evaluate) (2)**

Question 9

(a) Explain how does environment get affected by soil pollution? **(Analyse) (2)**

(b) 'Soil pollution brought changes in the health of the humans'. Explain how? **(Apply) (2)**

(c) What are the main preventive measures to combat pollution? What is its aim? **(Apply) (3)**

(d) Give three reasons about how earthquakes can be beneficial. **(Evaluate) (3)**

Question 10

(a) What is the temperature condition of tropical desert? **(Remember) (2)**

(b) Describe the areas experiencing tropical deserts. **(Analyse) (2)**

(c) Distinguish between mediterranean climate and temperate grasslands. **(Recall) (3)**

(d) Based on the given below picture, answer the following questions **(3)**

(i) Identify the type of region shown in the picture. **(Recall)**

(ii) Why is this region called the 'granaries of the world'? **(Analyse)**

(iii) How does the variation in temperature affect the ecosystems of this region? **(Apply)**

Question 11

(a) Distinguish between high tide and low tide. **(Analyse) (2)**

(b) State the types of ocean currents. **(Remember) (2)**

(c) With reference to tides and currents, answer the following **(3)**

(i) How salinity is responsible for causing the current? **(Analyse)**

(ii) Explain how ocean currents affect marine life? **(Analyse)**

(iii) Define the Labrador current. **(Understand)**

(d) Give a reason for each of the following **(3)**

(i) Warm currents produce a milder climate. **(Analyse)**

(ii) The Eastern coast of the USA is comparatively cold. **(Analyse)**

(iii) Warm ocean currents influence the climate of coastal regions. **(Analyse)**

Question 12

(a) Why did some countries choose more than one time zone? **(Apply) (2)**

(b) 'France has the maximum time zones in the world.' Why? **(Analyse) (2)**

(c) Distinguish between the lines of latitude and lines of longitude. **(Analyse) (3)**

(d) With reference to longitude, answer the following **(3)**

(i) State two characteristics of lines of longitudes. **(Understand)**

(ii) What is prime meridian? Explain with examples. **(Understand)**

Answers

2

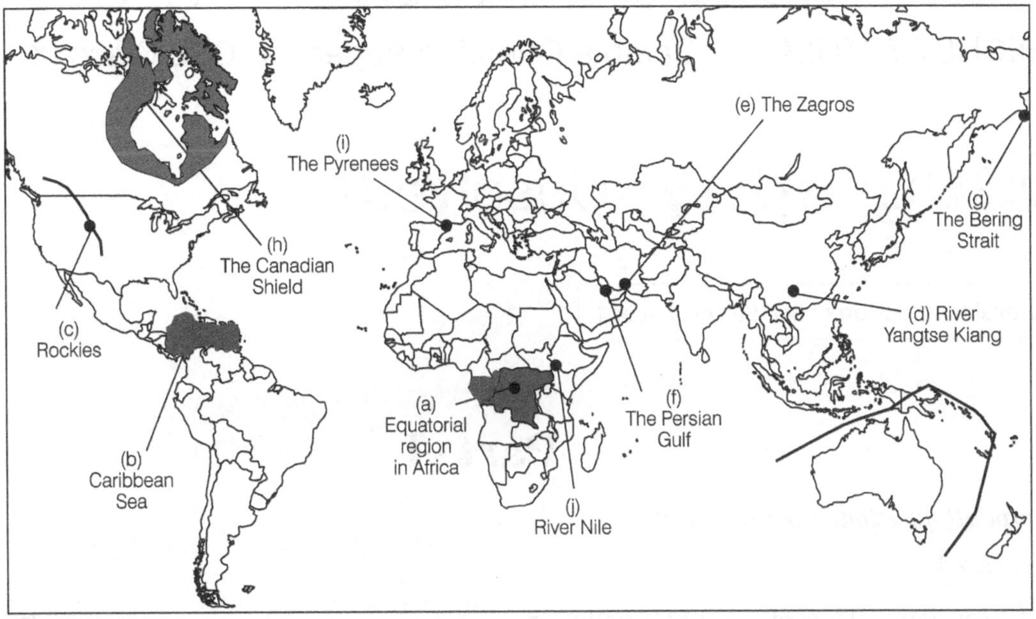

3 (i) (a) The Sun is located overhead the Tropic of Cancer.
(ii) (c) Sedimentary rocks
(iii) (c) erosion
(iv) (a) Barometer: Air Pressure
(v) (a) Both A and R are true and R is the correct explanation of A.
(vi) (c) Gutenberg discontinuity
(vii) (d) High tide
(viii) (a) Eutrophication
(ix) (d) Sedimentary rock
(x) (a) Equatorial low pressure belts

SAMPLE QUESTION PAPER 2

A HIGHLY SIMULATED Sample Question Paper for ICSE Class IX

Geography (Unsolved)

General Instructions : See Sample Paper 1

Part - I

(30 Marks)

Attempt all questions from this part

Question 1

(a) Mention any two effects of air pollution. **(Remember) (2)**

(b) How gravitational force is important for atmospheric pressure? **(Analyse) (2)**

(c) Give a reason for each of the following. **(Analyse) (2)**
(i) Collision of plates causes earthquakes.
(ii) Seismic waves effect the water bodies on Earth.

(d) Mention any two effects of the tides. **(Understand) (2)**

(e) Differentiate between positive and negative effects of weathering. **(Analyse) (2)**

Question 2

On the outline map of the world provided **(Recall)**

(a) Shade and name the roof of the world. **(1)**

(b) Mark and label the Great Dividing Range. **(1)**

(c) Locate, shade and label the Brazilian highlands. **(1)**

(d) Shade and label the Tundra region in Europe and Asia. **(1)**

(e) Locate, shade and label the North Sea. **(1)**

(f) Shade and label the Gulf of Carpentaria. **(1)**

(g) Shade and label the Strait of Gibraltar. **(1)**

(h) Locate and label the River Niger. **(1)**

(i) Shade and label the Black sea. **(1)**

(j) Locate and label the River Ob. **(1)**

Question 3

Choose the correct answers to the questions from the given options. **(10)**

(i) .... refers to a self-regulating and self-sustaining unit of the biosphere. **(Recall)**

(a) Ecosystem (b) Food cycle

(c) Biome (d) Ecology

(ii) The movement of the Sun and the celestial bodies from East to West is caused by **(Analyse)**

(a) The Earth's revolution around the Sun

(b) The Earth's rotation on its axis

(c) The gravitational pull of the Moon

(d) The Earth's tilt

(iii) Oxidation: Chemical weathering **(Remember)**

(a) Carbonation: Biological weathering

(b) Plants: Mechanical weathering

(c) Granular disintegration: Physical weathering

(d) Hydration: Erosion

(iv) Prime Meridian passes through which city? **(Recall)**

(a) Paris (b) London

(c) Birmingham (d) Liverpool

(v) **Assertion (A)** Physical weathering also known as mechanical weathering. **(Analyse)**

Reason (R) Main factors responsible for physical weathering are temperature changes and moisture only.

(a) Both A and R are true and the R is the correct explanation of the A.

(b) Both A and R are true, but the R is not the correct explanation of the A.

(c) A is true, but the R is false.

(d) A is false, but the R is true.

(vi) Stratosphere: Ozone layer **(Remember)**

(a) Troposphere: Weather (b) Mesosphere: Earthquakes

(c) Exosphere: Precipitation (d) Thermosphere: Air pressure

(vii) The given below picture shows a dense forest. Identify the natural region represeted in this image. **(Apply)**

(a) Tundra

(b) Equatorial region

(c) Savanna

(d) Temperate grasslands

(viii) **Assertion (A)** Geysers are a reliable source of renewable energy. **(Analyse)**

Reason (R) Geysers erupt at regular intervals but not provide continuous supply of hot water.

(a) Both A and R are true and R is the correct explanation of A.

(b) Both A and R are true, but R is not the correct explanation of A.

(c) A is true, but R is false.

(d) A is false, but R is true.

(ix) If an earthquake has a magnitude of 5.0 on the Richter scale, what level of intensity is expected? **(Apply)**

(a) Minor damage, rarely felt

(b) Severe damage, felt over a large area

(c) Unnoticeable, no damage

(d) Moderate damage, felt in the surrounding area

(x) .... causes condensation to occur in the atmosphere. **(Recall)**

(a) Increase in temperature

(b) Loss of heat

(c) Increase in air pressure

(d) Decrease in altitude

Part - II

(50 Marks)

Attempt any five questions from this part

Question 4

(a) Mention any two characteristics of Stratosphere. **(Understand) (2)**

(b) What are the causes of ozone layer depletion and how do chlorofluorocarbons (CFCs) contribute to it? **(Analyse) (3)**

(c) With reference to atmosphere, explain the following terms **(Understand) (2)**

(i) Stratosphere (ii) Exosphere

(d) With reference to composition and structure of the atmosphere, answer the following **(3)**

(i) Name the four layers of the Earth. **(Remember)**

(ii) Why is the atmosphere known as the blanket of the Earth? **(Evaluate)**

(iii) State any two causes of Global warming. **(Understand)**

Question 5

(a) Why are lines of latitude called parallels of latitude? **(Analyse) (2)**

(b) 'The lines of latitude form one of the coordinates of the grid system.' Explain any three uses of latitudes. **(Apply) (3)**

(c) Discuss about Indian Standard Time (IST). **(Understand) (2)**

(d) How International Date Line is important for us? **(Apply) (3)**

Question 6

(a) What is the distance of Earth from the Sun on aphelion and perihelion? **(Remember) (2)**

(b) Explain the direction of rotation and revolution of the Earth? **(Analyse) (2)**

(c) State the three phases of the Sun. **(Remember) (3)**

(d) How inclination of the Earth's axis causes day and night? Explain. **(Analyse) (3)**

Question 7

(a) Mention any two characteristics of the Earth's crust. **(Understand) (2)**

(b) 'The crust of Earth is only one percent of Earth's mass, yet it is the largest reservoir of resources for humankind.' Justify the statement. **(Evaluate) (2)**

(c) Give a reason for each of the following **(Analyse) (3)**

(i) The lower mantle is hotter and denser than the upper mantle.

(ii) The Mohorovicic discontinuity is an important boundary in Earth's structure.

(iii) The inner core is solid, despite the extremely high temperatures.

(d) "The Core of the Earth is also known as Nife." Explain. **(Analyse) (3)**

Question 8

(a) State the two types of plateaus? **(Remember) (2)**

(b) Mention any two types of depositional plains. **(Remember) (2)**

(c) Explain how are the fold mountains formed? **(Analyse) (3)**

(d) Simmi is a geologist and she is studying a new mountain range which is formed by tectonic collisions. When she went on excursion, she observed the folded rock layers, fault lines, rugged terrain, valleys and possible volcanic or earthquake activity. **(3)**

(i) Explain how the landscape changed during the early stages of mountain formation? **(Analyse)**

(ii) Analyse the geographical features which Simmi observed after the mountain range has fully formed. **(Analyse)**

Question 9

(a) Mention any two characteristics of igneous rocks. **(Understand) (2)**

(b) 'Sedimentary rocks are formed from materials derived from other rocks.' Analyse the statement. **(Analyse) (2)**

(c) With reference to rocks, answer the following **(Remember) (3)**

(i) What are sills and dykes? **(Understand)**

(ii) State any two characteristics of metamorphic rocks. **(Analyse)**

(iii) How are sedimentary rocks formed? **(Analyse)**

(d) Distinguish between rocks and minerals. **(3)**

Question 10

(a) Explain any two constructive effects of the volcanoes. **(Understand) (2)**

(b) Give two examples of sleeping volcanoes. **(Recall) (2)**

(c) A volcano in eastern Indonesia has erupted at least a thousand times this month, according to an official report on Sunday, as efforts are under way to evacuate thousands of villagers.It was one of 1,079 eruptions by the volcano recorded since 1st January by Indonesia's Geological Agency. "The ash was grey with moderate to thick intensity, drifting South-West. A loud rumbling sound was heard all the way to Mount Ibu Observation Post," the agency said. **(3)**

(Source: The Hindu, Date: 20th January, 2025)

(i) How does volcanicity lead to volcanic eruptions? **(Analyse)**

(ii) Why is it unusual to predict volcanic eruptions? **(Evaluate)**

(iii) Describe the two types of volcanoes, giving an example of each type. **(Understand)**

(d) Why volcanic eruptions may lead to ejection of materials in all forms? **(Evaluate) (3)**

Question 11

(a) Mention any two man-made causes of earthquakes. **(Understand) (2)**

(b) How the Richter scale is used for measuring the intensity of earthquake? **(Apply) (2)**

(c) Describe the destructive effects of earthquakes. **(Understand) (3)**

(d) Explain the main earthquake belt of the Earth. **(Understand) (3)**

Question 12

(a) Mention any two types of physical weathering. **(Remember) (2)**

(b) Explain any two agents of biological weathering with example. **(Analyse) (2)**

(c) Discuss the process of chemical weathering. **(Understand) (3)**

(d) Based on the given below picture, answer the following questions **(3)**

(i) Identify the type of dune shown in the image. **(Recall)**

(ii) Explain this dune. **(Analyse)**

(iii) Where these types of dunes are found? **(Understand)**

Answers

2

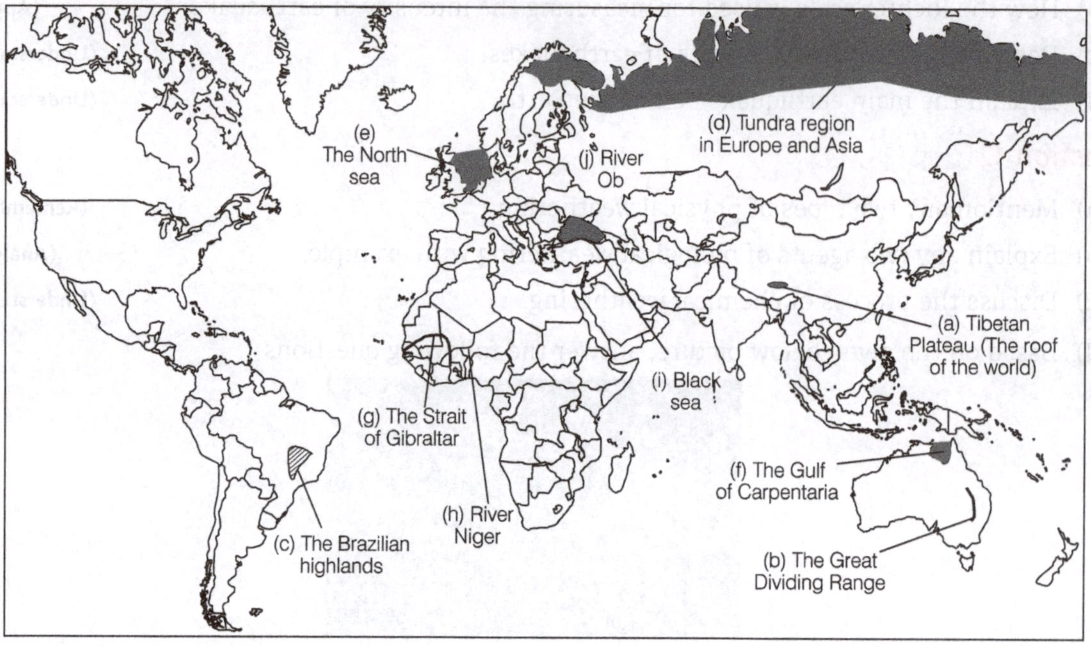

3 (i) (a) Ecosystem

(ii) (b) The Earth's rotation on its axis

(iii) (c) Granular disintegration : Physical weathering

(iv) (b) London

(v) (c) A is true, but the R is false

(vi) (a) Troposphere : Weather

(vii) (b) Equatorial region

(viii) (c) A is true, but R is false.

(ix) (d) Moderate damage, felt in the surrounding area.

(x) (b) Loss of heat

SAMPLE QUESTION PAPER 3

A HIGHLY SIMULATED Sample Question Paper for ICSE Class IX

Geography (Unsolved)

General Instructions : See Sample Paper 1

Part - I

(30 Marks)

Attempt all questions from this part

Question 1

(a) Describe the impact of ocean currents on the following. **(Understand) (2)**

(i) Navigation (ii) Fishing

(b) Differentiate between summer and winter solstice. **(Analyse) (2)**

(c) State any two characteristics of young fold mountains. **(Understand) (2)**

(d) How do rivers work as the source of denudation? **(Analyse) (2)**

(e) How wind forms different types of landforms? **(Analyse) (2)**

Question 2

On the outline map of the world provided **(Recall)**

(a) Shade and label the Tropical Monsoon region in South Asia. **(1)**

(b) Shade and label the Gulf of Mexico. **(1)**

(c) Mark and label the Mongolian plateau. **(1)**

(d) Mark and label the Andes. **(1)**

(e) Mark and label the River Irrawaddy. **(1)**

(f) Mark and name the strait, which connects the Andaman sea to the South China sea. **(1)**

(g) Locate and label the River Darling. **(1)**

(h) Shade and label the Caspian sea. **(1)**

(i) Shade and label the Gulf of Guinea. **(1)**

(j) Locate and label the River Colorado. **(1)**

Question 3

Choose the correct answers to the questions from the given options. **(10)**

(i) Which of the following landforms is typically formed in the lower course of a river, where the river is slower and has a wider channel? **(Understand)**

(a) V-shaped valley (b) Waterfall (c) Delta (d) Rapid

(ii) If the tide height is 20% higher than the normal tide, which type of tide does this refer to? **(Apply)**

(a) Spring tide (b) Neap tide

(c) Diurnal tide (d) Semi-diurnal tide

(iii) What type of landform is represented in picture given below **(Apply)**

(a) Block mountain (b) Residual mountain

(c) Young Fold mountain (d) Old Fold mountain

(iv) What is the reason behind acid rain? **(Remember)**

(a) Water pollution (b) Noise pollution

(c) Soil pollution (d) Air pollution

(v) Earth is slightly flattened at the .... **(Recall)**

(a) North Pole (b) Middle

(c) South Pole (d) North and the South Poles

(vi) Seismology is useful for geologists because **(Apply)**

(a) it is the study of earthquakes, seismic waves and related phenomena.

(b) it is the study of geological and geophysical phenomena of the Earth.

(c) it provides information about minerals.

(d) All of the above

(vii) Polar regions :Low insolation **(Remember)**

(a) Temperate regions: High insolation (b) Frigid regions: Constant insolation

(c) Tropics : High insolation (d) Torrid regions: No insolation

(viii) **Assertion (A)** The Tropical Monsoon type of climate is found in Southern Asia with onshore wet monsoons in the summer. **(Analyse)**

Reason (R) Tropical agriculture is dependent on natural rainfall and a large labour force.

(a) Both A and R are true and the R is the correct explanation of the A.

(b) Both A and R are true, but the R is not the correct explanation of the A.

(c) A is true, but the R is false.

(d) A is false, but the R is true.

(ix) The minimum distance between the Sun and the Earth occurs on .... day. **(Recall)**

(a) 22nd December (b) 23rd September

(c) 4th July (d) 3rd January

(x) .... layer of the atmosphere protects us from meteors? **(Recall)**

(a) Mesosphere (b) Stratosphere

(c) Troposphere (d) Ionosphere

Part - II

(50 Marks)

Attempt any five questions from this part

Question 4

(a) State any two features of the Earth that make it a unique planet. **(Understand) (2)**

(b) 'Our Earth is the only planet that supports life.' Explain the statement with examples. **(Analyse) (2)**

(c) With reference to Earth as a planet answer the following **(3)**

(i) Mention any two proofs that define Earth as spherical in shape. **(Analyse)**

(ii) Explain the term ecosystem. **(Understand)**

(iii) What is a solid crust? **(Remember)**

(d) Give reasons for each of the following **(Analyse) (3)**

(i) The vertical rays of the Sun provide more heat at the equator.

(ii) Temperature decreases from the equator to the poles.

(iii) Hot deserts have high temperature range.

Question 5

(a) Name the uppermost layer of the atmosphere and give its importance. **(Understand) (2)**

(b) Explain any two impacts of global warming on agriculture. **(Evaluate) (2)**

(c) Explain any three layers of atmosphere. **(Understand) (3)**

(d) Virat is doing research about the Stratosphere, which is located between 18 and 50 km above the Earth. **(3)**

(i) Why do jet aircrafts fly in the stratosphere? **(Apply)**

(ii) 'The Ozone layer lies in this sphere.' State any two natural causes of ozone layer depletion. **(Analyse)**

(iii) Mention any two characteristics of the stratosphere. **(Understand)**

Question 6

(a) Explain which region receives maximum insolation? **(Analyse) (2)**

(b) Explain the term terrestrial radiation. **(Understand) (2)**

(c) Distinguish between land breeze and sea breeze. **(Analyse) (3)**

(d) Give a reason for each of the following **(Analyse) (3)**

(i) The temperature is higher at the equator than at the poles.

(ii) The distance from the sea affects the temperature of a place.

(iii) Solar radiation plays important role in Earth's climate.

Question 7

(a) Mention any two factors that affect atmospheric pressure. **(Understand) (2)**

(b) 'The circum-polar low pressure belts are marked by violent storms in winter.' Explain this belt. **(Apply) (2)**

(c) With reference to atmospheric pressure and winds, answer the following **(3)**

(i) Mention the names of two types of barometer. **(Recall)**

(ii) What is anticyclone? **(Remember)**

(iii) State any two importance of jet streams. **(Understand)**

(d) Explain the factors affecting direction and velocity of the wind. **(Analyse) (3)**

Question 8

(a) What is precipitation? Explain its forms. **(Analyse) (2)**

(b) Distinguish between absolute humidity and relative humidity. **(Analyse) (2)**

(c) Based on the given below picture answer the following questions **(3)**

(i) Identify the type of cloud shown in the above image. **(Recall)**

(ii) Explain the cloud given in the above image. **(Analyse)**

(iii) Mention the forms of clouds. **(Remember)**

(d) Distinguish between convectional rainfall and orographic rainfall. **(Analyse) (3)**

Question 9

(a) What is air pollution? Mention any two source of air pollution. **(Remember) (2)**

(b) How nuclear tests add to the source of radioactive pollution? **(Analyse) (2)**

(c) 'Pollution in the cities is the price of growing affluence.' Justify the statement. **(Evaluate) (3)**

(d) Explain how has domestic waste led to the degradation of soil? **(Analyse) (3)**

Question 10

(a) Give one reason to explain each of the following **(Analyse) (3)**

(i) Physical weathering is more prevalent in desert regions.

(ii) Chemical weathering occurs more rapidly in tropical climates.

(iii) All the rivers do not form deltas.

(b) Mention any two works of river. **(Understand) (2)**

(c) Distinguish between block disintegration and exfoliation. **(Analyse) (3)**

(d) State the two characteristics of a river in the middle course. **(Understand) (2)**

Question 11

(a) The Amazon is at risk of reaching an irreversible tipping point. An estimated 17% of Amazon forests have been converted to other uses and an additional 17% degraded. The pressures on the Amazon are intensifying. We need to act now. Without the Amazon, we lose the fight against climate change. **(3)**

(Source: WWF, Date: 08th Oct, 2024)

(i) Identify the type of natural region as discussed in the above given passage. **(Recall)**

(ii) Give any two examples of natural vegetation of this region. **(Remember)**

(iii) Explain the agriculture activity of this region. **(Analyse)**

(b) Give an account of rainfall in equatorial region. **(Evaluate) (2)**

(c) What is tropical grassland? Explain the area and location of this grassland. **(Analyse) (3)**

(d) Explain the location and area of tropical deserts. **(Analyse) (2)**

Question 12

(a) State any two characteristics of the crust. **(Understand) (2)**

(b) Mention any two features of core. **(Understand) (2)**

(c) Explain any three major consequences of the movements of the Earth? **(Analyse) (3)**

(d) With reference to Earth's structure, answer the following **(3)**

(i) Why the Earth's crust undergoes many changes. **(Evaluate)**

(ii) Explain the composition of the Earth. **(Understand)**

(iii) What is Mohorovicic discontinuity. **(Remember)**

Answers

2

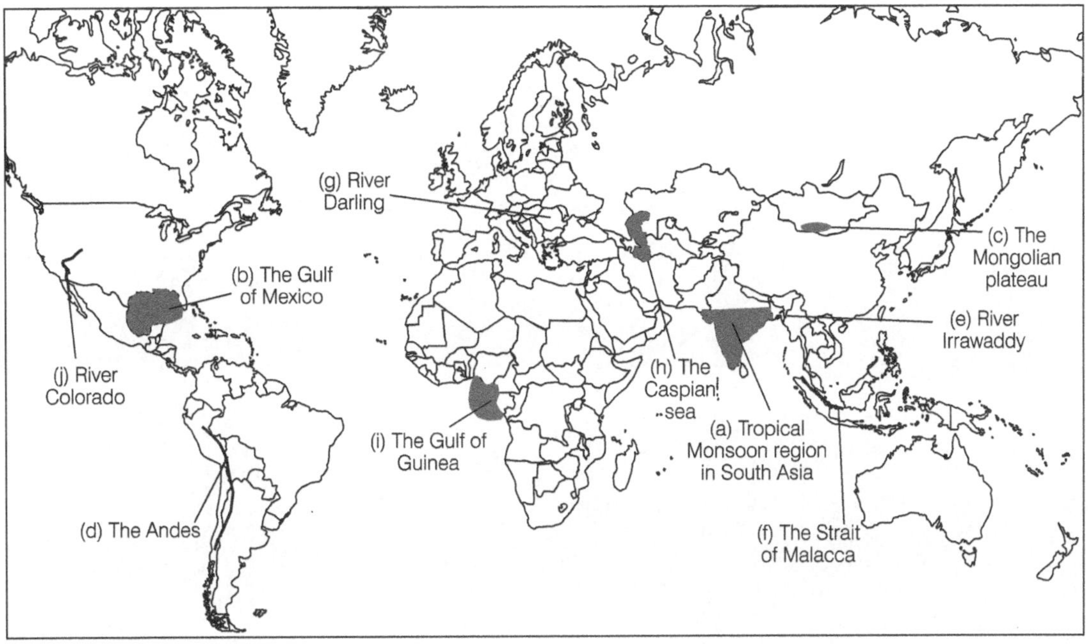

3 (i) (c) Delta

(ii) (a) Spring tide

(iii) (c) Young Fold mountain

(iv) (d) Air pollution

(v) (d) North and the South poles

(vi) (a) It is the study of earthquakes, seismic waves and related phenomena

(vii) (c) Tropics : High insolation

(viii) (b) Both A and R are true, but R is not the correct explanation of the A

(ix) (d) 3rd January

(x) (a) Mesosphere